THE
WISDOM GODDESS

Feminine Motifs in Eight Nag Hammadi Documents

Rose Horman Arthur

With Critical Translations of
ON THE ORIGIN OF THE WORLD
and **THE THUNDER**
by Richard L. Arthur

UNIVERSITY
PRESS OF
AMERICA

LANHAM • NEW YORK • LONDON

Copyright © 1984 by

University Press of America,™ Inc.

4720 Boston Way
Lanham, MD 20706

3 Henrietta Street
London WC2E 8LU England

ISBN (Perfect): 0-8191-4172-0
ISBN   (Cloth): 0-8191-4171-2

All University Press of America books are produced on acid-free
paper which exceeds the minimum standards set by the National
Historical Publications and Records Commission.

To the memory of my parents,
Trena Snyders Horman and John H. Horman,
who, in unison, served as my first and
foremost image of
The Wisdom Goddess

ACKNOWLEDGEMENTS

The critical translations of *On the Origin of the World* (II.5) and *The Thunder* (VI.2) from the Nag Hammadi Coptic documents found in Egypt nearly forty years ago were made by Richard L. Arthur, Th. D., who also helped with the other translations within the book.

Grateful acknowledgement is made for permission to use quotations from *The Nag Hammadi Library in English* edited by James M. Robinson, copyrighted in 1977 by E. J. Brill, the Netherlands, and reprinted by permission of Harper & Row, Publishers, Inc. The quotations are used for critical review and are compared with our own translations.

Professors and students at the Graduate Theological Union, Harvard Divinity School, the Chicago Cluster of Theological Schools, and several Nag Hammadi conferences have helped me in clarifying and substantiating my general thesis. A Harvard Divinity School appointment as Research/Resource Associate in Women's Studies in the Department of New Testament made it possible for me to devote a full academic year in a congenial atmosphere to this project.

Without the care, concern, and labors of persons too numerous to mention, this book would not be a reality. I choose to name, with profound gratitude, Karen Kolstad, Linda Manderud, Helen Arthur St. John, Malei Polu Veu, and Ellen Young, patient typists for numerous editions of a difficult text. I would also like to thank Helen Hudson of the University Press of America for editorial help in the preparation of the manuscript for publication.

If there are errors within this book, they are my responsibility. My hope is that they are minimal and that they will be corrected by the next generation of Nag Hammadi, New Testament, Gnostic, or Women's Studies enthusiasts. Thanks are due in advance to those who read *The Wisdom Goddess* and give constructive criticism.

TABLE OF CONTENTS

THE WISDOM GODDESS: Feminine Motifs in Eight Nag
Hammadi Documents attempts to show that within the Nag
Hammadi corpus there is a relative decline in the
prestige of personified Sophia (wisdom) from the
earlier non-Christian documents to the later Christianized and Christian documents. The introductory chapter
sets forth a basis for classification of the Nag
Hammadi tractates, as well as the methodology and
rationale for the study. The Sophia theme as it appears
in each of the eight documents is briefly sketched.

The second chapter is a comparison of the non-
Christian Apocalypse of Adam with the Christian tractate, the Exegesis on the Soul. In the Jewish-Gnostic
apocalypse, the "word of Gnosis" the salvific life-
giving principle, is given to Adam by the heavenly Eve,
whereas in the Christian document, the male spirit is
presented as the necessary agent of the feminine soul's
salvation.

In chapter three, a pagan letter, Eugnostos the
Blessed, and a parallel Christian revelatory discourse,
the Sophia of Jesus Christ, are compared. While in the
former, Sophia appears as an androgyne within a cosmological scheme, in the latter she is a fallen feminine
deity in need of the male spirit of Christ for her
salvation. Other persistent feminine motifs within
gnostic literature are considered, e.g., the fault of
the woman, and the soul imaged as feminine.

Chapter four details the differences in treatment of
feminine motifs in two related documents, On the Origin
of the World and The Hypostasis of the Archons. In the
former, the mythological presentation is almost entirely
set within feminine imagery, from the formation of the
world by Pistis Sophia and the creation of Eve before
Adam to the destruction of the world by the mindless
fury of an unnamed goddess. The comparison of feminine
motifs is followed by a presentation of linguistic
evidence that indicates that The Hypostasis of the
Archons is dependent in part on the Coptic text of On
the Origin of the World.

In the final chapter, The Thunder, a poetic non-
Christian tractate, is contrasted with the Christian
homily, the Gospel of Truth. It is suggested that the

title, BPONTH, "The Thunder," is derived from a corruption of two abbreviations, BRO, "Barbelo," and NTI, "God," i.e., "the divine Barbelo." This document is interpreted as an expression of a poetic work that also occurs in *On the Origin of the World*. The poem, for convenience, is entitled "The Song of the Woman." The final page of *The Thunder* is treated as a Christian addition devoted to praise of a monotheistic masculine deity. Feminine motifs, good and evil, prominent in the main portion of the work are completely absent here. The *Gospel of Truth* is interpreted as a reduction of earlier mythological gnosticism, and in it the feminine motifs function on a more abstract level. Here the soul and the prime cause of evil, Planē, "error," are still imaged as feminine while the positive element is the Father of Truth. The total impact of the comparisons tends to show that defeminization accompanied the Christianization of older gnostic traditions.

In the appendices fresh translations with critical notes are provided for *On the Origin of the World* (II.5) and *The Thunder, Perfect Mind* (VI.2), the two documents which, of the eight, are most feministic.

Most of the research for this book was done during the ten years I spent pursuing a doctorate at the Graduate Theological Union at Berkeley, California. Since 1979, however, the work has been completely updated, and while the documentation is limited to eight of the Nag Hammadi texts, the conclusion holds, so far as I have been able to ascertain, for the remaining texts.

"Now," writes Professor James M. Robinson in the introduction to *The Nag Hammadi Library in English* (1977), "the time has come for a concentrated effort, with the whole Nag Hammadi library accessible, to rewrite the history of Gnosticism, to understand what it was really all about, and, of course to pose new questions." This book represents an attempt to rethink the gnostic controversies almost exclusively on the basis of the new texts. Polemic aside, it seeks to view the feminine motifs from the vantage point of the author or editor of the text and to determine if there is censure or praise surrounding the particular motif.

TABLE OF TRACTATES

The following table lists the principal tractates of the Nag Hammadi Codices and of Berlin Codex 8502 which are investigated in this work, their codex and tractate numbers, and their page and line numbers from the Coptic manuscripts.

TEXTUAL SIGNS

[ ]   Square brackets indicate a lacuna in the manuscript.

⟨ ⟩   Pointed brackets indicate a correction of a
scribal omission or error, made by the translator.

( )   Parentheses indicate material which is useful
to the reader but not explicitly present in the
Coptic manuscripts.

{ }   Braces indicate superfluous letters or words
added by the scribe.

CHAPTER ONE

INTRODUCTION

The Nag Hammadi Library and Its Classification

In 1945 a collection of religious documents was
found in a jar within the caves near the modern city of
Nag Hammadi, Egypt.[1] It consists of twelve books plus
a single tractate which was found tucked inside the
front cover of codex six. Each book, except the tenth,
contains a group of quite short works so that one may
reckon a total of fifty-two tractates comprising about
one thousand one hundred and fifty large pages of which
nearly eight hundred are in good condition. All of the
documents are in the Coptic language, a form of old
Egyptian written in Greek capital letters, and all are
considered by scholars to be translations from earlier
Greek documents. They represent the work of different
scribes and authors, and, although they date from the
third or fourth century A.D., preserve traditions which
are much older. There are, for example, a fragment of
Plato's *Republic* (VI.5) and three versions of the
Apocryphon of John, some form of which was used by
Irenaeus in his work, *Against Heresies*, about 180 A.D.
The varied nature of the works makes it appropriate to
refer to the collection as a library.

Within the Nag Hammadi library are examples of quite
different forms of ancient literature. Side by side
are hymms of praise, philosophical essays, homilies, and
ecstatic utterances. There are acts, epistles, gospels,
and apocalypses analogous to those of the New Testament,
and wisdom literature comparable to that of the Old
Testament. There are several Hermetic tractates thought
to belong to Egyptian societies dedicated to the god
Hermes, as well as instances of "I am" aretalogies best
known from Isis inscriptions. Conspicuous by their
absence are books of an historical nature which could
give a clue to the origin or development of the library.
Also absent are manuscripts of biblical works, but there

---

1. For a good account of the discovery of the Nag Hammadi codices,
see John Dart, *The Laughing Savior* (New York: Harper & Row, 1976).

are abundant themes from both testaments, and even some
direct quotations. One looks in vain for the names of
the gnostic schools as preserved by the heresiologists,
although the names Valentinus (IX.56.2,5), Dositheos
(VII.118.10), and Basilides (IX.57.[8]) may refer to
gnostic leaders mentioned by the church fathers.[2] The
documents, in a general way, are related to the types
of religious and philosophical literature which the
fathers of the church, as well as the Neoplatonic
philosopher, Plotinus, found repugnant in the dis-
courses of groups which they labeled "gnostic".

Several reasons may be given for the lack of
exact correspondence between the data of the heresy
hunters and the contents of the Nag Hammadi texts. The
information given by the enemies of the gnostics is
polemic in nature while the Nag Hammadi texts appear to
be written by gnostics or by sympathizers. A second
reason for differing reports may be changes within the
gnostic systems, which, being syncretistic, did not remain constant in doctrine or scriptural exegesis. There
are the three copies of the *Apocryphon of John*, none of
which is identical with another and none of which agrees
completely with Irenaeus' descriptions of the Barbeloites.[3]

The lack of agreement between the Nag Hammadi texts
and the patristic accounts prohibits easy classification
of the documents according to the names of heresies
supplied by the church fathers. The *Apocryphon of John*
mentions Barbelo as an important goddess, and might be
expected to belong to the Barbeloites of Irenaeus. It,
however, also sets forth the glories of Seth and his
generation. Should the *Apocryphon of John* be classified
as belonging to the Barbeloites, to the Sethians, to
both, or to neither?[4] This difficulty, among others,
leads one to avoid the classifications of the fathers.

A more natural classification of the Nag Hammadi

---

2. Cf. Birger A. Pearson, "Anti-Heretical Warnings in Codex IX
from Nag Hammadi," *Essays on the Nag Hammadi Texts in Honour of
Pahor Labib*, ed. M. Krause (Leiden: E. J. Brill, 1974), pp. 145-54.
3. Cf. Irenaeus, *Against Heresies*, ed. A. Roberts and J. Donaldson,
vol. 1, *Ante-Nicene Fathers* (New York: Charles Scribner's Sons,
1925), I.xxix.
4. Cf. Irenaeus, *A. H.* I.xxix-xxx, for the doctrines of the Sethians and the Barbeloites.

documents is one according to their religious content:
non-Christian or Christian.[5] The non-Christian texts
can be subdivided into two kinds: documents which are
acquainted with the Old Testament or other Jewish
themes, and those which represent philosophical or
other ideas apart from Jewish motifs. An example of
the first is the *Apocalypse of Adam* (V.5) where the
prime characters are Adam and his son, Seth. An example
of the second is *Eugnostos the Blessed* (III.3; V.1) in
which the philosophical and religious content is not
recognizably Jewish.

The Christian documents can also be divided into
two groups: texts which were originally composed as
Christian, and texts which were "Christianized" by the
addition of new material. The *Gospel of Truth* (I.3;
XII.2) appears to have been authored by a Christian.
The *Sophia of Jesus Christ* (III.4; BG.3) is a clear
example of the second type, being a Christian update of
the pagan document, *Eugnostos the Blessed*. These two
documents are found adjacent to one another in codex
three. The *Sophia of Jesus Christ* is a Christian revelatory discourse formed by the addition of a frame narrative in which the resurrected Savior appears and
answers the disciples' questions with paragraphs drawn
from the letter of *Eugnostos the Blessed*. In this sense
Eugnostos may be classified as a pre-Christian document, although it does not necessarily originate in
pre-Christian times.

Hypothesis and Methodology

The documents to be compared in the following
chapters have been chosen primarily on the basis of the
classification "non-Christian" and "Christian." The
Apocalypse of Adam, a non-Christian Jewish text, is
compared with the *Exegesis on the Soul*, a Christian
tractate. *Eugnostos the Blessed*, a non-Christian
philosophical epistle is compared with its Christian
counterpart, the *Sophia of Jesus Christ*; the predominantly non-Christian *On the Origin of the World* is
compared with a similar Christian tractate, the
Hypostasis of the Archons. Finally, the non-Christian

---

5. See Werner Foerster, ed., *Die Gnosis*, Zürich: Artemis Verlag,
vol. 1 (1969), vol. 2 (1971); English translation, *Gnosis*, edited
by R. McL. Wilson, Oxford: Clarendon Press, vol. 1 (1972), vol. 2
(1974), 2:7-8.

aretalogy, *The Thunder*, is contrasted with the Christian homily, the *Gospel of Truth*. The objective in the analysis is twofold: first, to accentuate the feminine motifs; second, to draw conclusions regarding the relative status of the feminine motifs as exemplified in the two types of documents.

In all of the documents, we raise questions about "Sophia" (wisdom). In some texts Sophia appears as an hypostatized entity; in others as a mythological goddess; while in still others she is the archetype of the soul in need of redemption. Is the difference in the interpretation of Sophia to be accounted for on the basis of Christianization? In the documents in which Sophia is a personage within Jewish or gnostic myth, she is not a tragic figure in need of male redemption; rather, the fallen Sophia appears to be a specifically Christian soteriological motif.

In the non-Christian *Apocalypse of Adam*, Sophia is personified as an attribute of the eternal god (V.85. 16). Those who know the "words" of Sophia belong to the kingless generation of Adam's son, Seth. As such, Sophia is a salvific figure - her words save. In the *Exegesis on the Soul*, on the other hand, the soul is the subject of a discourse which appears to be based upon the myth of a fallen and repentant Sophia. The account boldly portrays the soul as a fallen woman. So long as she is with the Father she is virginal and bisexual, but when she falls into a body, she loses her virginity to faithless adulterers. Afterwards, she repents and calls upon the Father for help, whereupon he pities her and turns her sexual organs, exposed like male genitals, back to the inside. She receives her consort, her true bridegroom, and produces good children. In this Christian document, the salvific agent is male - his seed saves. The fallen syzygial nature of the soul, as expressed in this document, appears to be a result of the Christianization of an older Sophia myth.

In the *Letter of Eugnostos*, Sophia is presented as the syzygy of the Immortal Man (III.76.23-77.6) or of the Son of Man (III.81.21-33). In fact, it appears in this document that each heavenly aeon possesses a feminine partner, Sophia by name, and that the universe is an orderly series of bisexual creations. The pattern is significantly altered in the *Sophia of Jesus Christ*, where Sophia is found to be in rebellion against the "Father of the universe" (III.114.14-20), and her syzygy, the Christian Savior, is sent to be a cure for her fault and that of her children. The syzygial idea of the non-Christian document, *Eugnostos*, is picked up by the author of the *Sophia of Jesus Christ*, but now the feminine element is inferior and in need of "the breath of the great light of the male" (BG 120.4-5).

A more mythological figure of Sophia appears in *On the Origin of the World*. Here, she is a savior figure, personified as being at war with the archigenetor, Ialdabaoth. Her captain in the struggle is the Immortal Man, through whom she will destroy the archigenetor and his powers of evil. The Immortal Man is not presented as Jesus Christ, but seems to be the "Primal Man," a representative of humanity, by whom the reign of Sophia over the archons of fate is to be established. The myth of the destruction of the archons through gnosis given by Sophia is related to the Genesis account of the eating of the forbidden fruit. The non-normative hermeneutic suggests that by eating of the tree of gnosis, forbidden by the archigenetor, Adam and Eve become spiritually enlightened. Awakened to the deceitful character of the archigenetor, the first man disdains the pomp of the archons and renders praise to Sophia. Wisdom overcomes folly through the agency of the Immortal Man in this basically non-Christian document.

The *Hypostasis of the Archons*, Christian in outlook, builds upon the mythology of *On the Origin of the World* but varies it with regard to Sophia. The name "Sophia" is less frequent. Sometimes, it is disguised by codewords such as "authenticity" or "imperishability." Pistis Sophia is linked to the "mother of the abyss" (87.7) and is accused of accomplishing a work "without her partner" (94.7). Her work includes the foolish Samael (Ialdabaoth).

The report of Hippolytus concerning the Christian-gnostic doctrine of Valentinus records that Valentinus plagiarized from the Pythagorean philosophy with regard to the Monad, styling him "the Father of the All."[6] The Pythagoreans addressed the Mother, not the Father, as "the great soul of the world who gives birth, preserves, and renews. . . , the divine Goddess who bears along all souls in her mantle of light."[7]

---

6. Hippolytus, *The Refutation of All Heresies*, ed. A. Roberts and J. Donaldson, vol. 5, *Ante-Nicene Fathers* (New York: The Christian Literature Company, 1896), VI.xxiv.
7. The Pythagorean prayer is quoted in Eduoard Schuré, *The Great*

Hippolytus further reports the tenet of the duad to be the foundation of the Valentinian system of the emanation of aeons, and submits that in the Valentinian system, the youngest of the aeons, Sophia, wished to imitate the Father in producing offspring without copulation:

> She (Sophia) wished to emulate the Father and to produce of herself without a marital partner, that she might achieve a work in no way inferior to (that of) the Father.[8]

This Christianized erring Sophia, twenty-eighth and last of the aeons, appears to be a remythologization as well as a devaluation of the creative female principle, the universal goddess of the Hellenistic world.

From the report of Hippolytus one may infer that Valentinus knew the interpretation of Sophia as the agent of God's creative energy, the bridge between limited and unlimited existence. Valentinus taught, however, that Sophia had sought to surpass that role, and that her hybris in creating without a partner resulted in an abortive image of herself. Furthermore, Valentinus taught that for the restoration of the masculine form of the repentant Sophia as well as for the destruction of Ialdabaoth, the Father ordered the production of the aeon, Christ/Holy Spirit, thus completing the thirty aeons.[9] Here, the motif of the faulty Sophia is integrated within a Christian soteriology.

Tertullian relates that Valentinus built his system upon a previous one: "He found the seed of an older doctrine."[10] Probably the older gnostic system was one in which Sophia and the Immortal Man worked together for the overthrow of the destructive powers of fate.

Initiates, trans. by Fred Rothwell, vol. 2 (New York: McKay,1913), p. 92. The author states on p. 156: "Nobody can deny that Hellenistic civilization showed the highest respect for the feminine principle. The Great Mother and the other aspects of the Goddess received far more devotion and worship than Zeus - even as the Virgin Mother does in Catholic lands today. Over the city, Athena presided. The finest things of life were personified as Graces, Muses, Justice, Wisdom, Peace - all feminine. No other people has paid a higher tribute to the feminine principle."
8. Hippolytus, *Ref*. VI.xxv.
9. Hippolytus, *Ref*. VI.xxv, xxvi; cf. *ANF* V, p.86, n. 7.
10. Tertullian, *Adv. Valent*. 4, quoted in Foerster, *Gnosis*, 2:122.

The *Hypostasis of the Archons* with its stress upon Sophia's faulty creation, "alone without her partner" (94.7), and its high regard for the "will of the Father" (87.22; 88.11; 96.12), seems to represent a Christian reinterpretation of an earlier Sophia mythology. The positioning of the Son "over all and through all for ever and ever" (97.19-20) effectively replaces the Pistis Sophia of mythological gnosticism. These points are considered more fully in chapter four where the feminine motifs of *On the Origin of the World* are compared with those of the *Hypostasis of the Archons*.

In both *The Thunder* and the *Gospel of Truth*, the term "Sophia" occurs only once, but the contrast is remarkable. *The Thunder* seems to identify Sophia with an unnamed goddess, a deity whose pantheistic nature includes feminine and masculine characteristics - "I am the bride and the bridegroom" (13.27-29), and opposites in tension - "I am senseless and I am wise" (15.29-30). This deity is mythologically portrayed and probably stems from the goddess Barbelo. In Isis-like self-proclamation she says, "I am the Sophia of the Greeks and the Gnosis of the barbarians" (16.3-5).

By contrast, in the *Gospel of Truth*, Sophia is less personal: "His (the Father's) 'sophia' contemplates the Word, his teaching utters it" (23.18-21). In this Christian document one finds neither the great Sophia who overcomes the archons nor the fallen Sophia whose parthenogenic creation seems to necessitate a Christian savior. Nevertheless, the myth of an upper and a lower Sophia may still be seen lingering in the author's poetic presentation of Jesus Christ as the wisdom of the Father, and ΠΛΑΝΗ as personified error.[11] We quote here but one of the several passages which seem to equate error with the fallen Sophia. The author is reporting what happened when the Word (knowledge) came.

All the spaces were shaken and disturbed because they had no order nor stability. Error (ΠΛΑΝΗ) was upset not knowing what to do; she was grieved, in mourning, afflicting herself because she knew nothing. When knowledge drew near her - this is the downfall of her and all her emanations - error (ΠΛΑΝΗ) became empty, having nothing within her (26.15-27).

---

11. Contrast the wisdom of Christ in the *Gospel of Truth* I.19. 10-27 with the folly of personified error at I.26.15-27.

The last two documents, then, have been selected as beginning and end points in the comparison of Sophia motifs. From being identified mythologically in *The Thunder* with everything, male and female, good and evil, Sophia is reduced to two entities in the *Gospel of Truth*. She can be identified with Jesus Christ, the saving wisdom of the Christian faith, or she can be made the equivalent of error (ΠΛΑΝΗ), a fantastic distortion of Sophia which will vanish when the Father is revealed through his Son.

This summary of Sophia motifs appearing in four pairs of related documents should give the reader an idea of the method employed to establish the hypothesis that defeminization accompanied the Christianization of some of the gnostic texts.

Non-Christian and Christian Feminine Motifs

Besides the Sophia motif, there are a number of other feminine themes which appear to be treated pejoratively in the Christian gnostic texts. In general, these relate to interpretations of creation and to soteriology.

In the non-Christian tractate, the *Apocalypse of Adam*, the heavenly Eve, probably a disguised Sophia, teaches her partner "a word of knowledge (gnosis) of the eternal God" (V.64.12-13). The saving entity in the salvation plan is the feminine word of gnosis which is passed on to the Sethian generation, the earthly bearers of heavenly wisdom. The *Apocalypse of Adam* does not seem to know the distinction between spirit and soul which became an underlying assumption for the salvation scheme of Christian gnosticism.

In the Christian document, the *Exegesis on the Soul*, the Genesis 2.24 statement, "they will become a single flesh," is interpreted in such a way that the woman, apparently Eve, receives blame for going astray from the man. The quotation is used to substantiate the author's presentation of the soul as a feminine entity (ψυχη) which should repent. When she prays to the Father, he sends the bridegroom to the bridal chamber and in mystic sexual union the soul and her masculine counterpart again "become a single life" (II.132.35). The saving aspect of the soul is presented as masculine.

Genesis 3.16, "for the master of the woman is her

8

husband" (II.133.10), is quoted to underline the fallen condition of the soul and the salvific function of the male from whom she has strayed. The sexual imagery is emphatic: "This marriage has brought them back together again and the soul has been joined to her true love, her real master" (II.133.6-9). From him she receives "the seed that is the life-giving Spirit, so that by him she bears good children" (II.134.1-2). The distinction between soul and spirit is metaphorically presented as a split between the first man and woman, and the woman is made responsible for both the fall and repentance. Not feminine gnosis, but masculine seed, saves.

In chapter three we examine a pagan letter and a Christian revelatory dialog - two documents related on a literary level. The Christianized dialog copies from the *Letter of Eugnostos* for the major portion of the answers to questions raised by certain of the Savior's disciples. In the material which is common to both documents, one finds the idea of salvation by gnosis within a scheme which is not sexual. The gnostics have their place of repose in the "foreknowledge of the Unbegotten" (III.73.15). In the salvation scheme of the unique material of the *Sophia of Jesus Christ*, however, one sees again the distinction between soul and spirit. Sophia is the symbol of the soul and she is saved by conjunction with her spiritual male form, Jesus Christ. Even the title of the document probably reflects this idea, if we take the two phrases as personifications and understand "of" to mean "belonging to": the Sophia "belonging to" Jesus Christ.

Here, too, the myth of the arrogant demiurge, Ialdabaoth, appears. He is accused of imprisoning the light-drops of Sophia. From him the Christian Savior wrests the particles of Sophia "so that the masculine [multitude] may be completed" (III.118.6-7). The salvation plan is similar to that of the Christian tractate, the *Exegesis on the Soul*.

Both documents discussed in chapter four appear to contain some Christian elements. *On the Origin of the World* is basically, however, non-Christian and syncretistic, with the Christian elements found only at its beginning and ending. Within its complex middle portions, it presents the myth of Pistis Sophia making use of an Immortal Light-man to overcome the arrogant Ialdabaoth who claims to be the only god. There is no suggestion that the Light-man is the unique Savior, Jesus Christ. In the ending, however, one finds a type of

9

soteriology which closely resembles that of the Christian documents, the *Exegesis on the Soul*, and the *Sophia of Jesus Christ*. This scheme appears to be a Christian reinterpretation. Here one finds "the immortal Father" (II.124.5) and the "blessed little guileless spirits" (II.124.10) who belong to a fourth race, kingless and perfect, which is above all other races of mankind. Through these spirits, the "fault of the woman" which appears in the author's cosmology and soteriology (II. 99.30; 124.6) is to be overcome.

We endeavor by literary analysis to show that the extremities of *On the Origin of the World* are the work of the final author. His reworking of the gnostic myth subordinates Sophia by considering her and her progeny to be psychic and in need of the spiritual logos (masculine) for their salvation.

The *Hypostasis of the Archons* is also a composite document. We conclude that parts of it are dependent upon a Coptic copy of *On the Origin of the World* and that the *Hypostasis of the Archons* contains a patriarchalized and defeminized tradition derived from *On the Origin of the World*.

The two tractates discussed in chapter five are not related in any direct literary manner. *The Thunder* is a feminist document which by its form and content must have been associated with Barbelo, a feminine deity known from other documents of the Nag Hammadi corpus. It is of particular interest not only for its frequent use of "I am" affirmations, similar to those of Isis inscriptions, but also for its initial section which is linked in a literary tradition to *On the Origin of the World* and the *Hypostasis of the Archons*. In the latter documents certain expressions of the unnamed goddess of *The Thunder* are presented as those of a divine Eve: "Therefore it is said of her that she said, 'I am a portion of my Mother, and I am the Mother. . . .'" (II.114. 6-9). A similar allusion is made to the same "Song of the Woman" in the *Hypostasis of the Archons* (II.89.14-17).

Syncretism on another level is noticeable in the ending of *The Thunder*. Here, a Father God, contextually different from the creator god, but echoing his words, "I am he who alone exists" (VI.21.18-19), is found. This monotheistic boaster is presented as supreme while the goddess of the major portion of the tractate is now presented as the embodiment of sin, passion, and

10

temporary pleasure.

By comparison with the mythological nature of the tractates just mentioned, the style and content of the *Gospel of Truth* is more amenable to modern sensibilities. Some of the imagery is clearly taken from the New Testament. On the other hand, there is no ready explanation for much of the imagery unless one knows the proto-gnostic myth of Pistis Sophia, Ialdabaoth, and the Light-man. We believe, with Jonas, that the *Gospel of Truth*, while avoiding crude anthropomorphisms, is nevertheless dependent upon mythology for its imagery and is not understandable without some previous knowledge of gnostic myth.

Some sections of the *Gospel of Truth* indicate that the author's conception of the soul was feminine. The author seems to be involved in a type of poetic "remythologization" in which he associates the wisdom goddess with a deficiency to be filled by the Christian Savior.

Our comparison of four sets of Nag Hammadi tractates with regard to their uses of feminine imagery strives to give evidence of a trend toward defeminization of the mythology of creation and redemption in Christian gnostic works in contrast to the more overt feminine constituents of the non-Christian gnostic works.

Feminine Motifs and Gnosticism

The study of the feminine motifs in the Nag Hammadi documents is important for an understanding of the religious phenomenon called gnosticism. The documents provide an abundance of original material from the classical period of the growth of these so-called heresies and reveal the gnostics' own attitudes toward feminine religious motifs. The polemical-minded church fathers wanted their readers to believe that gnosticism developed as a pollution of Christian doctrine, that Simon Magus, whose name is mentioned in the New Testament, was its first proponent, and that Simon as well as his followers, were determined to "draw away the minds of the inexperienced and take them captive."[12] The study of the gnostics' own documents gives the scholar a chance to test the accuracy of the heresiolo-

---

12. Irenaeus, Preface to *A.H.*

gists' reports and to separate gnostic ideas from the polemics of the fathers.

This study also gives occasion to verify the definitions of gnosticism made by modern writers. Until the turn of the twentieth century, scholars generally viewed gnosticism as a Christian heresy.[13] One of the more confident advocates of this position today is Simone Pétrement who views even the non-Christian forms of gnosticism as post-Christian.[14] Most modern scholars, however, having taken into account the twentieth century discoveries, are apt to consider gnosticism as a religion in its own right.[15] Following the view first proposed by Anz in 1897, this group maintains that gnosticism predated Christianity.[16] Few scholars any longer doubt that certain so-called gnostic motifs developed prior to Christianity, but the debate continues regarding gnosticism as a distinct religion.[17]

Hippolytus, in the second century of the Christian era, reports that gnosticism took its beginning "from the wisdom of the Greeks, from the conclusions of those who have formed systems of philosophy, and from would-be mysteries and the vagaries of astrologers."[18] This potpourri of origins seems to fit the evidence from Nag Hammadi and to lead to the description of gnosticism as

---

13. Among scholars who have viewed gnosticism as a Christian heresy are A. Harnack, H. Leisegang, F. C. Burkitt, C. Schmidt, J. Munck, and A. D. Nock.
14. Simone Pétrement, "Le Colloque de Messine et le problème du gnosticisme," *Revue de Métaphysique et de Morale 72* (1967), pp. 344-73.
15. The view that gnosticism is a religion in its own right is expounded by Hans Jonas in the first edition (1934) of *Gnosis und spätantiker Geist*, vol. 1 (Göttingen: Vandenhoeck and Ruprecht, 3rd ed., 1964).
16. The theory of a pre-Christian origin for gnosticism and the situation of scholarship regarding it is well summarized by Edwin Yamauchi, *Pre-Christian Gnosticism* (Grand Rapids: Wm. B. Eerdmans, 1963) pp. 21-28.
17. An enlightening study of the debate regarding the origins of gnosticism is given in chapter 8 of *The Bible in Modern Scholarship*, ed. J. Philip Hyatt (New York: Abingdon Press, 1965), pp. 252-93, in which the paper of Gilles Quispel, "Gnosticism and the New Testament," read at the 100th meeting of the Society of Biblical Literature, Dec. 29-30, 1964, is responded to by Robert McL. Wilson and Hans Jonas.
18. Hippolytus, *Ref.* I, Preface.

a movement in the interpretation of vital motifs rather
than as a religion per se. "Nowhere do we find a pure
form of gnosticism, always it is built on earlier, pre-
existing religions or on their traditions."[19]

That many of the basic motifs are Judaic in origin
is becoming increasingly clear as the Nag Hammadi documents are researched. James M. Robinson noted this:

> This persistent trend in the scholarship of the
> twentieth century has been carried one step
> further by the Coptic gnostic codices from near
> Nag Hammadi, which reflect in some of their trac-
> tates, such as the *Apocalypse of Adam* and the
> *Paraphrase of Shem*, what seems to be non-Chris-
> tian gnosticism, a gnostic or semignostic Juda-
> ism, in some cases localized in the Jordan region
> and interacting with baptismal movements.[20]

The term "gnosticism", or any close equivalent, lacks
within the Nag Hammadi texts. The word derives from the
Greek γινωσκω, which means "I know". The fathers of the
church and Plotinus, writing against the sects whose
members they called "Gnostics", maintained that the members claimed for themselves a secret "knowledge" which
made them superior to others.

The content of the secret "gnosis", according to one
Valentinian formulation, is self-knowledge with regard
to the questions: "Who were we, who have we become;
where were we, where have we been cast: whither do we
hasten, from what are we freed; what is birth, what rebirth."[21] Part of this formula is found within the *Gospel of Truth* in a section which seems to describe a
gnostic in terms of obedience to God:

> Having knowledge he does the will of Him who
> called him; he wishes to please him; he receives
> rest. Each one's name becomes his own. He who
> thus shall know understands whence he came and
> whither he goes (I.22.9-15).

---

19. H. J. W. Drijvers, "The Origins of Gnosticism as a Religious
and Historical Problem," *Nederlands Theologisch Tijdschrift* 22
(1968), p. 331, as quoted in E. Yamauchi, p. 185.
20. James M. Robinson and H. Koester, *Trajectories through
Early Christianity* (Philadelphia: Fortress Press, 1971), p. 264.
Cf. also James M. Robinson, "The Coptic Gnostic Library Today,"
New Testament Studies 14 (1968), pp. 356-401.
21. Clement of Alexandria, *Excerpta e Theodoto*, I.78.2.

The knowledge of God, as manifested through his me-
diator, Jesus Christ, seems to be constitutive of gnosticism in Christian texts. On the other hand, the secret gnosis in non-Christian texts often pertains to a
feminine deity, called Sophia, who links created and
noncreated being. The gnostic condition depends upon a
pneumatic relationship with her who is at once the content of knowledge and the agent by which her worshipper
attains gnosis.

Is there any evidence in pre-Christian writings to
suggest that the followers of Sophia considered themselves more spiritual than other men and worthy of the
term "gnostic"? In an article in the *Harvard Theological Review*, R. Horsley pursued the pertinence of
Philonic literature as a possible background for the
distinctions of spiritual status among the Corinthians,
viz., "pneumatics" and "psychics".[22] He discovers in
Philo traces of a concept of two grades of humanity
among the people who reverenced Sophia. Horsley tries
to show that the language of religious status in both
Philo and in Paul's first letter to the Corinthians
involves Sophia, and concludes that the "pneumatics" of
I Corinthians are the high-born children of Sophia.
According to Horsley, it was Paul who made the identification of Sophia with Christ.

M. Jack Suggs, approaching the subject of Sophia
through the hypothetical "Q" document, concluded that
Matthew was responsible for those innovations which
made Jesus no longer the last and greatest of Wisdom's
children, but Sophia herself.

> For Q, Wisdom sends forth her prophets - from
> the first generation to this generation which
> has rejected Jesus and John. However, it would
> not greatly overstate the case to say that *for
> Matthew* Wisdom has "become flesh and dwelled
> among us" (John 1:14).[23]

In searching for the origins of gnosticism, it is
necessary to remember that speculation on Sophia is very
much older than Pauline or Matthean Christology.[24]

---

22. Richard A. Horsley, "Pneumatikos vs. Psychikos, Distinctions
of Spiritual Status Among the Corinthians," *Harvard Theological
Review* 69:3-4 (1976), pp. 269-88. See especially p. 284, n. 34.
23. M. Jack Suggs, *Wisdom, Christology, and Law in Matthew's
Gospel* (Cambridge: Harvard University Press, 1970), p. 57.
24. The source of the feminine imagery for Sophia has to be sought

When Philo writes of man's becoming divine by union
with Sophia, he is not to be interpreted as presenting
a new theological development but a trend in sophialogy
which was forming already before the book of Proverbs
was written. In Proverbs 1-9 Sophia speaks as a Wisdom teacher and likens herself to a gushing spring in
causing her spirit to overflow upon those who need her
instruction. The Sophia myth was worked out different-
ly in various gnostic circles. Sophia is sometimes a
revealer, but sometimes she is also represented as a
fallen being who needs redemption from the prison of
the world. She becomes the model for the soul whose
fate is like unto hers. Knowledge of Sophia's fall,
repentance, and redemption helps the soul to disengage
herself from the world and awaken to her true selfhood
so that even as a fallen and redeemed figure Sophia may
have a soteriological function. Those who belong to her
share her understanding of humility and exaltation.

Besides the Sophia motif and its correlatives, there
are numerous other feminine motifs which, when considered together, suggest that a kind of feminist theology
pervades the Nag Hammadi texts. For convenience these
motifs may be summarized under seven topics: the Godhead, Creation, Fall and Redemption, Incarnation,
Church, Eschaton, and Discipleship.

The godhead is sometimes represented by the mother
figure alone, as in the Sophia myth of *On the Origin of*

---

in the interaction between Judaism and pagan goddess cults asso-
ciated with wisdom. The thesis of Hans G. Conzelmann in "Die
Mutter der Weisheit," in *Zeit und Geschichte*, pp. 225-34, ed.
Erich Dinkler (Tübingen, 1964), and available in English in *The
Future of Our Religious Past*, ed. James M. Robinson (New York:
Harper & Row, 1971), that Isis is the source of the Jewish Sophia,
is given support by reason of the feminine aretalogies, styled
like Isis inscriptions, in Jewish-oriented Nag Hammadi documents.
The analysis of hypostatizations of divine attributes in the
ancient Near East by Helmer Ringgren, *Word and Wisdom* (Lund: H.
Ohlssons, 1947) suggests caution in attributing the personified
wisdom's background to any one ancient goddess, but Burton L. Mack,
Logos und Sophia (Göttingen: Vandenhoeck & Ruprecht, 1973), and J.
Bergman, "Ich bin Isis: Studien zum memphitischen Hintergrund der
griechischen Isisaretalogien," *Acta Universitatis Upsaliensis,
Historia Religionum* 3 (1968), support the probability of Isis
mythology as source of the imagery both for the figure of Sophia
and the figure of the kingly child of Sophia in the Jewish wisdom
tradition.

the World, and sometimes in conjunction with the father god, viz., the "Metropator" in the *Apocryphon of John*. The *Gospel of Philip* relates that the Christians, by reason of their conversion, accepted a father God: "When we were Hebrews we were orphans and had only our mother, but when we became Christians we had both father and mother" (II.52.21-24).

Creation is the work of Sophia in many Nag Hammadi documents. The non-Christian tractate, *Eugnostos the Blessed*, calls Sophia ΠΑΝΓΕΝΕΤΙΡΑ, "creatrix of the universe" (III.82.5). At Nag Hammadi, the Genesis story of creation is often exegeted in a non-normative manner. In *On the Origin of the World*, Eve, daughter of Sophia, exists before Adam and gives him life. She says to him: "Adam, live! Rise up upon the earth!" (II.116.2-3). Adam rises and says to her: "You will be called 'Mother of the Living' because you are the one who gave me life" (116.6-8).

As for the fall and redemption, the gnostic radical solution is intriguing. Eve did not sin. She was taught gnosis by the serpent, which was itself a pneumatic, feminine creature called "the Instructor(ess)" (*Hyp. Arch.* 89.31-32; 90.11). The feminist theology does not deny that a curse followed upon the first parents' disobedience to the great archon, but the remedy is feminine. The archon is overcome by the daughter of Pistis Sophia, according to the *Hypostasis of the Archons*:

> And Zoe, the daughter of Pistis Sophia, cried out and said to him, "You are wrong, Saklas," the interpretation of which is Ialdabaoth. She breathed into his face, and her breath became for her a flaming angel; and that angel bound Ialdabaoth; he cast him down to Tartaros, at the bottom of the Abyss (95.5-13).

A second feminine redeemer appears in the *Hypostasis of the Archons* in the person of Norea. The gnostics were not so foolish as to leave unanswered the question as to where Adam's sons found their wives. Eve bears a daughter, apparently named Norea. She is a soteriological figure called a "saving virgin (ΠΑΡΘΕΝΟC ΝΒΟΗΘΕΙΑ) for generations of generations of mankind" as well as "the virgin whom no power has defiled" (91.35-92.3).

The incarnation includes a feminine personage accord-to a marriage mystery set forth in the *Gospel of Philip*:

"If I may utter a mystery, the Father of the All united with the virgin who came down" (71.3-5). Here it is the feminine figure who descends in order to reveal the mystery of the bridal chamber. R. McL. Wilson suggests in his commentary on the *Gospel of Philip* that the author possibly thought of Mary as descending for the purpose of union with the supreme god in view of Jesus' conception.[25] This accords with Irenaeus' report of the doctrine of the Ophites and Sethians:

> But Jesus, inasmuch as he was begotten of the Virgin through the agency of God, was wiser, purer and more righteous than all other men. Christ united to Sophia descended into him, and thus Jesus Christ was produced.[26]

The church is a feminine symbol in orthodox Christianity, but the Nag Hammadi document, *On the Origin of the World*, places this entity distinctly in the eighth or feminine sphere and does so in a context quite primitive. The church, with the cherubim and the seraphim, is one of Sabaoth's creations and is modeled after "the church of the eighth sphere" (105.22-23). *Eugnostos the Blessed* and the parallel passage in the *Sophia of Jesus Christ*, name "Church" as the male part of the heavenly androgyne, Church/Life, which is the model for the church below (*Eug.* III.87.4-5; *SJC* III.111.6-8).

The eschaton is symbolized in some Nag Hammadi documents as the abolishing of sexism. The *Gospel of Thomas*, logion 22, reads:

> Whenever you make the two one, and when you make the inside as the outside, and the outside as the inside, and the side above as the side below, so that you make the male and the female into that identical one, so that the male will not act the male and the female will not act the female . . . then you shall enter the [kingdom] (37.25-35).

The *Gospel of Philip* expresses the same idea in referring to the separation of the first parents:

> When Eve was still in Adam death did not exist. When she was separated from him death came into

---

25. Robert McL. Wilson, *The Gospel of Philip* (New York: Harper & Row, 1962), p. 146.
26. Irenaeus, *A.H.*, I.xxx.12.

being. If he again becomes complete and attains
his former self, death will be no more (68.22-26).

The *Gospel of Philip* also praises Christ as one who
came to repair the division through the sacrament of
the bridal chamber which reunites the separated man and
woman:

> If the woman had not separated from the man, she
> would not die with the man. His separation be-
> came the beginning of death. Because of this,
> Christ came to set aright the separation which
> was from the beginning and again unite the two,
> and to give life to those who died as a result
> of the separation and unite them. But the wom-
> an is united to her husband within the bridal
> chamber. Indeed those who have been united in
> the bridal chamber will no longer be separated.
> Thus Eve was separated from Adam because she
> was never united with him in the bridal chamber
> (70.9-22).

Although the eschaton may be described in terms of
human marriage, the author of the *Gospel of Philip*
knows that the form of union in the hereafter is not
properly portrayed with the marriage metaphor: "Whereas
in this world the union is one of husband and wife - a
case of strength and weakness - in the aeon the form of
the union is different, although we refer to them by
these names" (76.6-9).

Discipleship in the Nag Hammadi documents is not the
privilege of men only. In the *Sophia of Jesus Christ*,
there are seven women students who are said to have followed Jesus along with the twelve disciples. "After he
had been raised up from the dead, his twelve disciples
and seven women were studying (ΜΑΘΗΤΕΥΕ) with him . . ."
(III.90.14-18). Reference is made in the *Gospel of
Philip* to three holy women who were Jesus' constant
companions:

> There were three who always walked with the Lord:
> Mary his mother, and her (sic) sister, and Magda-
> lene, the one who was called his consort. For
> Mary is his sister, and she is his mother, and
> she is his twin (59.6-11).

The last saying in the *Gospel of Thomas* is often explained incorrectly as saying that only men are the
legitimate disciples of Jesus:

Simon Peter said to them, "Let Mary depart from among us, because women are not worthy of the Life." Jesus said, "Behold, I myself shall guide her so that I may make a man of her, so that she too may become a living spirit like unto you men. For every woman who will make a man of herself shall enter the kingdom of heaven" (51.18-26).

This saying is to be viewed in the context of a school-debate, where the antifeminine remark of Peter is corrected by Jesus. Mary is not to leave the discipleship on account of her being a woman. Jesus himself will "make a man of her." The Coptic probably reflects the Greek ανδριζω, which means "make brave and strong," a word commonly used in early Christian paraenesis.[27]

This summary should serve to show that feminine imagery permeates much of Nag Hammadi literature and is not limited to the documents discussed in the following chapters. The conclusions drawn from the study of these eight documents need to be tested and examined in detail in the remainder of the Nag Hammadi collection.

---

27. For some similar correctable sayings of Peter in the synoptic gospels, cf. Mt. 16:22; 17:4; 18:21; Lk. 8:45; and 22.33.

CHAPTER TWO

FEMININE MOTIFS IN THE APOCALYPSE OF ADAM

AND IN THE EXEGESIS ON THE SOUL

The *Apocalypse of Adam* and the *Exegesis on the Soul* represent two completely different approaches to the Judaic tradition. The *Apocalypse of Adam* takes a thoroughly radical, "gnostic", approach to Genesis, equating the creator God with the arrogant archigenetor, and boldly reinterpreting the Genesis stories with new meanings. All of this is done with a minimum of Christian reference, so that this document shows itself to be one of the purest examples of Jewish-oriented gnosticism at Nag Hammadi. Feminine motifs, when they occur, are sympathetically treated.

The *Exegesis on the Soul*, on the other hand, is a conventional Christian homily, which makes use of Old Testament material in a familiar way. Texts from various Old Testament books are produced as "proof texts" to buttress the argument, the main point of which is that the soul is a feminine entity, an inferior substance standing in need of masculine "spirit" for her salvation.

The first document is representative of pre-Christian exegesis of Genesis by marginal sects of Judaea and Samaria. The second document illustrates a developed Christian gnosticism, still rooted in Judaism, but with an antifeminist bias that makes use of the Old Testament to "prove" male superiority. In it the Old Testament is used to show that "the master of the woman is her husband" (II.133.9-10), and the first woman "led man astray" (133.5).

Introduction to the Apocalypse of Adam (V.5)

The *Apocalypse of Adam*, to his son Seth, is the

21

fifth tractate in codex five of the Nag Hammadi library.[1] Although there is much apocalyptic literature which pertains to both Adam and Seth, this twenty-two page Coptic document was unknown until its discovery at Nag Hammadi in 1945.[2] Its apocalyptic themes are esoteric, and the fragmentary nature of the last three or four lines of each page adds to the difficulties of discerning the meaning of this strange revelation. Dating to the fourth century, A.D., the manuscript contains material which is undoubtedly much older. For our purposes the document may be divided into three sections, the middle one of which contains an excursus that appears to be only incidentally related to the apocalypse proper.

The Beginning (*V.64.5-67.14*). The author of the *Apocalypse of Adam* purports to present the dying words of the nine hundred year old Adam to his especially graced son, Seth.[3] A midrashic account based on Genesis, the apocalypse explains Adam's glorious state in paradise, his fall into the power of the archigenetor, and the origin of the Sethian race. Adam's revelation recalls the unity of spirit which once existed between himself and Eve in the aeon from which they came. More exalted than the god who formed them, they had been like the great eternal angels, but upon their fall from paradise on account of the wrath of the archigenetor, they were separated into two aeons. The separation caused the loss of glory and the lack of "first knowledge" (ΓΝWCΙC ΝϢΟΡΠ) of the God of truth.[4] This knowledge,

---

1. The tractate was first published by Alexander Böhlig and Pahor Labib, *Koptisch-gnostische Apokalypsen aus Codex V von Nag Hammadi im Koptischen Museum zu Alt-Kairo* (Halle-Wittenberg: Wissenschaftliche Zeitschrift der Martin-Luther-Universität, 1963), pp. 86-117.
2. The relationship of the *Apocalypse of Adam* to other apocryphal literature bearing Adam's name is not well defined, but even a cursory view of the Nag Hammadi corpus shows that Adam and Seth were important figures in gnostic thought.
3. According to the septuagint, Adam begot Seth at age 230 and lived thereafter for 700 years. According to *On the Origin of the World* (II.121.22-23), Adam lived 930 years, 70 of his allotted 1,000 being taken from him by the unrighteous archons. The seven-hundredth year of Seth (V.64.4) is the year of Adam's death, an appropriate time for the transfer of the revelation from Adam to Seth.
4. The term "first knowledge" occurs so frequently in texts related to the *Apocalypse of Adam*, that one may suppose it to be a gnostic

however, reentered the Sethian race by reason of the revelation which Adam gives to Seth. Adam himself received that revelation from three heavenly visitors who charged him to rise from the sleep of death and listen to "the words" concerning the Sethians. Although the creator god, whom Adam serves in fear and slavery, seeks to prevent the transfer of the revelatory words, they are, nevertheless, delivered to Seth before Adam's death.

The Apocalypse Proper (V.67.14 - 85.18). Adam reports to Seth the revelation of the three alien visitors concerning the destiny of Seth and his race. He foretells the persecutions which the Sethians will have to endure at the hands of the creator god. In the act of harassing them, the archigenetor, here called Saklas, will cause a flood with the intention of destroying all men except Noah and his family who are to be regarded as Saklas' friends. Adam relates that the plan will fail of its intended effect because angels will come to deliver the Sethians. When, after the flood, the gnostic generations will reappear on earth, Saklas will accuse Noah of bearing them against his express command, but Noah will confess that the gnostics have come about through the God of truth and through gnosis, not through any generative influence on his part.

Adam further relates that Saklas will give the earth to Noah who will divide it among his three sons, Ham, Japheth, and Shem. Noah will counsel his sons to serve god, the almighty Saklas, in fear and servitude. The Sethians, meantime, will be brought into a land where they will live with angels for six hundred years during which time four hundred thousand descendants of Ham and Japheth will abide with them sinlessly. Having been thwarted in his attempt to destroy the gnostics and their influence by means of the flood, Saklas will send a fire upon the earth, but again the gnostics will be rescued. An illuminator will come to deliver from death the gnostics among the descendants of Ham and Japheth, and, working signs and wonders in the name of Seth, he will shame the archontic powers who will be able only to punish his flesh.

According to Adam's revelation, a final conflict with

---

theologoumenon. Here, it seems to represent the gnosis first given by the heavenly Eve to Adam before Adam's separation from her. Cf. *Apocryphon of John*, BG 28.6,8; 29.13; 31.20; 34.19; 36.19; *Eugnostos* III.73.15; and the *Gospel of the Egyptians* III.42.10.

23

the powers of darkness will ensue during which a cloud of darkness will come upon mankind. Then the people will call blessed and immortal those who "have known God in a knowledge of truth" (83.12-14). The gnostics, because of their faithfulness to the unwritten word delivered by angelic beings, will bear unfailing fruit.

A long, poetic excursus apparently of independent origin from the rest of the document, stands within the revelation proper. It concerns an account of thirteen kingdoms each of which relates the origin of an illuminator. Each stanza ends with the refrain: "thus he came upon the water." The excursus is followed by a claim of "the kingless generation" (82.19-20) that its illuminator came from a great aeon causing a knowledge (ΓΝΩϹΙϹ) of the "undefiled of truth" (82.23-24) to come into being, so as to enlighten the whole aeon.

The Ending (85.19-31). The *Apocalypse of Adam* ends with a repetition of the claim that the revelation is that of Adam to Seth and is to be passed on to Seth's posterity. The apocalypse itself is then described as

> the holy baptism of those who know the eternal knowledge (ΓΝΩϹΙϹ) through those born of the word and the imperishable illuminators who came from the holy seed: Yesseus, [Maz]areus, [Yesse]-dekeus, [the Living] Water" (85.24-32).[5]

The title is appended, as is common practice in the Nag Hammadi documents.

Syncretism in the Apocalypse of Adam

The various motifs in the *Apocalypse of Adam* must be reckoned as a syncretistic blend. There are, however, no explicit references to Christianity. Böhlig claims that the text directs one to a pre-Christian presentation of a savior figure. He writes:

> The text is undoubtedly gnostic and also a Sethian writing. It must, however, strongly

---

5. See Alexander Böhlig, Frederik Wisse, and Pahor Labib, *Nag Hammadi Codices III,2 and IV,2: The Gospel of the Egyptians* (Leiden: E.J. Brill, 1974), p. 194, for a discussion of Yesseus, Mazareus, Yessedekeus. The words are probably a corruption in Greek of "Jesus of Nazareth, Jesus, the Righteous."

24

be doubted whether it has been created only by
Sethians in the strict sense; it points more-
over, to a pre-Christian origin out of Jewish-
Iranian Gnosticism.[6]

In reviewing Böhlig's edition, K. Rudolph drew attention to the non-Christian nature of the *Apocalypse of
Adam*:

> The importance of this document resides espe-
> cially in the fact that it is obviously a non-
> Christian, indeed, probably a pre-Christian
> product.[7]

J. M. Robinson argues that the *Apocalypse of Adam* and
the *Paraphrase of Shem* supply the necessary evidence to
support Bultmann's hypothesis of a pre-Christian gnostic
redeemer myth.[8] R. Kasser agrees that the *Apocalypse of
Adam* could derive from pre-Christian times. He writes:

> One finds here nothing, in effect, which re-
> calls Christianity, at least not directly or
> openly; so that this work, or one or the other
> of its principal components, could well go back
> to pre-Christian times or to some non-Christian
> (heterodox Jewish) milieu contemporary with the
> most obscure periods of primitive Christianity.[9]

G. MacRae suggests that should one start with the
premise that the author of the *Apocalypse of Adam* knew
the New Testament, he might be able to find traces of
Christianity, but considers it most unlikely that any
second-century Gnostic would have eliminated all traces
of Christ or other New Testament personages.[10]

On the other hand, E. Yamauchi, marshalling the views
of the above-mentioned scholars, attempts to refute them
by means of New Testament allusions which he considers

---

6. Alexander Böhlig, *Mysterion und Wahrheit* (Leiden: E. J. Brill,
1968), p. 149.
7. Review of Böhlig and Labib, "Koptisch-gnostische Apokalypsen aus
Codex V," by K. Rudolph in *Theologische Literaturzeitung* 90 (1965),
col. 361.
8. Robinson, *Trajectories*, p. 234, n. 4.
9. Rodolphe Kasser, "Bibliothèque gnostique V: *Apocalypse d'Adam*,"
Revue de Théologie et de Philosophie 16 (1967), pp. 316-317.
10. George W. MacRae, "The Coptic-Gnostic *Apocalypse of Adam*,"
Heythrop Journal 6 (1965), p. 32.

numerous and transparent. He makes use of reviews by
J. Daniélou, R. Haardt, A. Orbe, and H. Schenke which
conclude that the allusions to the Illuminator - the
working of signs and marvels, the opposition of the
powers who will not see him, the punishment of his
flesh, and the descent of the Holy Spirit upon him -
are references to Jesus Christ.[11] Yamauchi's argument
against the pre-Christian nature of the *Apocalypse of
Adam* concludes:

> ...Böhlig's far-reaching thesis that the
> *Apocalypse of Adam* by reason of Iranian and
> Mandaean parallels is a document of non-
> Christian and pre-Christian Gnosticism is
> simply a hypothesis which is built on too
> many precarious assumptions.[12]

Study of the *Apocalypse of Adam* can be aided by com-
paring it with the *Gospel of the Egyptians* with which
it has much in common. Two examples of commonality
suffice here - the names of the illuminator-saviors,
Micheu, Michar, and Mnesinous (V.84.5-6; cf.III.64.15-
16) and the phrase "Yesseus [Maz]areus [Yesse]dekeus"
(V.85.30-31; cf.III.64.10-11; 66.10). There is little
doubt that the *Gospel of the Egyptians* has been second-
arily Christianized, and it is very probable that these
names, which appear in the contexts of spells or man-
tras, could have been added to the end of an otherwise
non-Christian document to lend it a Christian character.
Only minor linguistic changes are needed to suggest the
names "Jesus, the righteous" and "Nazareth." This
apparent addition does not, however, change the basic
nature of the *Apocalypse of Adam*, a syncretistic document, in which the Jewish characteristics predominate.
Regarding these and the dating of the syncretism, G.
MacRae offers the following:

> The Redeemer myth of the *Apocalypse of Adam*
> grew out of late Jewish speculations that were
> fostered by the syncretistic atmosphere of the
> Near East around the time when Christianity
> made its appearance.[13]

Robinson takes particular note of the Jewish background evidenced in the "form" of the *Apocalypse of
Adam* which is like that of the *Testament of the Twelve*

---

11. Yamauchi, p. 110, n. 43.
12. Ibid., p. 115.
13. MacRae, "The Coptic Gnostic *Apocalypse of Adam*," p. 34.

Patriarchs, and in the frequent use of phrases descrip-
tive of "words of wisdom."[14] For example, Adam tells
Seth to listen to his *words* (64.3-6), specifies Eve's
role in teaching him a *word* of knowledge of the eternal
God (64.12-13), hears *words* from the three visiting
strangers (66.9-10), and delivers these same apocalyptic *words* to Seth. Noah's pronouncement to his sons
begins: "My sons, listen to my *words*" (72.18-19). The
saving, unwritten, angel-borne words are specifically
called "the *words* of imperishability and truth" (85.13-
14). The *Apocalypse of Adam* concludes with a section
which shows that "revelation" and "word" (ΛΟΓΟC) are
related concepts:

> These are the revelations which Adam showed
> forth to Seth his son. And his son taught
> them to his seed. This is the secret gnosis
> of Adam, which he gave to Seth, which is the
> holy baptism of those who know the eternal
> gnosis through those begotten of the *word*
> (ΛΟΓΟΓΕΝΗC) and the imperishable luminaries
> who came forth from the holy seed (85.19-29).

Continuing his form-critical analysis of the "logoi
sophōn" with reference to the *Apocalypse of Adam*,
Robinson comments: "Here those 'with wisdom,' called
'luminaries,' could well be a gnosticized and mytholo-
gized development of the concept of the sages as bearers
of the saving 'words.'"[15]

In the *Apocalypse of Adam*, the salvific words of wisdom, brought by Sethian illuminators, as well as the
foolish words of Saklas, delivered by Noah to his sons,
are set within narratives drawn from the Old Testament.
Besides the Jewish influences, there are Iranian and
Hellenistic motifs. Böhlig notes relationships to
Jubilees, the Mandaean Ginza, and the Manichaean Homilies.[16] Others find motifs in the *Apocalypse of Adam*
that go back to the Persian *Avesta* and to Zoroastrian-
ism.[17]

---

14. Robinson, *Trajectories*, p. 107.
15. Ibid., p. 108.
16. See Böhlig, *Koptisch-gnostische Apokalypsen aus Codex V*, pp.
86-95.
17. Cf. Andrew K. Helmbold, *The Nag Hammadi Gnostic Texts and the
Bible* (Grand Rapids: Baker Book House, 1967), p. 87 and references
there.

Within the genre of apocalyptic literature, the
Apocalypse of Adam represents an early stage of Jewish
and Christian gnostic literature. The Apocalypse could
be dated as early as the first or second century, A.D.
A. Helmbold summarizes its character:

> This Apocalypse seems to be a typically Sethian
> Gnostic production revealing some of the rela-
> tionship of ideas between the Great Gnostics,
> the Mandeans, and the Manichaeans. It shows
> the pregnostic Iranian, Jewish, and Hellenistic
> sources which are syncretized in Gnosticism.
> In the syncretism, gnosis (knowledge) stands
> forth as the means of salvation.[18]

Eve. The feminine motifs in the *Apocalypse of Adam*
center around three basic themes: creation, fall, and
redemption of mankind. These themes are treated within
the context of the myths of Genesis, albeit with a non-
normative hermeneutic in respect to the existential
questions for which, Clement of Alexandria reports,
gnosis promises answers: "Who were we? Who have we
become? Where were we? Where have we been cast?
Whither do we hasten? From what are we freed? What is
birth? What rebirth"?[19] These ultimate questions being
central to the *Apocalypse of Adam*, it is our concern to
note here the feminine motifs used in answering them.

To the first question, "Who are we?", Adam replies
in his own name and that of his partner that they are
beings of a more exalted nature than Saklas and his
powers. Their exaltation was due to Eve's spiritual
status, that is, to her "gnosis" of the true God. Eve
gave Adam a "word of knowledge" so that, united as a
syzygial pair, they were superior to the creator god.
Adam's praise of Seth's gnostic mother is related in
the Apocalypse:

> Listen to my words, my son Seth. When god had
> created me out of the earth along with Eve your
> mother, I went about with her in a glory which
> she had seen from the aeon from whom we had
> come forth. She taught me a word of knowledge
> (ΓΝWCΙC) of the eternal God. And we were like
> unto the mighty angels of eternity, for we
> were higher than the god who created us and

---

18. Ibid.
19. Cf. Clement of Alexandria, *Excerpta e Theodoto*, I.78.2.

the powers which were with him - those which we
knew nothing of (64.5-19).

The second question for which gnosis promises the
answer concerns the fall of mankind. To the question,
"Who have we become?", the *Apocalypse of Adam* states
bluntly: "We became two aeons" (64.23). This unnatural
state of division came about by reason of the rage of
the chief archon who found Adam and Eve more knowledgea-
ble than himself. He separated Adam from the bringer of
gnosis, the heavenly Eve. Gnosis left Adam and apparently returned to "the seed of some great aeons" (65.
4-5). Here, "the seed" probably refers to the heavenly
Sethians who are to bring the saving gnosis again to
the earth.

The blame for the separation of man from his gnostic
counterpart is placed squarely on the foolish god,
Saklas.

> Then god, the ruler of the aeons and the powers,
> divided us in his rage. Then we became two
> aeons. And that glory which was in our heart
> abandoned us, thy mother Eve and me - along with
> that first gnosis that blew within us (64.20-
> 28).

As distinct from the normative hermeneutic of the
story in Genesis in which Adam and Eve fall into sin by
reason of eating from the tree forbidden by God, the
Apocalypse of Adam considers the fall of mankind as a
separation of the man from her who *knew* better than he.
Man's syzygial relationship is sundered, male and female rent symbolically in two. The feminine principle
of gnosis, given by the heavenly Eve to Adam, left him
and returned to the upper spheres.

The third question for which gnosis supplies an
answer, "Where have we been cast?", is not so clearly
answered in the *Apocalypse of Adam* as it is in some
other gnostic documents. One may infer, however, that
the first parents are no longer in a paradisaic state
of knowledge when God withdraws from them and they act
in a non-gnostic manner. The *Apocalypse of Adam* relates
that they began to act like humans in serving the creator god and no longer like immortals in acknowledging
the eternal God. Adam reveals to Seth the change from
heavenly knowledge to earthly knowledge:

> After those days the eternal knowledge (ΓΝШCIC)
> of the God of truth withdrew from me and thy

mother Eve. From that time forth, we learned
about dead things, like humans. Then we recognized the god who had created us. For we were
not strangers to his powers. And we served him
in fear and bondage. And after these things we
became darkened in our heart (65.9-23).

The last questions of gnosis concern soteriology:
"Whither do we hasten, from what are we freed, what is
birth, what rebirth?" In the final passages, the
Apocalypse affirms that the gnostics, having overcome
all persecutions, will come into everlasting life.
"They shall live forever" (83.14-15), because they have
been freed from corrupting desire (83.16). "Birth"
seems to imply man's coming into being through the
archigenetor, but rebirth is salvation by gnosis. The
gnosis of rebirth is like unto that which the heavenly
Eve once possessed and gave to Adam in the aeon from
which the first couple originated.

Sophia. The word "Sophia" occurs but once in the
Apocalypse of Adam. This is in the concluding words of
the secret teaching of the dying Adam, in the phrase
"wisdom (Sophia) of gnosis." Throughout the tractate,
gnosis is set forth as the means of salvation, a gnosis
obtained through the secret words of which the *Apocalypse of Adam* is itself an example:

> For these words of the eternal God which have
> been preserved were not put in the book nor are
> they written down, but angelic (beings) will
> bring them, which (words) will not be under-
> stood by all the generations of mankind. For
> they will be on a high mountain upon a rock of
> truth. Therefore, they will be named, "the
> words of Imperishability and Truth" to those
> who know the eternal God in a Sophia of Gnosis
> and a teaching of angels forever (85.3-18).

In the above passage the personified "Sophia" appears
to be associated with saving gnosis. A personified
wisdom is also recognizable in the account of the heavenly Eve teaching Adam the "word of gnosis" (64.12-13).

*The Goddess of the Sethians According to
Epiphanius, Irenaeus, and Hippolytus*

In chapters thirty-nine and forty of *Panarion,* Epiphanius' "Medicine Chest," the author claims to have had
personal acquaintance with the Sethians and to have

learned much about them from their writings. He reports that the Sethians trace their descent from Seth, the son of Adam, and ascribe to him everything virtuous and just, going so far as to call him Christ and asserting that he is Jesus.

According to Epiphanius, the Sethians taught that the angels had a falling out over the two sons of Adam and caused Cain to kill Abel, whereupon the one whom they call "the Mother and Female" prevailed over the warring angels and caused Seth to be born. In him she planted a seed of her power and thus was instituted the elect race, through which would come the destruction of the powers of the angels who shaped the world. The name of Sophia does not appear in the report, but rather the phrases "Mother of all," and "Mother on high."

Certain characteristics of Epiphanius' report concerning the Sethians make it likely that "the Mother and Female" about whom he is speaking is to be associated with the feminine principle of gnosis in the *Apocalypse of Adam*. According to Epiphanius, this female principle is also the celestial sender of Jesus, the new Seth.

> But from Seth, from his seed and descending from his race, there came the Christ himself, Jesus, not by (human) birth but miraculously appearing in the world; and he is Seth himself, who both then and now visits the human race, being sent from the Mother on high.[20]

The flood story is found in both the *Apocalypse of Adam* and Epiphanius' report about the Sethians. Although the narratives do not agree in detail, they both suggest that it was a female principle who resolved to save the Sethian generation. In the *Apocalypse of Adam*, the "revelation of gnosis which came from thy mother Eve" (69.14-17, Böhlig)[21] is pitted against the power of the "pantocrator" when he decides to "destroy all flesh" by the flood (69.1-11). Epiphanius reports that the Sethians taught that the Mother took notice of the wickedness among the mixed races of Cain and Abel and resolved to purify the seed of men. She chose Seth and

---

20. Epiphanius, *Panarion*, XXXIX.iii.5 in Foerster, ed., *Gnosis* vol. 1, p. 295.
21. The text is uncertain. MacRae gives "the life of the knowledge that came from me and Eve." Both readings are possible. In the opening passage of the *Apocalypse of Adam*, it is Eve who teaches Adam the revelation of gnosis which she saw.

displayed him in purity and in him alone she put the
seed of her power and purity."[22] Then, seeing the dis-
orderly passion of angels and men, she sent the purifying flood.

> The same Mother and female (deity) went and
> brought on a flood and destroyed every insur-
> rection of all men of the opposing race, in
> order, of course, that the pure and just race
> deriving from Seth should alone remain in the
> world, for the institution of the higher race
> and of the spark of justice.[23]

The report of Irenaeus concerning the Sethians also
notes the potent place of the mother deity in the begetting of the gnostic race and in the salvation of
mankind.[24] According to Irenaeus' report, it was by
the forethought of Sophia that Seth was begotten and
then Norea. Through them the mother carefully preserved the spark of light which was peculiarly her own.
When the archigenetor sent the flood, Sophia opposed
him and saved some of her favorites by means of the
sprinkling of light which proceeded from her, and
through them the world was again filled with mankind.
Irenaeus knows the myth of Sophia's attempt to overcome Saklas, the same deity who opposes Eve in the
Apocalypse of Adam. He also knows a more detailed
myth of Saklas' arrogant words and Sophia's answer concerning the Immortal Man. Irenaeus knows, too, the
Genesis midrash of the heavenly Eve, although he tends
to identify or confuse her with Sophia and Prunikos.
The church father's report describes a Christian
Sethian group whose traditions have moved far beyond
the Genesis accounts.

The Sethians, according to Hippolytus, supported
their doctrines by an allegorical interpretation of
scripture, but Hippolytus maintained that their tenets
really derived from the earliest period of Greek philosophy. "Wherefore," he writes, "one may reasonably
assert that the Sethians celebrate rites among themselves, very closely bordering upon those orgies of the
'Great Mother' which are observed among the Phlia-
sians."[25] A long tradition of Mother Goddess specula-

---

22. Epiphanius, *Pan.* XXXIX.ii.7.
23. Epiphanius, *Pan.* XXXIX.iii.1.
24. Irenaeus, *A.H. I.xxx.*
25. Hippolytus, *Ref.* V.xv.

32

tion is probably basic to the midrash in the *Apocalypse of Adam*. Here the creator god is dubbed Saklas, "folly," and the conflict of Ialdabaoth and Sophia (Wisdom) is anticipated by that of Saklas and Eve. The Immortal Man of standard gnosticism has his counterpart in Seth. On the other hand, the church fathers' reports of the Sethians seem to concern a Christianized sect which recognized Jesus as Seth incarnate.

Feminine Motifs in the Excursus on the Successive Kingdoms (V.77.27-83.4)

Within the *Apocalypse of Adam* there is a poetic excursus which does not appear to belong to the apocalypse proper. Its subject is the origin of twelve illuminator-saviors, who appear miraculously through agencies such as birds, rocks, and clouds. These lowly beginnings contrast with the high origin of the thirteenth Illuminator, that of "the kingless generation." Of this generation it is reported that God chose its illuminator out of all the aeons and "caused a gnosis of the undefiled one of truth to come to be [in] him" (82.21-25).

In some of the kingdoms, feminine motifs are involved. The first kingdom tells of a mother, the third of a virgin's womb, the sixth of a woman who became pregnant from desire for flowers, the ninth of one of the nine muses who became pregnant from her own desire, and the eleventh of a daughter who became pregnant by her own father. These stories, culled from various mythologies, are reminders of times of feminine deities prior to Christianity's triumph.

The most interesting of the folk prophecies in terms of feminine motifs is that of the fourth kingdom. In it Solomon is associated with an army of demons who seek after a virgin for his sexual delight. He does not defile this virgin because another is given him in her stead. The *Apocalypse of Adam* is not the only Nag Hammadi text in which Solomon is treated as less than heroic.[26] In the *Testimony of Truth*, Solomon is reported to have built Jerusalem by means of the demons (IX.70.6-9). In the *Second Treatise of the Great Seth*,

26. See Søren Giversen, "Solomon und die Dämonen," *Essays on the Nag Hammadi Texts in Honour of Alexander Böhlig*, ed. Martin Krause (Leiden: E. J. Brill, 1972), pp. 16-21.

Solomon is said to be a laughing-stock "since he thought that he was a Christ, having become vain through the Hebdomad, as if he had become stronger than I and my brothers" (VII.63.11-15). In the tractate, *On the Origin of the World*, the reader is referred to the *Book of Solomon* to find the names and functions of the forty-nine androgynous demons brought forth by the "sons of Death" (106.30-107.3). It would appear that the proverbial wisdom of Solomon is being treated as folly in these tractates in comparison with the true wisdom of Sophia.[27]

The undefiled virgin is an important feminine motif in the Nag Hammadi documents. The *Hypostasis of the Archons* says of Eve's daughter (Norea?): "She is the virgin whom no power hath defiled" (II.92.2-3). The *Gospel of Philip* says of Mary:

> Mary is the virgin whom no power hath defiled. She is a great anathema to the Hebrews, who are the apostles and the apostolic men - this virgin whom no power hath defiled (II.55.27-32).

The motif of the virginal birth appears in prophecies three and four of the *Apocalypse of Adam*.

> The third Kingdom saith of him: He came into being from a virgin womb. He was cast out of his city, he and his mother. He was taken to a desert place and nourished there. He came and received glory and power, 'and thus he came upon the water.'
> The fourth Kingdom saith of him: He came into being...virgin...her, he and Phersalis and Sauel, and his armies which had been sent forth. And Solomon himself sent forth his army of demons to seek after the Virgin. And they were not able to find her whom they sought after. But the virgin who was given to them - she it was who was brought. And Solomon took her.
> The Virgin became pregnant. She brought forth the child in that place. She nourished

---

27. The polemic against Solomon may reflect Samaritan roots of Sethian gnosis. The Samaritans fit the description of "the kingless generation" in that they never recognized the Davidic dynasty and to this day remain a theocracy. For Samaritan theology, see John MacDonald, *The Theology of the Samaritans* (London, 1964).

him in a border of the desert. When he had
been nourished, he received glory and power
from the seed by which he was begotten. 'And
thus he came upon the water.' (78.18-79.19).

This motif of the virgin birth in the kingdom-prophe-
cies does not seem to have originated within Jewish
speculation. Rather, the juxtaposition of prophecies
three and four seems to imply a line of development
whereby an alien idea (prophecy three) has been developed
and given an Old Testament context by a hostile allusion
to Solomon. We seem to be in the presence of a pre-
Christian syncretism in which foreign ideas are being
assimilated by a Jewish sect.

Conclusion

The chief feminine motifs in the *Apocalypse of Adam*
may be summarized under the headings Eve and Sophia.
Before the creation of man by the archigenetor, Eve
lived with Adam in a glorious aeon. It was she who had
seen the glory of the superior aeon and who had taught
Adam the gnosis of the true God. By reason of the
gnosis which Eve shared with her partner, the human
couple was greater than the creator god and equal to the
eternal angels in honor.

The separation of Eve from Adam is the original sin in
the *Apocalypse of Adam*. Unlike normative hermeneutic of
Genesis which blames Eve, the *Apocalypse of Adam* blames
Saklas for the fall of mankind. The *Apocalypse of Adam*
suggests that the salvific feminine principle of gnosis
re-entered humanity via the children of the first
mother, Eve. When Eve's son Seth appears in the world,
he does so as the seed of a higher aeon. Through the
revelation of gnosis, he learns the plan for saving mankind through his generations.

The importance of the *Apocalypse of Adam* lies in its
presentation of a fundamental conflict between the
creator god and the feminine spirit typified by Eve.
This conflict is set entirely within a Judaic context,
without Christian elements, and seems to present a long-
standing polemic against the biblical Jehovah as well
as the Davidic dynasty. The evidence points to hetero-

35

dox Judaism as the point of origin for these interpretations.[28]

Introduction to The Exegesis on the Soul (II.6)[29]

The *Exegesis on the Soul*, like the *Apocalypse of Adam*, has its title at the beginning and the ending. Unlike the *Apocalypse of Adam*, it is written in good, idiomatic Coptic, is well preserved, and appears to be a whole document rather than a collection of independent parts.[30] The theme, which is the fall, repentance, and salvation of the soul, is approached from many sides and exemplified by a long allegory based on quotations from the Bible as well as Homer's *Odyssey*.

Succinctly, the document describes the soul as a virginal, bisexual entity which once lived with the father God. In some way, not explained in the text, the feminine part of the soul fell into a body and became a dispossessed and incomplete being. When the soul repents and appeals for help, the father sends her male counterpart so that through this reunion the soul's identity will be restored. The author exhorts repentance and prayer to the father God that he may send the soul's male partner.

The anonymous *Exegesis on the Soul* must have had a Greek vorlage, perhaps written as early as 200 A.D., but only this one Coptic copy survives.[31] Certainly the author knew both the Old and New Testaments, as his many quotations attest. Apart from the biblical images,

---

28. See A. F. J. Klijn, *Seth in Jewish, Christian and Gnostic Literature* (Leiden: E. J. Brill, 1977), pp. 29-32, for a discussion of the Samaritans as "the sons of Seth."
29. The first edition of the *Exegesis on the Soul* was published by M. Krause and P. Labib, *Gnostische und hermetische Schriften aus Codex II und Codex VI*, Abhandlungen des Deutschen Archaologischen Instituts Kairo, Koptische Reihe, Band II, Weisbaden, 1971 (appeared 1972), pp. 133-49. For a useful introductory article, see G. W. MacRae, "A Nag Hammadi Tractate on the Soul" in *Ex Orbe Religionum*, (Supplements to *Numen*, XXI, Leiden, 1972), pp. 471-79.
30. See Frederik Wisse, "On Exegeting the *Exegesis on the Soul*," *Les Textes de Nag Hammadi*, ed., Jacques E. Ménard, (Leiden: E. J. Brill, 1975), pp. 68-81.
31. See William C. Robinson, Jr., Introduction to *The Exegesis on the Soul* (II,6) in *The Nag Hammadi Library*, p. 180.

one might see the *Exegesis on the Soul* as a Platonic or
Pythagorean exposition on the exile and return of the
soul to her homeland. The Christian nature of the document is evident in the use of the New Testament and
Christ's name.

The *Exegesis on the Soul* may be divided into two
parts: the first, a short narrative; the second, a pro-
longed allegory based on a pneumatic exegesis of sacred
scripture. The first lines of the text limit the
subject and supply the imagery for the entire allegory,
viz., the soul as feminine.

> The wise ones who lived before us gave a femi-
> nine terminology to the soul. Truly, she is
> feminine by nature as well. She even has a
> womb (II.127.19-22).

Both the narrative introductory section and the
allegory are divided into three sections, the last of
which presents a climax.[32] The narrative section
expands on the theme in a rather conventional fashion
without any reference to scriptural or Homeric passages. W. C. Robinson's claim that the quotations are
non-integral to the narrative and that their omission
"leaves a narrative which, while not entirely clear, is
relatively intact" does not seem correct.[33] On the
contrary, as F. Wisse states, "the narrative depends
for its contents on the quotations."[34] The structural
correspondence is shown below.

Subject Matter	Narrative	Allegory
1. The Soul's Fall and Resultant Troubles	127.19-128.26	129.5-131.16
2. The Soul's Repentance and Pleas for Mercy	128.26-129.2	131.16-137.15
3. The Soul's Assurance of Salvation	129.2-5	137.15-26

The first section (127.19-128.26) introduces the subject and reports the soul's origin and her fall from the
father's house into the hands of evil archons who treat
her with contempt and deceive her with worthless gifts.

---

32. Wisse, pp. 80-81.
33. See William C. Robinson, Jr., "The Exegesis on the Soul,"
Novum Testamentum 12 (1970), p. 104.
34. Wisse, p. 80.

Upon abandoning these adulterers, she retains only desolate widowhood and "feeble-minded children." The following topoi may be noted in the allegory: The soul's virginal existence in the house of her father (129.21-22), her fornication with evil powers (129.11-20; 130. 7), the deceptive favors she is given (130.2-5), her wantonness (129.15-20; 130.13-20), and her handicapped children of fornication (129.33-34). These details of the allegory are buttressed by the scriptural passages which follow them and do not belong to any known non-Christian myth of the soul.

In an effort to legitimate the sexual allegory, the author makes a reference to Paul's correspondence with Corinth, in which Paul explains his admonition, "Do not associate with prostitutes" (I Cor.5:9), as a warning against converse with evil archons.[35]

> I wrote to you in the letter, 'Don't mix with prostitutes - surely not the prostitutes of this world, or the covetous, or thieves or idolators - since then you would have to go out from the world (131.3-8).

The author of the *Exegesis on the Soul* points out that Paul is speaking "spiritually" when he tells the Corinthians not to mix with prostitutes. To prove this exegesis, the letter to the Ephesians (6:12) is alluded to:

> For our wrestling is not against flesh and blood, as he said, but against the world rulers of this darkness and the spiritual powers of evil (131.9-13).

The second section (128.26-129.2) summarizes the ideas of the repentance of the soul, her pleas to the father for help, and her restoration to her former place. These themes are elaborated and accompanied by proof texts in the allegory itself. In 131.16-137.15 the author details the spiritual nuptials and contrasts them to carnal ones. When the soul has intercourse with her beloved she receives life-giving seed from him and bears good children as opposed to those she bears with the archons. She receives the divine nature from

---

35. Wisse, (p. 72), considers this passage as crucial to the entire tractate since it gives Paul's sanction to the exegetical approach which the author uses.

the father, a blessing characterized as "the resurrection from the dead," "the ransoming from captivity," and "the ascent to heaven."

At two points within the allegory, the author interrupts the flow of symbolic language to remind the readers that it is fitting to pray, to repent, to confess sins, and to beseech the father with outstretched hands and without hypocrisy (135.4-15; 136.16-27).

The third section in the narrative consists of a short statement:

> When he (the Father) sees her (the soul) in such a state (i.e., repentant), then he will count her worthy of having mercy upon her, for many are the afflictions that have come upon her because she abandoned her house (129.2-5).

The theme of repentance is critical for the entire document, a fact witnessed by its position at the end of both the narrative and allegorical sections. In the latter, the author quotes Psalm 6.6-9, which relates that the Lord hears those who weep and pray. Upon this scriptural assurance the exegetical treatise is completed, and the author needs only to rephrase the psalm to convince his readers that "if we truly repent, God, who is long-suffering and great in mercy, will hear us" (137.22-26).

Feminine Motifs in The Exegesis on the Soul

The soul is expressly correlated with sexual imagery at the very beginning of the Exegesis on the Soul: "The wise ones who lived before us gave a feminine terminology to the soul." The Greek word for soul, ψυχη, linguistically feminine, is retained in the Coptic text and introduced by the feminine article "T‧" According to the Exegesis on the Soul, the soul is feminine by nature and has a womb; but she is bisexual in form while she is with the Father, the author of her virginity. In her heavenly, androgynous condition, the soul's womb is properly inward but when she leaves her perfect husband it suffers harm and is exposed "like male genitals" (131.19-132.2).

The author's choice of the androgyne to represent the complete man reflects the understanding of man as transcending sexuality. To think correctly of man, accord-

39

ing to the *Exegesis on the Soul,* is to image him in
terms of unity, not polarity. Such a concept of man is
found in Plato's *Symposium* and later in Philo of
Alexandria. Influenced by Plato's concept of a primeval
androgyne, Philo understood Genesis 1:26, "Let us make
man" as referring to the "idea," the blueprint of man.
This idea, incorporeal, immortal, and neither male nor
female is in the divine image. By contrast, man on
earth is bodily, mortal, both male and female, in accord
with Genesis 2.

In Eastern Christianity, from the earliest period,
there was a tendency to relate man's sexual polarity to
his fallen condition, and to blame the fall upon sensu-
ality, primarily sexual lust. A similar view was
recently espoused by the mystic theologian of the
Russian Orthodox Church, Nicholas Berdyaev, who likewise
used Plato's myth of the androgyne as the basis of an
anthropological metaphysic. Berdyaev viewed man as a
divided sexual being, in a constant state of disharmony,
dissatisfaction, and passion. Original sin is man's
division into two sexes, and the fall involves the loss
of human virginity. Sex is the source of life, but it
is correspondingly the source of death. According to
Berdyaev, man is a disharmonious invalid chiefly because
he has lost his original androgeneity.[36] A similar
elaboration of the myth of the androgyne is found in
some representatives of Jungian psychology.[37]

The author of the *Exegesis on the Soul* does not present an account of the fall of the soul but states
simply that "she fell into the hands of many robbers"
when "she fell into a body and came to this life" (127.
25-27). Only the female part of the androgyne fell,
for the author explains that the robbers made her believe that they were her real husband. They defiled
her and caused her to produce "dumb, blind, and deformed"
offspring (128.24-25). The metaphor of the prostitution
of the soul is emphasized by long quotations from Jeremiah (3:1-4) and Hosea (2:2-7), and by a shorter one
from Ezekiel (16:23-26) which seems especially appro-

---

36. Paul K. Jewett, *Man as Male and Female,* (Grand Rapids: Williams
B. Eerdmans Publishing Co., 1975), pp. 24-28, gives a concise
statement of the history of the androgynous idea.
37. See *Psyche and Symbol,* a selection from the writings of C. G.
Jung, ed. by Violet S. deLaszlo, (New York: Doubleday & Co., Inc.,
1958). Cf. pp. 9-60 on the "anima" and "animus," the self, and
Christ as symbol of the self.

priate in view of the "bridal chamber" motif which the author employs later.

> It happened after much wickedness, said the
> Lord, you built yourself a brothel and made
> yourself a beautiful place in the square. And
> you built yourself brothels on every street
> and you wasted your beauty, and you spread
> your legs in every alley, and you multiplied
> your harlotries. You prostituted yourself to
> the sons of Egypt, those who are your neigh-
> bors, men of great flesh (130.11-20; cf.
> Ezek. 16:23-26).

What the passage meant to the original writer does not concern the author of the *Exegesis on the Soul*, for he uses it for the sake of his allegory. Thus, the phrase "men of great flesh" is said to mean "the fleshly and the sensual, and the things of the earth, by which the soul has been defiled here" (130.22-24). Among the soul's defilements are mentioned bread, wine, oil, clothing, and "the other folly which surrounds the body" (130.24-27).

The fallen soul is imaged as a prostitute and the repentant soul is imaged as a bride. Whereas adulterers had defiled her before she repented, the soul's real husband is now sent to her by the Father. Her celestial better half is imaged as male, as husband, as first-born brother, and as bridegroom.

> From heaven the Father sent her her man, who is
> her brother, the first-begotten. Then 'the
> bridegroom came down to the bride' (132.7-10).

Although the author of the *Exegesis on the Soul* does not expressly condemn the soul for her fall, there is little doubt that he holds her responsible. Nothing is said about the archons creating man on earth as a dis-harmonious entity. Rather, the soul is blamed for her sorry condition. Apparently the author knows the Pauline interpretation of Genesis which blames Eve for Adam's sin.

> For they were originally joined to one another
> when they were with the Father before the woman
> led astray the man who is her brother (133.3-6:
> cf. I. Cor. 11:3 and I Tim. 2:14.

The author distinguishes two Adams, the one who is the soul's true love, her real master, who gives her the life-giving seed, "her brother, the first-begotten" (132.8-9), and another Adam, the brother whom she is reported to have led astray (133.5-6). Indeed, the soul could have been allegorized as a male who fell from his feminine counterpart had not the normative hermeneutic of Genesis made Eve the cause of Adam's sinning.

Gen. 3:16, referred to in 1 Cor. 11:3 and in Eph. 5:23, is understood by our author to refer to the celestial brother, the bridegroom of the soul.

> This marriage has united them to one another
> again, and the soul has been joined to her true
> love, her real lord, as it is written: 'For
> the lord of the woman is her husband' (133.6-
> 10).

The vast difference between spiritual and carnal marriage is noted and supported by another passage from Genesis which is interpreted as referring to heavenly marriage.

> For that marriage is not like carnal marriage.
> Those who had intercourse with one another were
> satisfied with that intercourse. And as if it
> were a burden they left behind them the annoy-
> ance of physical desire and they did not
> [separate] from each other, but [...] this
> marriage. But [when] they united [with one
> another], they became one life. Wherefore
> the prophet said (Gen. 2:24) concerning the
> first man and the first woman: 'They shall
> become one flesh' (132.27-133.3).

The myth of the fallen, repentant, and espoused feminine soul is similar to the myth of the fallen and repentant Sophia in such documents as the *Gospel of Philip* II.59.30-32, the *Sophia of Jesus Christ* (III. 114.14-18) and the *Apocryphon of John* (II.9.25-35). On this basis, one would hardly go wrong in suggesting that the *Exegesis on the Soul* thinks of Christ as the soul's true consort.

> But the Father is kind and good. He hears the
> soul that calls upon him and sends her the
> light of salvation (135.26-29).

Neither the name "Christ" nor the name "Sophia" appears in the tractate, but in the above passage, Christ may well be intended by "light" and Sophia may stand for the repentant "soul."

42

One may regard the *Exegesis on the Soul* as presenting an interpretation of the soul as a divided entity, neither complete light nor darkness, but a middle ground over which both light and darkness vie for control. The light particle has somehow entered the middle sphere, which in the *Exegesis on the Soul* is called the place of deception, where Aphrodite reigns, until upon the soul's repentance, she enjoys a spiritual wedding. Aphrodite occurs in the ending of the *Exegesis on the Soul*, and the author has nothing good to say of her. She is introduced with a quotation from the *Odyssey*, which the author has chosen as pertinent to his allegory. In this Homeric passage, Helen blames Aphrodite for beguiling her away from her home, her daughter, and her "beautiful" husband.

Apparently, Helen is a type of the fallen soul for our Christian author.

> Again [Helen] [...] saying '[...] turned away from me. It is to my house that I want to return.' For she sighed, saying (*Odyssey* IV. 261-264), 'It is Aphrodite who deceived me. She brought me out of my village. My only daughter I left behind me, and my good, understanding, beautiful husband.' For when the soul abandons her perfect husband—because of the deception of Aphrodite which consists in the begetting of this place—then she will be injured (136.35-137.9).

The passage which suggests that Aphrodite is in charge of the place of deception and another which calls Egypt "the house of bondage" (137.12-13) may give a clue to the historical origin of the treatise. Aphrodite was identified with Isis in parts of the Mediterranean world, particularly in Egypt, and may have been held in high esteem by those whom the author wished to convert to his type of Christianity. To our author, however, this goddess stands for deception and bondage. Repentance with regard to such a condition is the first step in the return of the soul to its home, even as repentance from Isis proclivities may be said to have preceded the Israelites' return from the bondage of Egypt (137.11-15).

That the *Exegesis on the Soul* relies upon male-dominated societal norms for its imagery is evident from two biblical citations alluding to patrilocal marriage. The Psalmist is quoted (Psalm 45:10-11):

43

> Hear, my daughter, and see, and incline thine
> ear and forget thy people and thy father's
> house. For the king has desired thy beauty;
> for he is thy lord (133.15-20).

This text fits well the Christian author's image of
heaven as the home of the bridegroom. The soul is
urged to forget the house of her earthly father with
whom things went badly for her, but to remember her
Father who is in the heavens (133.25-28).

The second passage is God's order to Abraham to leave
the land of Ur (Gen. 12:1): "Come out from thy (masc.)
land and thy (masc.) kinsmen and from thy (masc.)
father's house" (133.29-31). This command is reinter-
preted to refer to the feminine soul who has been de-
tained in the house of her earthly father. The societal
norm which the author makes a fundament of the allegory
is patrilocal marriage, in that the soul is required to
leave her own family and go to that of her husband.

Summarily, the allegory in the *Exegesis on the Soul*
treats most of the feminine elements pejoratively. The
soul, responsible for her own condition, is in bondage
until the patriarchal god delivers her, completes her,
and raises her to her original bisexual condition.
Allegorically, the soul is fallen and feminine while
her brother is unfallen and masculine. The supernatural state of oneness is reattained through the
coming of the soul's husband in the sacrament of the
bridal chamber. Patriarchal motifs surrounding the
marriage metaphor suggest male-dominated societal norms
and anti-goddess, patriarchal religion, which is height-
ened by the polemic against Aphrodite, who is seen as
a threat to marital stability.

*Comparison of the Feminine Motifs in The Apocalypse
of Adam with Those in The Exegesis on the Soul*

The *Apocalypse of Adam* is a non-Christian, perhaps
pre-Christian, revelatory discourse stemming from
peripheral Judaism. The *Exegesis on the Soul* is a
Christian allegorical essay which attempts to substantiate the author's idea of the soul predominantly
through biblical quotations. The *Apocalypse of Adam*
shows a high regard for feminine motifs; the *Exegesis
on the Soul* presents a basically pejorative view. The
differences may be summarized under the following categories: deity, fall of the soul, and soteriology.

In the *Apocalypse of Adam* the supreme being is not presented as masculine. Phrases such as "God the eternal" and "God of Truth" need not be linked to sexual imagery as with most Christian documents. We have tried to show that the main deity of the *Apocalypse of Adam* is either Sophia or a type of deity to whom the characteristic Jewish wisdom features were ascribed. By contrast, in the *Exegesis on the Soul*, the supreme being is the Father God of Christianity. Although the main characters in the document are the feminine soul and her saving male partner, the term "father" in reference to the Christian God appears twenty-one times. The frequency of the term and the theologoumenon, the "will of the Father," which thrice appears without any apparent reason (131.28; 132.24, 134.6), leads to the tentative conclusion that the author is as much concerned with stressing the potency of the father god as the repentance of the feminine soul.

In the *Apocalypse of Adam*, the fall of humanity is due to the jealousy of the archons over the superior nature of the first humans. The foolish archons struggle with a Wisdom goddess for control of Adam and Eve. The metaphors for the opposing forces are more often phrased in terms of light and darkness, death and life, gnosis and ignorance, than with sexual terminology. Nevertheless, the Genesis account of creation and fall with its sexual imagery is integrated into the narrative in such a way that the masculine creator god, Saklas (folly), opposes the wise Eve.

In the *Exegesis on the Soul*, the fall pertains to an individual psyche rather than to humanity in general. The soul is responsible for her own fall, viz., her separation from her spiritual partner. The heavenly Man is described as bisexual and the fall is expressed as the feminine deserting the masculine. This imagery is psychological rather than mythological in nature, but the choice of the female as the fallen entity is based upon more than the linguistic gender of ψυχη.

The Greek story of Psyche and Eros may be compared for its treatment of Psyche (soul) and Aphrodite.[38] The princess Psyche is said to have been so beautiful that Aphrodite, being jealous, instructed her son Eros to punish her. Soon afterward, Psyche's father was

---

38. See "Eros and Psyche," *Larousse Encyclopedia of Mythology*, (New York: Prometheus Press, 1959), p. 132.

commanded to conduct his daughter to the top of a mountain where she became the prey of a monster. Suddenly, however, she is wafted to a magnificent palace, where in the darkness, a mysterious person who claims to be her destined husband, joins her. She cannot see his face, but she knows him as a delightful lover. He always leaves before daybreak and makes her promise never to attempt to see him. Psyche's sisters, consumed by envy, taunt her, saying that if her lover refuses to let her see his countenance, he must be some hideous monster. One night Psyche lights a lamp so as to see him clearly. No fearful monster is there, but rather the charming Eros whom Aphrodite has sent to punish Psyche. Eros, awakened, reproaches Psyche for lack of faith, and vanishes along with the palace. Psyche is left alone. Pursued by Aphrodite's wrath, Psyche overcomes every obstacle by a mysterious help. Eros, touched by the repentance of his paramour whom he has never ceased loving, goes to Zeus and begs that Psyche be allowed to rejoin him. Zeus not only consents but confers immortal life upon Psyche. Aphrodite forgets her deceptive schemes, and the marriage takes place on Olympus with great festivity.

The allegory in the *Exegesis on the Soul* is similar to that of the Psyche and Eros tale. Like Psyche, the soul is responsible for her separation from her lover. When the soul (ψυχη) repents, she receives both her husband and eternal life.

The theme of the separation of the androgyne in the *Apocalypse of Adam* and the *Exegesis on the Soul* presents an interesting comparison. According to the *Apocalypse of Adam*,

> God, the ruler of the aeons and the powers,
> divided us (Adam and Eve) in his rage. Then
> we became two aeons (V.64.20-23).

According to the *Exegesis on the Soul*, the separation is the fault of the woman.

> For they were originally joined to one another
> when they were with the Father before the
> woman led astray the man who is her brother
> (II.133.3-6).

Original sin is thus connected with sexuality, and the woman is the temptress. That lust and worldly begetting is the cause of the separation of the bisexual

46

soul is made clear in the explanation of the role of
Aphrodite:

> For when the soul abandons her perfect hus-
> band because of the deception of Aphrodite
> which consists in the begetting of (in?) this
> place - then she will be injured (137.5-9).

The soteriological plan of the *Apocalypse of Adam* is
based upon some kind of similarity between an undefil-
able feminine principle and transcendental generative
forces which are described as aeons. The theory
includes the implicit recognition of the divine nature
of the feminine principle. When that principle made its
first appearance within humanity it did so through Eve.
That Eve is the prototype of the gnostic saviors is
clear from the beginning of the *Apocalypse of Adam*:
"She taught me a word of knowledge (ΓΝWCIC) of the
eternal God" (V.64.12-14).

The mention of three divine visitors coming to Adam
in a dream (V.65.24-29) is reminiscent of the three
angels who visited Abraham before the birth of Isaac,
an episode commented upon by Philo in *Quaestiones in
Genesin* IV.35. Philo uses the word "trinity" of these
visitors in a way that implies that there was speculation in his community about the plurality of the deity.[39]
The allusion in the *Apocalypse of Adam* can also be seen
as a reference to a higher type of deity, one that is
intent upon opposing the archontic creator of the world.

The *Apocalypse of Adam* records the tension between
these three revealers and the creator god. The feminine
principle in some way is linked to these mysterious
higher aeons. Although the creator god, in an attempt
to rid himself of Eve's progeny "to whom has passed
the life of gnosis" (69.13-15), caused a great flood,
he was unable to extinguish the superior race. Noah
confessed that that generation came into being, not
through him but through gnosis (71.21-72.1). These
gnostics, like Isaac, are engendered miraculously after
the visit of the three angels.

In the *Apocalypse of Adam*, the "imperishable seed"
signifies a salvific force which makes its influence
felt so that mankind will not utterly perish with the
wayward world. And the elect race are clearly said to

---

39. See Erwin Goodenough, *By Light, Light,* New Haven: Yale University Press, 1935), pp. 147-48.

be "not alien to them," viz., the angels and the imperishable seed (V.76.2-6). In the *Exegesis on the Soul*, one gets a different picture of the same soteriological motif. Here, salvation is expressed by the metaphor of male seed from a transcendent Father who works primarily on the individual soul rather than upon the universe. The soul is described as feminine and in need of redemption. Her salvation comes from the Father by means of an agent explicitly imaged as male. The female is put into the position of inferiority, so that it is necessary for her to be complemented in order to be as once she was, virginal and androgynous.

To accentuate the degradation of the female soul and her need for the masculine "light of salvation" (II.135.29), the author quotes *I Clement* 8.3:

> If your sins reach from earth to heaven, and if they be red as scarlet and blacker than sackcloth, and if you turn to me with all your soul and say to me, 'My father,' I will hear you like a holy people (II.135.32-136.4).

Plainly the regenerative force is masculine. In this type of psychology, the spirit which regenerates the soul is crassly depicted as male seed:

> And when she had intercourse with him she received from him the seed that is the life-giving Spirit, until by him she bears good children and nourishes them. For this is the great, perfect marvel of birth. And so this marriage is made perfect by the will of the Father (II.133.34-134.6).

The sexual language used to portray the condition of the non-regenerate soul is rather grotesque at one point. The womb of the soul is said to be on the outside like male genitals.

> As long as the soul keeps running about everywhere, copulating with whomever she meets and defiling herself, she exists in the suffering she deserves to receive. But when she perceives the straits she is in and weeps before the Father and repents, then the Father will have mercy on her and he will make her womb turn away from outward things and will turn it again inward, so that the soul will regain her proper character.

48

For they (the souls) are not like women.
For the womb of the body is within the body
like the other internal organs, but the womb
of the soul is around the outside like the
male genitals, which are external.

Then, when the womb of the soul turns herself inward, according to the will of the
Father, she is baptized and immediately purified from the defilement outside which had
been pressed upon her (II.131.13-31).

The second paragraph of the passage just quoted is
possibly an explanatory gloss. It appears that a
literal-minded male reader took exception to the strong
feminine imagery, and corrected it by adding the explanation that the soul's womb was formed like a male.
The continuation, however, in the third paragraph makes
it plain that the author was speaking metaphorically,
and the terms "outward" and "inward" refer to the focus
of the womb's attention, which, indeed, should properly
be "inward." To compare the soul to a woman with an
exterior womb, like the male genitals, is indeed unusual. Perhaps the author himself sensed the strangeness
of the metaphor, for he adds another metaphor that is
not so shocking - that of clothes being washed and
turned inside out to be cleaned (131.31-34).

In the *Apocalypse of Adam*, the saving illuminators
are regularly described as parthenogenetically conceived. In the *Exegesis on the Soul*, however, this
primitive religious doctrine is expressly contradicted.

But since she is a female, by herself she is
powerless to beget a child. From heaven the
Father sent her her man, who is her brother,
the first-begotten. Then 'the bridegroom came
down to the bride' (132.6-10).

Basically, the earlier view of the feminine soul as
akin to life, gnosis, generation, wisdom, and the higher
aeons has been entirely reconstructed in the type of
Christian gnosticism exemplified by the *Exegesis on the
Soul*. By means of the very common Christian division of
body, soul, and spirit, a new view of the soul as
feminine and inferior to spirit has been presented. Of
course, within this predominantly patriarchal system
it is no accident that the superior element, the spirit,
is depicted as masculine. This type of imagery is not
restricted to the *Exegesis on the Soul*; it is a frequent
theme in the Christian gnostic documents of the Nag

Hammadi collection. One could suggest that this pattern provided a convenient method for downgrading earlier feminine motifs in the gnostic tradition. Themes such as the impossibility of the feminine to conceive by herself, of the dependency of Sophia upon Christ, of "the fault" of the psychic woman, and the regenerative force of the male spirit, are common and basic in developed Christian gnosticism.

CHAPTER THREE

FEMININE MOTIFS IN EUGNOSTOS THE BLESSED

AND IN THE SOPHIA OF JESUS CHRIST

Introduction to Eugnostos the Blessed
(III.3 and V.1 and to The Sophia of
Jesus Christ (III.4 and BG 8502.3)

Eugnostos the Blessed, though written in epistolary
form, is a religio-philosophical essay concerning the
transcendent God. The beginning and ending of the
letter are written in the first-person style, but the
entire middle section reads like a textbook on the
astrophysical evolution of the universe.

The *Sophia of Jesus Christ* takes the form of a
revelatory discourse purportedly given by the resurrected Savior, Jesus Christ, to his disciples in
Galilee. Despite the different forms, the documents
are two versions of the same original. Each is found
in two versions among the Nag Hammadi and Berlin codices.[1] Both copies of *Eugnostos* were found in the Nag
Hammadi collection (III.70.1-90.13; V.1-17). One ver-

1. Walter C. Till, *Die Gnostischen Schriften des Koptischen
Papyrus Berolinensis 8502* (Berlin: Akademie-Verlag, 1955), con-
tains the Coptic text and German translation of the *Sophia of
Jesus Christ*, as well as treatment of textual differences with
respect to the codex-three copies of the *Sophia of Jesus Christ*
and *Eugnostos the Blessed*. Martin Krause, *Die Gnosis*, 2 vol.
(Zurich: Artemis Verlag, 1969, 1971) 2:24-29, presents another
German translation, the accompanying footnotes for which are on
pp. 153-160. An English translation of Krause's work by R. McL.
Wilson is found in *Gnosis*, vol. 2, pp. 24-39. Douglas Parrott, in
the *Nag Hammadi Library*, pp. 206-228, provides an English translation in parallel columns of *Eugnostos the Blessed* and the *Sophia
of Jesus Christ* of Nag Hammadi, codex three. Parrott employed the
codex five version of *Eugnostos* and the Berlin codex version of the
Sophia of Jesus Christ where pages were missing in codex three.

sion of the *Sophia of Jesus Christ* follows *Eugnostos* as
the fourth tractate in Codex III (90.14-119.18), and the
other is the third tractate in codex Berolinensis 8502
(77.8-127.13). All the copies are in Coptic, but they
apparently derive from Greek originals. A Greek fragment of the *Sophia of Jesus Christ*, corresponding to
III.97.16-99.10 and BG 88.19-91.14 survives as papyrus
Oxyrhynchus 1081.[2]

In an important study of the two documents, M. Krause
presented strong evidence through literary analysis
that the *Sophia of Jesus Christ* is dependent on
Eugnostos.[3] He found that the unique material of
Eugnostos agrees contextually with the material which is
common to both documents, but that the unique material
of the *Sophia of Jesus Christ* does not agree with the
material common to both documents. He, therefore, concluded that *Eugnostos* was the primary document and that
the movement in the secondary *Sophia of Jesus Christ* is
towards Christianization. By the use of a Christian
frame story, the *Sophia of Jesus Christ* shaped the cosmogonic material of *Eugnostos* into a series of dialogues
between Jesus and his disciples. In examining the
documents' parallels, one may learn a great deal about
how a non-Christian document could be modified to
accommodate it to Christianity.

The main themes of *Eugnostos* seem to be based on the
existence of a transcendent being who inhabits a super-
celestial sphere along with his androgynous image, the
Immortal Man. From the Immortal Man there evolves an
androgynous son, called the Son of Man, and from the
latter another androgyne called the Son of the Son of
Man. These beings exist together in ineffable joy, and
subsequent evolutions proceed from them. The author
states:

> And the Immortal Man is full of every imperish-
> able glory and ineffable joy, while his entire
> kingdom rejoices continually (V.8.18-22).

How important Eugnostos considers his instruction
may be gleaned from the introductory remarks, when,

----

2. The Greek fragment of the *Sophia of Jesus Christ* in papyrus
Oxyrhynchus is incomplete but can be read with the help of the
Coptic copy. Cf. Till, *BG 8502*, p. 216.
3. Martin Krause, "Das literarische Verhältnis des Eugnostos-
briefes zur Sophia Jesu Christi" in *Mullus: Festschrift für
Theodor Klauser*, (Munster, 1964), pp. 215-23.

after summarizing the inconsequential views of the philosophers, he concludes:

> Whoever, then, is able to achieve the solution of these three opinions that I have just described and attain by means of another view to reveal the God of truth and be in harmony with everyone because of it, he is an immortal in the midst of mortal men (III.71.5-13).

In closing the letter, Eugnostos predicts that a revealer will come who need not be taught and who will teach everything "joyously and in pure knowledge" (III. 90.7-11). The *Sophia of Jesus Christ* apparently considers the prophecy to have been fulfilled in Jesus Christ, whom it specifies as the ultimate revealer. It reports that Jesus has come from the celestial spheres to sunder the power of the archons and to teach us how to avoid their entanglements (BG 121.13-17).

Some examples of the changes made in the *Sophia of Jesus Christ* with respect to *Eugnostos* will be discussed later, but for introductory purposes it is sufficient to observe that the myth of the fallen Sophia and that of the resurrected Jesus as the unique Savior are found in the *Sophia of Jesus Christ* but are lacking in *Eugnostos*. Significant Middle Platonic philosophical ideas which are common to both *Eugnostos* and the *Sophia of Jesus Christ* intimate that the original was composed during the first two centuries of the Christian era.[4]

Three fundamental questions arise in the mind of the reader with regard to the content of the documents. Is the transcendent God presented as alone and unknowable? Why are the roles of Sophia so varied? How can one account for the complicated message and structure of the *Sophia of Jesus Christ* in comparison with the relatively simple content and structure of *Eugnostos*? Each of these questions is related to feminine motifs and will be discussed separately in the next sections.

The Deity and Feminine Motifs

The nature of the deity is, for the gnostics, no less a mystery than the trinitarian formulations of orthodox Christianity. Irenaeus reports diverse opinions among certain gnostics with regard to the deity:

---

4. Parrott, *NHL*, p. 207.

Some declare him to be without a consort, and
neither male nor female, and, in fact, nothing
at all; while others affirm him to be masculo-
feminine, assigning to him the nature of a
hermaphrodite; others, again, allot Sigē
(silence) to him as a spouse, that thus may be
formed the first conjunction.[5]

In the opening passage Eugnostos states that whatever exists by reason of itself or by itself alone has
a monotonous life, thus implying that the God about
whom he teaches is not alone: "For that which derives
from itself alone leads an empty existence" (III.71.
1-3). He then gives an apologia for a transcendent
deity characterized as incomprehensible, unknowable,
immortal, eternal, unbegotten, faultless, blessed, and
nameless. He is called "the Father of the All" (III.
73.2-3), but more correctly "Forefather" (III.74.22-23),
because "the Father is the 'Archē' (APXH) of that which
is revealed" (III.74.23-75.1). Here, the old feminine
hypostasis, APXH, seems to have been replaced by a
"second father."

The ineffable character of the Forefather apparently
does not constitute a lonely state. Heavenly powers
are with him and he rules over them even before they
are visible. Transcendence and community are compati-
ble:

> Ere anything was revealed of that which is re-
> vealed - the majesty and the authorities that
> are in him - he ruled over all things of the
> universe without anything ruling over him. For
> he is all mind, thought, and reflection, dis-
> cretion, reason, and power. All of them are
> equal in power, the sources of the universe.
> And their entire kind until their end exists in
> the primary knowledge of the Unbegotten One
> (III.73.3-16).

As an exception to the single state of the Forefather, there is a second father, a mirror image of him,
coterminous with him, but not equal to him in power.
With the second father is also a multitude of mirror
images, a race known as "the generation without kingship" and "the children of the Unbegotten Father"
(III.75.13-23).

---

5. Irenaeus, A. H. I.xi.5.

Other exceptions to the single nature of the Forefather seem to include powers known as "Eidea," "Archē,"
"Pistis," and "Sophia." These aspects of the deity, to
be translated as "idea," "beginning," "faith," and
"wisdom," are of feminine linguistic gender in Greek and
appear as loanwords in the Coptic texts where they are
preceded by the Coptic feminine definite article. The
terms may represent speculation regarding feminine
aspects or emanations of the transcendent God.

Such speculation about the feminine aspect of the
deity was common in early Christianity. Even Irenaeus
relates that God made all things by his Word and adorned
them by his Wisdom, employing Prov. 8.22-25, to support
his own Christology.

> The Lord created me the Archē of his ways for
> his works. He established me from everlasting,
> in the Archē, before he made the earth, before
> he established the depths, and before the
> foundations of waters came forth. Before the
> mountains were set in order, and before all the
> hills, he begot me.[6]

"*Eidea*" *in Eugnostos the Blessed and in The Sophia of
Jesus Christ*. Eugnostos informs the reader that "Eidea"
belongs completely to the Father. She is hypostatized
as one who knows suffering, and as such, is reminiscent
of Isis, and the Jewish Wisdom figure.

Eug. III.72.6-13

With him (the Father)
there is an Eidea (*EIDEA*)
that is his alone. Not as
the Eidea which *we* have
received nor as *we* have seen
it, but an Eidea foreign
and far superior to all
things and nobler than
the universes. She sees
all suffering and perceives
herself through *herself*
alone.

*SJC BG 84.17-85.9
(III.94.24-95.7)*

With him (the Father)
there is an image (*EINE*)
that is his alone. Not as
you have seen, nor as
you have received
but an image foreign
and superior to all things
and nobler than the
universes. *He* perceives
on all sides and sees
himself through *himself*
alone.

---

6. Irenaeus, *A.H.* IV.xx.2-3.

Instead of the Greek feminine term *EIDEA* which is common to *Eugnostos III* and the *Sophia of Jesus Christ III*, the Berlin codex uses the Coptic masculine *EINE*, "image." The difference is probably significant, for in the Berlin codex *EINE* is to be identified with Jesus Christ, the "image" of the Father.[7] The historicized and Christianized nature of the Berlin codex version is observable in the use of the pronoun "you," which causes the revelation to appear to be directed to the disciples. The change from *EIDEA* and "we" in Eugnostos to *EINE* and "you" in the *Sophia of Jesus Christ* (Berlin codex) follows shortly another passage which significantly changes the imagery of the deity. Whereas *Eugnostos* relates that no one knows the deity except himself, the *Sophia of Jesus Christ* parallel adds "and the one to whom he wills to reveal himself, through me who came forth from the first light" (BG 83.13-17; III. 94.10-13).

The variant "all suffering" (Eug. 72.12; SJC III.95. 6) and "on all sides" (BG 85.7) ultimately goes back to a Coptic dialecticism.[8]

2ICE-NIM, in Sahidic, "all suffering," has been corrected in both Codex III copies to *2I-CA-NIM*, "on all sides." The double correction implies that "all suffering" was once the established reading. If the texts had previously existed in a Subachmimic dialect, we would have had *2ICENIM* (Subach.), which has both meanings, depending upon the word division. Although the original meaning of the passage is obscure, it is certain that at one time the figure of a universal sympathetic goddess was found here.

"Eidea" in The Apocryphon of John. In the *Apocryphon of John*, the term *EIDEA* twice occurs in passages which suggest its meaning to be that of an hypostatized entity similar to Sophia. *EIDEA* is described as an aeon on the same level as Wisdom (Sophia) and Love (Agape).

---

7. Cf. BG 8502.92.13-16 where the Savior is identified with the EINE, "image" of God. Cf., also, the parallel in III. 100.2-4.
8. The text of *Eugnostos* III.72.12 and the *Sophia of Jesus Christ* III.95.6 have both been corrected from *2ICE*, "suffering," to *2I CA (NIM)*, "on (all) sides." In Achmimic, *2ICE* would be ambiguous since it may have both meanings.

Apocryphon of John II.8.12-16

And the third light is Daveithai, who is installed over the third aeon. And three other
aeons are with him: Sophia, Agape, Eidea.

The first words of the revealer in the *Apocryphon of
John* make use of the term "Eidea" in a way that suggests
that "Eidea" can be a name or aspect of the revealed
trinity.

Apocryphon of John II.2.10-17

Why are you afraid? Are you a stranger to this
Eidea (*EIDEA*)? That is, Do not be timid. I am
the one who is with you always. I am the
Father. I am the Mother. I am the Son. I am
the undesecrated and undefiled one. I have come
to reveal that which is, and that which has
been, and that which shall come to pass.

Here, the "Eidea" signifies the revealer, perhaps in a
feminine aspect, and is indirectly a form of the deity
itself. The feminine nature of the revealer occurs
again at the end of the Berlin version of the *Apocryphon*:

And once again this Mother came before me.
This is what she has done in the world: she
has established her seed over it (BG 8502 76.
1-5).

The simple English translation "semblance," employed in
The Nag Hammadi Library, does not do justice to the
implications of the term "Eidea."

In all of the extent versions of the *Apocryphon of
John*, the revealer figure has become identified with
Jesus. Typical is the secondary ending in codex two in
which it is related that the revelation was given by
Jesus to John: "And the Savior gave it to him (John)
so that he should write it down and keep it safe. . .
and immediately he became invisible before him" (31.32-
32.3). The ending of the *Sophia of Jesus Christ* in BG
8502 is very similar: "These things the blessed Savior
said and became invisible to them" (BG 126.17-127.2).
The identification of the hypostatized feminine "Eidea"
with the Savior in the *Sophia of Jesus Christ* is a
typical process in the Christianization of gnostic documents. An example from the New Testament will show the

57

importance of the concept for early Christian theology:
in the Epistle to the Hebrews, Jesus' relationship to
God is defined as "the effulgence of his glory and the
exact image (χαραχτηρ) of his nature" (Heb. 1:3).

  "*Archē*" *in Eugnostos the Blessed and in The Sophia of
Jesus Christ.* A somewhat different situation exists in
the two documents with respect to the term *APXH*, "beginning," "rule," "aeon" (fem.). The phrase "from the
beginning," or "in the beginning," seems sometimes to be
used in a purely temporal sense and at other times refers to a personified *APXH* endowed with generative
power. In this latter usage, an identification with
Sophia can be intended, in that the *APXH* can mystically
mean the feminine being from which God formed the world.
This ambiguity shows up in the following passages.

Eug. III.86.24-87.9   *SJC BG 111.2-112.4 (III.*
                                111.2-12)

Therefore, the church of   Therefore, the church of
the Eighth revealed   the Eighth, which was re-
itself as androgynous.   vealed as androgynous,
It has been named in   has been named in part
part masculine and   masculine and in part
in part feminine.   feminine. The masculine,
The masculine was named   in fact, was called
Church and the feminine   Church, but the feminine
Life so that it should   Life, so that it should
be manifest that from   be manifest that from
a woman the life in   *the woman* the life of
all the aeons came   all the aeons came
into being, every   into being. And every
name being taken   name was taken
from the beginning (APXH.)   *from this APXH.*

  "From the beginning," in *Eugnostos*, here could be
understood purely in a temporal sense. However, a new
personal interpretation is intended in the *Sophia of
Jesus Christ*, mirrored in the agential word for "from,"
NTOOTC, and in the addition of the demonstrative "this."

  A mystical sense of the term *APXH* also seems to be
present in *Eugnostos*. On two occasions this document
introduces new material with the words, "This is
a(nother) beginning (*APXH*) of knowledge" (III.74.19-20;
76.13).[9] The second reference seems to make an allu-

---

9. For this formula as an introduction to collections of sayings

sion to the Sophia of Prov. 8:22-23 by the words: "the
first who was revealed before the universe."

Eugnostos III.76.13-24

This is another APXH of knowledge, by the hand
of *the Begotten One, the first who was revealed
before the universe*. In the infinite realm,
there is a self-grown, self-constructed father
who is full of shining, ineffable light. This
one (masc.) understood the APXH so that his
image should come into being as a great power.
Immediately, the APXH of that light revealed an
immortal, androgynous man.

By scrupulously avoiding the personified APXH in his
translation, D. Parrott gives us an unwieldly version:

Eugnostos III.76.13-24 (Parrott)

Another subject (APXH) of knowledge is this,
under the heading of *the begotten. Before the
universe, the First was revealed*. In the
boundlessness he is a self-grown, self-
constructed father who is full of shining,
ineffable light. In the beginning (APXH) he
decided to have his form come to be as a great
power. Immediately the beginning (APXH) of
that light was revealed as an immortal,
androgynous man. (our italics)

This translation does not yield any connection between
"the heading of the begotten" and that "self-grown,
self-constructed father," yet it is clear that the
passage is speaking of some kind of divine syzygy which
produced the Immortal Man. That APXH in *Eugnostos* can
have the meaning of a partner for the transcendent
deity is clear from an earlier passage:

Eugnostos III.71.13-18

The One who exists is ineffable. No APXH has
known him; no power, nor subordinate, nor any
force of nature from the foundation of the
world - except he himself alone.

---

in the Egyptian Wisdom tradition, see Robinson, *Trajectories*,
p. 110.

The apparent contradiction of this passage with the previous one can be explained on the view that the transcendent deity is unknowable but knows all of the powers beneath him.

A similar connection between the terms ΑΡΧΗ and "name" is reported by Irenaeus in his attack upon Marcus. This heretic is supposed to have received the following special revelation concerning the origin of all things:

> When first the unoriginated, inconceivable Father, who is without material substance, and is neither male nor female, willed to bring forth that which is ineffable to Him, and to endow with form that which is invisible, He opened His mouth and sent forth the Word, similar to himself, who, standing near, showed Him what he Himself was, inasmuch as he had been manifested in the form of that which was invisible. Moreover, the pronunciation of His name took place as follows: - He spake the first word of it, which was the "Archē" [of all the rest].[10]

A footnote in the Roberts-Donaldson edition reports that the old Latin preserves the Greek word αρχη untranslated, implying that "ARCHĒ" was the first word which the Father spoke.[11]

"Archē" elsewhere in Codex II. The use of ARCHĒ as an hypostatized power is not limited to Eugnostos and the Sophia of Jesus Christ. Two passages from On the Origin of the World illustrate a similar usage:

On the Origin of the World 99.6-8; 100.14-16

From that day forth the rule (ΑΡΧΗ) of envy was manifest in all of the aeons and their worlds.

From that day forth was manifest the rule (ΑΡΧΗ) of the word, which attained unto gods, angels, and mankind.

---

10. Irenaeus, A. H. I.xiv.1.
11. See Roberts-Donaldson ANF, (1925 edition) vol. 1, p. 336, n. 4. For another connection between "beginning" (fem.) and "name", see the Gospel of Truth, I.38.6-9, where the "name" of the Father is said to be the Son.

In the *Apocryphon of John* the masculine archons are contrasted with the feminine *APXH*.

Apocryphon of John II.24.32-34

> And he (the Protarchon) installed the two
> archons over some *APXH* (pl.), so that they
> should rule over the grave.

"Archē" in Jewish sources. The gnostic usage of *APXH*
and particularly of the phrase "in the *APXH*" is probably
traceable to the incipit of Genesis in the Septuagint,
and as such is related to the Chokhma figure of the Old
Testament and the Jewish schools of Wisdom. In the
Palestinian Targum and in the Samaritan Liturgy, "the
beginning" became the equivalent of Wisdom-Sophia. "In
the beginning (αρχη) God created the heaven and the
earth" became "In his wisdom God created the heaven and
the earth." Wisdom was considered to be God's feminine
helper at creation.[12] The association of *APXH* and
Sophia with God's Son may have led to the Syriac version
of Gen. 1:1, "In his Son, God created the heavens and
the earth."[13]

"Archē" in the Fathers of the Church. The hermeneutic
in which the *APXH* of the opening of Genesis is taken to
refer to God's Son is also found in Justin's *Dialogue
with Trypho:*

> 'I shall give you another testimony, my friends,'
> said I, 'from the Scriptures, that God begat be-
> fore all creatures *a Beginning* [who was] a cer-
> tain rational power [proceeding] from himself,
> who is called by the Holy Spirit, now the Glory
> of the Lord, now the Son, again Wisdom. . ."[14]

---

12. Cf. Gilles Quispel, who notes the Palestinian Targum and the
Samaritan Liturgy in *Gnostic Studies I*, (Istanbul: Nederlands
Historisch-Archaeologisch Instituut in het Nabije Oosten, 1974),
p. 222. Quispel offers the suggestion that the transition from the
Jewish concept of wisdom to that of the gnostic concept of wisdom
took place in the school of Simon Magus.
13. See B. Bagatti, *The Church from the Circumcision*, trans. E.
Hoade (Jerusalem: 1971), p. 175. Cf. *The Epistle of Ignatius to
the Tarsians*, vi, (ANF, vol. 1), where the words of Prov. 8:27,30
referring to Wisdom are applied to Jesus Christ by Ignatius.
14. Justin Martyr, *Dialogue with Trypho, a Jew*, LXI (ANF, vol. 1).

According to Justin, all these names may be applied to Jesus, "since He ministers to the Father's will, and since He was begotten of the Father by an act of will."[15] Justin argues that one can indisputably learn from the "let us make" passage of Genesis that God "conversed with someone who was numerically distinct from Himself, and also a rational Being."[16]

The antiquity of the feminine imagery of the power known as ΑΡΧΗ is hardly to be denied. In listing passages from the Old Testament which he thinks the heretics perverted, Irenaeus recounts:

> Moses, then, they declare, by his mode of beginning the account of the creation, has at the commencement pointed out the mother of all things when he says: 'In the beginning God created the heaven and the earth' for, as they maintain, by naming these four, - God, Beginning, heaven, and earth, - he set forth their Tetrad.[17]

Irenaeus likewise blames the Valentinians for their false exegesis of the opening of John's Gospel. According to the Valentinians, the "Archē" is in the Father and of the Father, while the Word is in the "Archē" and of the "Archē."[18]

> For when John, proclaiming one God, the Almighty, and one Jesus Christ, the Only-begotten, by whom all things were made, declares that this was the Son of God, this the Only-begotten, this the Former of all things, this the true Light who enlighteneth every man, this the Creator of the world, this He that came to His own, this He that became flesh and dwelt among us, - these men, by a plausible kind of exposition, perverting these statements, maintain that there was another Monogenes, according to production, whom they also style "Archē."[19]

Another excerpt from Irenaeus shows clearly that "Archē" was an important hypostatization among the gnostics. Irenaeus is discussing the remarkable dis-

---

15. Ibid.
16. Ibid., LXII
17. Ireneaus, Α.Η. I.xviii.1
18. Ireneaus, Α.Η. I.viii.5.
19. Ireneaus, Α.Η. I.ix.2.

crepancies among gnostic leaders as to which aeonic being spoke the scriptures:

> For if anyone, wishing to test them do question one by one with regard to any passage those who are their leading men, he shall find one of them referring the passage in question to the Propator - that is to Bythus; another referring it to Archē - that is to the Only-begotten; another to the Father of all - that is to the Word.[20]

It is clear that Christian gnostic speculation on the term "Archē" is an important feature in the *Sophia of Jesus Christ*. This speculation apparently had pre-Christian roots in a feminine hypostasis which in *Eugnostos* makes up one half of a syzygy with "the begotten one," a term that probably signifies the creative Father (Eug. III.76.14).

The question of the loneliness and knowability of God needs to be answered separately for *Eugnostos* and the *Sophia of Jesus Christ*. In the pagan *Eugnostos*, God is described as unknowable but not alone, because there exists with him a multitude of mirror images of himself. In addition to this, in the Christianized *Sophia of Jesus Christ*, the reader is informed that God was unknown, "until now." With the coming of the Savior, he has been made known (BG 93.12; 101.17). The difference between the idea of God in *Eugnostos* and in *Sophia of Jesus Christ* shows up in the following passage.

Eug. III.71.13-18

SJC BG 83.5-19 (III.94.5-14)

The one who exists is ineffable. No ΑΡΧΗ has known him; no power nor subordinate, nor any force of nature from the foundation of the world - except he himself alone.

The one who exists, the ineffable one, exists without any ΑΡΧΗ having known him; neither has any power nor subordinate, nor any force of nature from the foundation of the world known him until now - except he himself alone, *and the one to whom he wills to reveal himself through me, the one who came forth from the first light. From now on he will reveal himself* through me. I am the great Savior.

---

20. Ireneaus, A.H. IX.xxxv .4

The second question which arises in the mind of the
reader of *Eugnostos* and the *Sophia of Jesus Christ* is
that of the varied roles of Sophia. Like the feminine
hypostases, "Eidea" and "Archē," Sophia is of supernatural origin and divine nature. In some passages in
the *Sophia of Jesus Christ*, she appears in a fallen
state, contesting with Ialdabaoth for the imprisoned
souls that she has sent into the world.[21]

The following expressions about (Pistis) Sophia are
peculiar to *Eugnostos*.

(1) "Now the First Man is 'Pistis'" . . (III.78.3-4).
In the parallel passage (III.102.20-21), the *Sophia of
Jesus Christ* pointedly omits this identification. One
may suppose that the *Sophia of Jesus Christ* did not
want to associate the Model Man (Christ) with "Pistis,"
who in developed gnosticism becomes identical with
Sophia, the fallen aeon.[22]

(2) "Then the Savior co-operated with his syzygy,
Pistis Sophia. He revealed six androgynous spiritual
beings. . . . The sixth is Pistis Sophia" (82.7-83.1).
This passage is omitted in the *Sophia of Jesus Christ*.
In the place of Eugnostos' catalogue of 360 powers, the
Sophia of Jesus Christ presents a version of the myth
of the *fallen* Sophia and the coming of the savior (BG
103.10-105.14).

Both *Eugnostos* and the *Sophia of Jesus Christ* know
of a Pistis of the invisible world who is found in the
visible world, but the Christian document specifies that
the visible things are "of the unbegotten father" (BG
90.12-13). This clarification may be the author's
attempt to distinguish the Christian creator from a
gnostic archigenetor.

Eug. III.74.12-19   *SJC BG 90.3-13 (III.98.12-
                              20)*

Now, if there is one who   The perfect savior said,
would believe on the words   Come

---

21. Cf. the *Sophia of Jesus Christ* III.107.24-25; BG 105. 5-7; and
BG 118.15-18.
22. In *Orig. World*, II.98.13-14 the designation "Pistis" is
explained by the name "Sophia." Cf. also *Hyp. Arch.* II.94.5-6.

which have been presented,
let him examine thoroughly
from that which is hidden
to the perfection of that
which is visible. And this
Ennoia will teach him
how Pistis of
the invisible
things has been found in
the visible things.

from these invisible things
to the perfection of that
which is visible. And she,
the emananation of the Ennoia,
will reveal to you how
Pistis of the invisible
things has been found in
the visible things *of the
unbegotten father.*

It is, of course, possible that "Pistis" here is simply
the word for "faith" and that both documents refer to a
kind of natural theology by which man can know about
God through created things. This explanation, however,
seems less likely than that which takes "Pistis" to be
an hypostatization similar to "Eidea," "Archē," and
"Sophia," since the hypostasized Pistis is also an
important figure in other Nag Hammadi documents.[23]

*Sophia Contrasted in Eugnostos and The Sophia of
Jesus Christ.* The name "Sophia" occurs in the first
line and also as part of the title at the end of the
Sophia of Jesus Christ. "Sophia," here is probably to
be understood as the personified aeon who as a type of
the fallen soul is redeemed by Christ, so that the
title may be interpreted as meaning "The Sophia who
belongs to Jesus Christ." On the other hand, in
Eugnostos "Sophia" appears as the name of the female
aspect of a being who is equally male and female, as the
following parallel shows.

Eug. III.76.21-77.6

*SJC BG 94.7-95.4 (III.101.
6-19)*

Immediately the ΑΡΧΗ
of that light revealed an
immortal, androgynous
man. His masculine name
is called 'the begetter of
[NOYC],' while his femi-
nine name is 'all-wise
Sophia, generatrix
(ΓΕΝΕΤΕΙΡΑ).' It is
also said of her that

Immediately the light of
that ΑΡΧΗ was revealed in
a first man, immortal and
androgynous, *in order that
through this immortal one
mankind should attain unto
salvation and awaken from the
sleep of oblivion by means of
the teacher who has been sent,
who is with you until the end*

23. Cf. *Orig. World* II.98.13-14; 99.2, 24, 29 et al. and the
Paraphrase of Shem VII. 26.3, 14, 15; 28.30; 30.2, 5 et al.

	of the misery of the robbers, his consort being the great Sophia who was appointed from the beginning within him as a syzygy through the self-begotten father.
she resembles her brother [and] her syzygy.	

The affective tone surrounding "Sophia" in *Eugnostos* is quite different from that in the *Sophia of Jesus Christ*. In accord with the cosmogony of *Eugnostos*, Sophia and her male partner in the spheres are equal; in accord with the soteriological plan of the *Sophia of Jesus Christ*, Sophia can be understood in two aspects: the immortal man's consort; and the faulty, incomplete soul. To make this clear we need to examine other passages concerning Sophia.

Eug. III.81.21-82.6	SJC BG 102.14-103.9 (III.106. 14-24)
Now the Son of Man co-operated with Sophia, his syzygy, and he revealed a grand, androgynous light. [They call his] masculine *name* 'savior, the begetter of all things.' His feminine *name* is called 'Sophia, universal generatrix (ΠΑΝΓΕΝΕΤΙΡΑ)' whom some call 'Pistis.'	The perfect savior said: The Son of Man co-operated with Sophia his syzygy, and he revealed *himself* in a grand, androgynous light. *On the one hand,* they call his masculinity 'savior, the begetter of all things,' *but on the other hand,* his femininity 'Sophia, universal generatrix (ΠΑΝΓΕΝΗΤΕΙΡΑ)' whom some call 'Pistis.'

The wording of the passages above is very similar, but there are three noteworthy differences. The first is the use of the reflexive form of the verb, "revealed," in BG 102.18, whereas the transitive verb is used in *Eugnostos*. The use of the reflexive implies that the Son of Man has revealed himself, whereas in *Eugnostos* the Son of Man is reported to have revealed a third androgynous man. A second difference is the use in the Berlin codex of the Greek particles μεν . . . δε, correlatives which indicate opposition much like English "on the one hand . . . but on the other hand." Here the particles distinguish the pre-eminent Savior from his consort Sophia. A third difference is that the word "name" in reference to the androgyne "savior-Sophia" is twice missing in the Berlin codex version. These changes support the idea that the *Sophia of*

Jesus Christ is more concerned with soteriology than cosmogonic androgynes.[24]

In the *Sophia of Jesus Christ* (BG 103.10-105.14; III.106.24-108.4) there is an allegory in which the soul, represented as a drop of light, is depicted as fettered in the darkness of the world. This light-drop is from Sophia, and like her is in need of redemption. The Savior comes to "justify" Sophia, and to awaken her children that they "should bring forth much fruit." At the conclusion of the allegory, the fallen nature of Sophia with respect to the Savior is clearly expressed: "that the other Sophia might be justified from that fault and that her children might no longer suffer lack but attain unto honor and glory" (BG 105. 5-11).

In *Eugnostos* 88.7-8 Sophia is called "the silence" and "the syzygy" of the immortal man, but in the parallel in the *Sophia of Jesus Christ* it is the immortal man who is himself designated "the silence."

Eug. III.88.3-11	*SJC BG 113.11-114.2*
All of the immortals which I have just described have all of their authority from the power of the immortal man *and Sophia, his syzygy,* who was called "the silence" because in reflection without words she perfected her imperishable majesty.	But the immortals which I have just described have authority from the power of the immortal man who was called "the silence." Through reflection without words he perfected his universal majesty.

That in the original reading the "silence" belonged to Sophia is indicated by the curious aporia in the parallel passage in the codex-three version of the *Sophia of Jesus Christ*: "through reflection without words *her* [sic] universal majesty was perfected" (III.112.9-11).

Sophia in the Codicil of The Sophia of Jesus Christ (BG 117.8-127.10; III.114.7-119.17). This brings us to

---

24. The codex-three copy of the *Sophia of Jesus Christ* reads more closely in this passage with *Eugnostos* III than with the Berlin codex copy of the *Sophia of Jesus Christ*.

a consideration of the codicil, that important section
of the *Sophia of Jesus Christ* which occurs after the
parallel material from *Eugnostos* has been completed.
The beginning of the codicil has Mariamme asking Jesus
a question concerning the disciples' origin, destiny,
and activity. The texts of the two versions differ
considerably in their presentations of the Savior's
answer. The codex three version contains about six
additional lines, effectively replacing Sophia by "the
father of the universe" and affirming that Sophia had
decided "by herself alone to cause these things to come
into being without her man." Apparently, Sophialogy
was a fertile field for speculation, and the unique
material of codex three seems to contain anti-Sophia
themes beyond those of the Berlin codex version. The
development corresponds in some ways to the Sophialogy
of the *Apocryphon of John* and the *Hypostasis of the
Archons*.

Two possibilities exist to explain the difference
between the versions: either the Berlin codex omitted
the material in question, or it was added by an editor
of the codex three version. The first view was that of
Till, who, unfortunately did not substantiate his
claim.[25] The second possibility - that the passage in
question was added in the updating of the document -
can be argued in two ways. First, with regard to subject matter, it will be shown that within the context
of the *Sophia of Jesus Christ* and other early gnostic
documents, the reading "Mother of the universe" is to
be preferred over "Father of the universe" as the creator of the veil between the immortals and those below.
Second, the motif of the folly of the woman in creating
"without her partner" appears to be an interpolation in
accord with Christian gnostic theology.

SJC BG 117.17-118.11   *SJC III.114.12-24*

The perfect savior said   The perfect savior said
to them: I want you to   to them: I want you to
understand that Sophia,   understand that Sophia,
the mother of the uni-   the mother of the universe, will reveal her   verse,
goodness. He (?) will
be revealed with his
mercy and incomprehen-
sibility.

---

25. Till, *BG 8502*, p. 277.

He created that veil between the immortals and those that came into being after them.	*the syzygy, decided by herself alone to cause these things to come into being without her man.* But when the father of the universe decided that he should reveal his inconceivable goodness, he created that veil between the immortals and those that came into being after them.

The italicized material in the codex three version appears to be a distinctive Nag Hammadi interpolation. The Coptic of both texts is difficult and corrupt, but the reader will be struck by the unusual notion of the Father of the universe creating a veil such as he is purported to have done in the codex three version. The Berlin codex text is obscure, but one thing is certain, it does not contain the phrase "Father of the universe." The gender of the pronouns, always a source of difficulty in Coptic, and of particular confusion when they refer to androgynes, must not be given too much weight. In view of the fact that another passage in the Berlin codex version (120.14-121.1) joins the concepts of the Mother Sophia and the veil, it is possible that the text originally read, "She created that veil. . ." in accord with the beginning of the passage in which Sophia is the subject. We give here the other passage in the *Sophia of Jesus Christ* and three passages from other documents which connect the veil motif with Sophia.

Sophia of Jesus Christ BG 120.14-121.1

And ⟨all⟩ these things came to pass in the will of our Mother Sophia so that the curtains of that place should be co-ordinated. . .

The parallel in codex three is lacking (III.115-116), but both *On the Origin of the World* and the *Hypostasis of the Archons* represent a tradition which knows Sophia as the maker of the veil.

Orig. World II.98.16-23	*Hyp. Arch.* II.94.5-10
And immediately her (Sophia's) will was manifest as a heavenly image, possessing an	Sophia, she who is called Pistis, wanted to make a work by herself, without

unimaginable magnitude, being in the midst of the immortals and those that came into being after them, even as the heaven is a veil separating mankind from that which is above.

her partner. And her work became a heavenly image. There is a curtain between those above and the aeons which are beneath.

In addition to the above passages, the Codex II-IV version of the *Apocryphon of John* associates the veil with the Mother.

> *Apocryphon of John II.13.32-36*
>
> . . . but when the mother understood that the veil of darkness had come into being imperfectly and she knew that her partner had not agreed with her, then she repented. . .

When the passage in codex three which we are discussing (114.12-24) is compared with other texts related to the "veil," one concludes that the original version of the *Sophia of Jesus Christ* did not include the concept of the Father of the universe creating the veil, but that this motif is a later addition in the Nag Hammadi version.[26]

The phrase "Father of the universe" does not often occur in the marginally Christian documents of the Nag Hammadi collection. Probably the phrase did not appear at all in the original text of the *Apocryphon of John*. It is relatively certain that the only occurrence in the Codex II-IV version is redactional. Compare the Berlin codex parallel with it.

Ap. John BG 48.1-4

Ap. John II.14.19-24

The holy perfect father, the first man, ⟨taught⟩ him in the form of a man.

. . . the holy Metropator, and the perfect one, the perfected Pronoia, the icon of the invisible, that is, *the father of the universe*, he through whom all things came into existence, - the first man - for in a masculine form he revealed his image.

---

26. Cf. also the *Sophia of Jesus Christ*, BG 118.15-119.4 where the

In the Nag Hammadi version, the phrase "Father of the universe" is unnecessary for the sentence, and even the introductory ΕΤΕ ΠΑΪ ΠΕ, "that is," marks it as an editorial expansion. We should also note that the maleness of the image is pertinent only to a sex-related soteriological scheme.

A consideration of other Nag Hammadi texts criticizing parthenogenic creation shows that this was a favorite target of anti-Sophia polemic. The occurrence of this motif at the beginning of the codicil in codex three should not surprise us. The Nag Hammadi author wanted to include the statement that "Sophia, the mother of the universe, the syzygy, decided by herself alone to cause these things to come into being without her man," i.e., without her savior, in order to introduce the soteriological plan of the codicil with its syzygy doctrine of opposites in tension. Here Sophia is the feminine and fallen type of the soul, and as she is saved by conjunction with her male and spiritual aspect, so souls are saved by being joined with "that (male) spirit and breath, that the two should be one, as it was in the beginning" (BG 122.8-12; III.117.1-3).

Summarily, the evidence of the passage concerning the creation of the veil and Sophia's fault in producing parthenogenetically indicates that III.114.15-21 at the beginning of the codicil is an interpolation. The interpolation seems designed to downgrade Sophia in order to magnify her savior. The proposed fault of Sophia is a logical precondition for the task of the savior in the syzygial soteriology of the *Sophia of Jesus Christ*. That same fault has no logical place within the cosmogonic system of aeonic androgynes developed in *Eugnostos the Blessed*.

The Complicated Structure of The Sophia of Jesus Christ.

The third problem which arises in the mind of one who compares *Eugnostos* with the *Sophia of Jesus Christ* is the complicated structure of the latter document. Complications originated when the author of the *Sophia of Jesus Christ*, in using the source document, *Eugnostos*, combined it with a soteriological plan that produced a

---

veil apparently comes into being as a result of the lower Sophia's struggle to attain the pleroma.

conglomerate of ideas whose ingredients are nearly inseparable. The codicil, however, presents the basics of the soteriological system unmixed with images from *Eugnostos*. By examining the codicil, one may be able to disentangle the motifs which relate directly to soteriology and recognize the changes wrought upon the cosmogonic plan of Eugnostos.

Feminine Motifs within the Codicil of The Sophia of Jesus Christ. Some of the motifs in the codicil are familiar from the presentations of the fathers of the church. The feminine ones, related to ideas presented in the first seven chapters of the first book of Irenaeus' *Against Heresies*, can be discussed under four headings: the soul imaged as feminine; Sophia's fault; Ialdabaoth's prison for feminine souls; and different destinies for humans.

(1) The soul imaged as feminine. According to Irenaeus who reports that his information is from the commentaries of certain followers of Valentinus, the heretics distinguished three kinds of humans: the "hylics" of material nature; the "psychics," ensouled but not enspirited; and the "pneumatics," ensouled and enspirited. The hylics are not saved; the psychics have free choice with regard to their destiny - either destruction or the Ogdoad, a place midway between destruction and the pleroma; the pneumatics, by nature righteous, enter into the pleroma.

Again, according to Irenaeus, the heretics considered themselves to be the pneumatics, the spiritual seed of the mother Achamoth. Their final destiny was to be associated with her, so that when she enters the pleroma as the consort of the Savior, they become fit brides for the angels who serve the Savior.[27]

The first discussion in the codicil revolves around the term ΤΑϯΛΕ, "drop," a word of feminine gender. The text surrounding the word is difficult, and the translation by D. Parrott in *The Nag Hammadi Library* does not clarify. Parrott's translation reads:

Sophia of Jesus Christ BG 118.18-120.3 (Parrott)

And these became a curtain of a spirit. From <the>aeon above the effluences of light, just

---

27. Irenaeus, *A. H.* I.vii.1.

as I said already, a drop from the light and the spirit *came down* to the lower regions of the Almighty of chaos, so that *he* might reveal their molded forms from that drop, because it is a judgment on him, the Prime Begetter, who is called 'Yaldabaoth.' That drop revealed their molded forms through the breath *{or a living soul.* It was withered and it slumbered in the ignorance of the soul. (our italics)

The difficulties in this translation are twofold. First, Ialdabaoth is credited with revealing "their molded forms (ΠΛΑϹΜΑ)" from the drop. Such a translation does not agree with related texts which state that the pneumatics become manifest in the plasma, and thus, they, not Ialdabaoth, make manifest the plasma of the archons. The passage should be compared to the ending of *On the Origin of the World* which relates that when the immortal Father "wished to dispossess the archons of destruction through their plasma (pl.), he sent your images down into the world" (II.124.7-10). Also relevant is the passage in *Hyp. Arch.* 96.33-34, "when the true Man is revealed in their plasma (pl.)."[28] The next-to-last sentence also clearly states that it is the drop which "revealed their molded forms." That the first portion of the passage is corrupt can be discerned from the fact that in the Coptic, beginning with " *(which)* came down", the remainder of the sentence is an incomplete relative clause. As a plausible emendation, we suggest a feminine subject for the verb "reveal," viz., ΕϹΕΟΥWΝ2, "so that *she* might reveal." The Greek verb in the original text would not have specified the gender. We should also note that in the earlier passage of the *Sophia of Jesus Christ*, it is clearly stated that the drop was sent forth by Sophia (BG 104.15-18).

A second difficulty with Parrott's translation concerns the phrase ΕΥΨΥΧΗ ΕϹΟΝ2, translated as "for a living soul." The text states that "the drop revealed their (the archons') plasma through the breath (ΝΙϤΕ)." The word ΝΙϤΕ can also be the participial use of the verb, "breathing," thus making the sentence an obvious reference to the Genesis account of God's breathing into Adam the breath of life. In gnostic hermeneutic the breath is Sophia's, imparted unknowingly by Ialdabaoth, and supplies the highest element for Adam. The phrase ΕΥΨΥΧΗ ΕϹΟΝ2 mirrors exactly the last phrase of Gen. 2:7,

---

28. See footnote 25 in Chapter four, p. 108.

εισ ψυχην ζωσαν, "into a living soul."[29] A better translation might read:

Sophia of Jesus Christ BG 118.18-120.3 (Arthur)

But these became a veil of spirit from the aeons
above the effulgences of light.
As I have said before (103.10-15) - a drop
from the light and the spirit *which* came down to
the lower regions of the Almighty one of chaos -
so that <it (fem.)> might reveal their plasma
by that drop being a judgment to him, the Archigenetor, who is called "Ialdabaoth." That drop
revealed their plasma by means of "*the breathing into a living soul.*" It cooled and slept on
account of the oblivion of the soul.

The theme of the soul as a bride occurs in the codicil
in much the same way as in the *Exegesis on the Soul.*
The word ΝΟΥ2Β is used in BG 122.7 to indicate a kind of
yoking as in marriage. Moreover, the allustion to Gen.
2:24, "that the two of them should become a single one
as it was from the beginning" is also made in *Ex. Soul*
II.133.3-8, where it is explained that spiritual marriage
has joined the soul with her bridegroom.

Sophia of Jesus Christ BG 122.5-13

For this reason, then, I (the savior) have come
to this place, so that they (the psychics)
should be *yoked* with that spirit, and the
breath, and that the two should become a single
one, as it was from the beginning, so that you
should bring forth much fruit. . .

The codicil understands that the psychic ones are
under the domination of Ialdabaoth. They are imaged as
feminine, while the spiritual ones, the offspring of the
Savior, are to become yoked to them as in marriage, thus
completing the original androgyne which was symbolized
by the first union - "so that the two should become a
single one."

(2) *Sophia's fault.* The fault of Sophia is recognized
by both Irenaeus and the author of the *Sophia of Jesus
Christ* as an important feature of gnostic theology. In
fact, Irenaeus reports two faulty Sophias: the one, an

---

29. Cf. *Hyp. Arch.* 88.15-16 ΑΠΡωΜΕ ΕΤΜΜΑΥ ϢωΠΕ ΑΥΨΥΧΗ ΕϹΟΝ2, "that
man became a living soul."

aeon, is degenerate on account of passion; the second, called "Achamoth", is at fault because of an innate opposition of her nature to knowledge. Moreover, Achamoth, according to Irenaeus, is said to have desired to return to him who gave her life, and from that desire derived souls, even that of the demiurge. Irenaeus reports of Achamoth:

And when she could not pass by Horus on account of that passion in which she had been involved, and because she alone had been left without, she then resigned herself to every sort of that manifold and varied state of passion to which she was subject; and thus she suffered grief on the one hand because she had not obtained the object of her desire, and fear on the other hand, lest life itself should fail her, as light had already done, while, in addition, she was in the greatest perplexity. All these feelings were associated with ignorance. And this ignorance of hers was not, like that of her mother, the first Sophia, an Aeon, due to degeneracy by means of passion, but to an [innate] opposition [of nature to knowledge]. Moreover, another kind of passion fell upon her (Achamoth) namely, that of desiring to return to him who gave her life. This collection [of passions] they declare was the substance of the matter from which this world was formed. For from [her] desire of returning [to him who gave her life], every soul belonging to this world, and that of the Demiurge himself, derived its origin.[30]

In the codicil, the "fault of the woman" motif follows closely upon the passage concerning the creation of the veil. Sophia (BG 118.1-2) is here burdened with "the fault of the woman," and is said to come into being while personified error wars against her.

Sophia of Jesus Christ BG 118.7-18

He (?) created that veil between the immortals and those that came into being after them, so that the inevitable should follow upon every aeon, and the chaos, so that the fault of the woman should be made manifest, and that she

---

30. Irenaeus, *A. H.* I.iv.1-2.

should come into being contending with error
(ΠΛΑΝΗ).

(3) *Ialdabaoth's prison for feminine souls.* According-
ing to Irenaeus, when the demiurge fashioned his psychic
man, Achamoth is said to have deposited within this man,
without the demiurge's knowledge, a spiritual seed which
she had brought forth as a result of her contemplation
of the angels of the Savior.

> But they further affirm that the Demiurge him-
> self was ignorant of that offspring of his
> mother Achamoth, which she brought forth as a
> consequence of her contemplation of those
> angels who waited on the Savior, and which was,
> like herself, of a spiritual nature. She took
> advantage of this ignorance to deposit it (her
> production) in him without his knowledge, in
> order that, being by his instrumentality
> infused into that animal soul proceeding from
> himself, and being thus carried, as in a womb
> in this material body, while it gradually
> increased in strength, it might in course of
> time become fitted for the reception of per-
> fect rationality.[31]

The codicil identifies "Ialdabaoth" (BG 119.16) with
the Archigenetor, that is, the demiurge. It affirms
that Ialdabaoth, who in several Nag Hammadi documents
boasts that he alone is God, has been overcome by the
Savior. The disciples are to continue awakening the
imprisoned souls so that the latter will finally judge
their captors, the archons. The Savior relates of himself:

Sophia of Jesus Christ BG 125.10-126.16

> But I, I have come from the First who was
> sent, so that I should reveal to you that
> which was from the beginning, concerning the
> arrogance of the Archigenetor and his angels,
> for they say of themselves that they are gods.
> But I have come to rebuke them for their blind-
> ness that I may teach everyone the God who is
> over the universe. You, now, trample down
> their caverns, cut down their game-plan
> (ΠΡΟΝΟΙΑ), break in pieces their yoke, and

---

31. Irenaeus, A. H. I.v.6.

awaken that which is mine. For I have given you authority over all things as children of the light to trample their power under your feet.

(4) *Different destinies for mankind.* Both Irenaeus and the codicil of the *Sophia of Jesus Christ* relate that with regard to mankind material substance must perish, spiritual substance returns to the pleroma, and psychic substance will go to an intermediate place. For psychic men, continence and good works are essential that they may enter the intermediate habitation. For the spiritual and the perfect, good works are not essential, because by nature the pneumatics are destined for gnosis and the pleroma. In this world, the immature spiritual seed of the pneumatics is brought to perfection.

> There being thus three kinds of substances, they declare of all that is material . . . that it must of necessity perish, inasmuch as it is incapable of receiving any 'afflatus' of incorruption. As to every animal existence . . . they hold that, inasmuch as it is a mean between the spiritual and the material, it passes to the side to which inclination draws it. Spiritual substance, again, they describe as having been sent forth for this end, that, being here united with that which is animal, it might assume shape, the two elements being simultaneously subjected to the same discipline . . . . They further hold that the consummation of all things will take place when all that is spiritual has been formed and perfected by Gnosis and by this they mean spiritual men who have attained to the perfect knowledge of God and been initiated into these mysteries by Achamoth. And they represent themselves to be these persons. . . .[32]

The destiny of souls as portrayed in the codicil of the *Sophia of Jesus Christ* is complex. The text appears to be duplicated in some fashion, and there are multiple accounts of the destinies of souls.

---

32. Irenaeus, A. H. I.vi.1,4.

77

For he who knows the father in pure gnosis
shall pass on to the father and shall find rest
for himself in the unbegotten father. But he
who knows him faultily shall pass on with the
fault and (not?) find rest for himself in the
Eighth. And he who knows the immortal spirit,
which is the light, in silence through reflection and good-will within the truth, let him
bring me some symbols of the invisible one, and
he shall become light in the spirit of silence.
He who knows the Son of Man in gnosis and
agapē, let him bring me a symbol of the Son of
Man, and he shall pass on to that place - with
those who are in the Eighth.[33]

The ascent of the soul to the upper spheres as suggested in the above passage is characteristic of the
endings of gnostic revelatory documents, as for example,
On the Origin of the World, the *Hypostasis of the
Archons*, the *Apocryphon of John*, the *Apocalypse of Paul*,
the *Gospel of Mary*, and *Poimandres*. Jonas has stressed
the wide variety and importance of the ascent motif
throughout gnosticism.[34] For our purposes, it is sufficient to note the place of the feminine in the ascent
of the soul. In the passage given above, she is typified by "the silence." In the codex three parallel, the
Greek loanword СІГН is used, which in some gnostic
systems is a feminine hypostasis ranking as the partner
of Bythus, "the abyss."

The "symbols" brought to the Savior may represent
passwords which in gnostic systems are used by the soul
to escape the archons as it passes through the spheres.
A good example is found in the *Apocalypse of Paul* (V.2)
which records that Paul, travelling in the Spirit,
recites the proper words and ascends to the tenth heaven
where he finds his fellow spirits. Another example from
the Nag Hammadi documents is found in the Hermetic tractate, the *Discourse on the Eighth and Ninth* (VI.6). By
incantations, the soul journeys successfully through
seven planetary spheres and finally enters the realms of
true bliss, the Eighth and the Ninth.

---

33. This translation makes use of some of the Greek loanwords in
the codex three parallel.
34. See Hans Jonas, *The Gnostic Religion*, 2d ed. rev. (Boston:
Beacon Press, 1963) pp. 165-69.

The codicil seems to preserve a tradition in which personified Silence protects the soul as it passes through the spheres (BG 123.13). Irenaeus attributes such a teaching to disciples of a certain Marcus. The soul is saved by affiliation with a deity called either "Redemption" or "Silence," who after listening to the pleading of the soul, helps it escape the judging archon.

For they affirm, that because of the *Redemption* it has come to pass that they can neither be apprehended, nor even seen by the judge. But even if he should happen to lay hold upon them then they might simply repeat these words, while standing in his presence along with the *Redemption*: "O thou, who sittest beside God, and the mystical, eternal Sigē (silence), thou through whom the angels (mightiness), who continually behold the face of the Father, having thee as their guide and introducer, do derive their forms from above, which she in the greatness of her daring inspiring with mind on account of the goodness of the Propator, produced us as their images, having her mind then intent upon the things above, as in a dream, - behold, the judge is at hand, and the crier orders me to make my defense. But do thou, as being acquainted with the affairs of both, present the cause of both of us to the judge, inasmuch as it is in reality but one cause." Now, as soon as the Mother hears these words, she puts the Homeric helmet of Pluto upon them, so that they may invisibly escape the judge. And then she immediately catches them up, conducts them into the bridal chamber, and hands them over to their consorts.[35]

Feminine Motifs outside the Codicil of The Sophia of Jesus Christ. It may be of benefit here to review the question with which we began this section, namely that of the complicated structure of the *Sophia of Jesus Christ* compared with that of *Eugnostos*. We suggested that the difficulties came about when the author of the *Sophia of Jesus Christ* superimposed a Christian soteriology upon a pagan cosmogony. In the codicil the author presented his own views, and these approximate those of the heretics described in the first seven chapters of Irenaeus' first book of *Against Heresies*.

---

35. Irenaeus, *A. H.* I.xiii.6.

Although the codicil represents the longest single section without parallel in *Eugnostos*, there are some other important passages not found in *Eugnostos* which contain significant feminine imagery. We now turn our attention to this material for an examination of the same four themes we have discussed in the codicil.

(1) *The soul imaged as feminine*. We have already considered the allegory of the soul as a light-drop in the codicil of the *Sophia of Jesus Christ*, but the figure also occurs at the beginning of the long independent section in BG 103.10-107.8 (=III.106.24-108.25). The allegory of the light-drop does not occur at all in *Eugnostos*, so it may therefore be considered a redactional motif in the *Sophia of Jesus Christ*. An interesting indication of this type of redaction shows up in the codicil at BG 119.4-5 where the author remarks, "As I have said before - a drop from the light and the spirit which descended . . ." The following is the first occurrence of the allegory of that drop in the *Sophia of Jesus Christ*.

Sophia of Jesus Christ BG 103.10-16

Everyone who comes into the world was sent forth by this one (ΠΑΕΙ) like unto a drop from the light into the world of the Pantocrator.

In this passage, the "Pantocrator" is probably Ialdabaoth rather than the supreme deity. The referent of the drop metaphor is "everyone who comes into the world," that is, souls from above. The identity of the sender of the drop remains unstated at this point. The Coptic masculine pronoun ΠΑΕΙ probably refers to the aeonic being of the previous paragraph, the Savior-Sophia, an androgyne also present in the *Eugnostos* source at this point (III.82.1-6 = III.106.17-24). The *Sophia of Jesus Christ* seems to treat the androgyne as a separated entity in which the feminine part needs redemption by the masculine part. Accordingly, in this context, the "drop from the Light" represents the soul from Sophia. This is made clear a few lines further on in the text.

Sophia of Jesus Christ BG 104.13-105.2

I (the savior) raised it (the drop) up, so that it should bring forth much fruit through me, that is, that drop that was sent forth by Sophia, that it should be complete and not suffer lack, but that it should be fructified by me.

80

(2) *Sophia's fault.* The fault of Sophia also appears
in the continuation of the allegory of the light-drop.
The Savior relates his task and gives reasons for his
warfare with the archons.

Sophia of Jesus Christ BG 105.2-4

I am the great savior - in order that his (the
father's) glory should be revealed, that the
other Sophia might be justified from that fault,
so that her children might no longer suffer lack
but attain unto honor and glory, and that they
might ascend to their father and know the way
of the words of the light (of masculinity).

The parallel in codex three adds to the last line of the
above passage the sexualizing phrase "of masculinity"
(III.108.5). This addition can be understood as pro-
ceeding from the image of the children of Sophia as feminine light-drops which need male completion in order to
be fruitful. Sophia herself is to become one with the
masculine savior in order to be justified from the
fault.

(3) *Ialdabaoth's prison for feminine souls.* The name
"Ialdabaoth" does not occur in *Eugnostos*, although it
appears in the *Sophia of Jesus Christ* in the codicil.
In the main body of the *Sophia of Jesus Christ* reference
is made to "the robbers" and "those over chaos."[36] In
Eugnostos on the other hand, there is no mention of evil
powers nor of a necessity to be saved from them, except
perhaps one instance of personified Planē, "error,"
pictured as waging war with Sophia.[37] Within the allegory of the light-drop, in the *Sophia of Jesus Christ*, a
being occurs who is said to "guard it with his hand."
He is the Pantocrator, "the Almighty." At first this
figure does not appear to be inimical, but the continuation of the allegory makes it clear that he has

---

36. Cf. "robbers" in BG 94.18-19, 104.12; 121.3, 16-17); and "those
over chaos" 109.12-13. Other references to evil powers in the
Sophia of Jesus Christ include "king over this miserable creation"
(BG 95.15-17); "Pantocrator" (BG 103.15); "oblivion of the authorities" (BG 106.2-3); "hebdomad" (BG 109.1); "Powers which are called
gods" (BG 112.7-9); "Ialdabaoth" (BG 119.16); "the ones without
mercy" (BG 122.1).
37. Cf. *Eugnostos* III.77.8-9. See the following section, *Soteriological Motifs in Eugnostos and The Sophia of Jesus Christ* for a
discussion of this passage, p. 85.

imprisoned the light-drop, and that the Savior must rescue it from him. He is associated with the chain of oblivion, as well as with misery, vanity, and blindness, all features reminiscent of the arrogant Ialdabaoth, and this is probably what is meant.

Sophia of Jesus Christ BG 103.10-104.12

Everyone who comes into the world was sent forth by this one, like unto a drop from the light into the world of the Pantocrator *who guards it* (lit. "them") by his hand. And his chain of oblivion bound it in the will of Sophia so that this thing should be manifest to the world of misery on account of his vanity, and blindness, and ignorance. For he was given a name.
But I, I came forth from the upper realms, in the will of the great light. I loosed that creation. I tore through the business of the robbers' grave.

An allusion to Ialdabaoth is to be seen in the phrase, "he was given a name." The parallel in codex three reads, "he named himself" (III.107.11). Traditions for both of these expressions occur in a narrative in *On the Origin of the World* where Ialdabaoth receives his name from Pistis Sophia, and is also said to have named himself (*Orig. World* II.100.9-24).

The continuation of the allegory in which the Savior is pictured as loosing the lower creation in order to rescue the light-drop makes it clear that the drop has been imprisoned by the hostile ruler of this world.

(4) *Different destinies for mankind*. The conclusion (BG 105.14-106.10) of the allegory of the light-drop gives some indication of the different destinies allotted to different classes of mankind. The "fleshly" (CAPKINOC) ones are identified with the "fearful fire" and "defiled intercourse," but the elect ones will be removed "far from the oblivion of the powers." The message of the allegory is similar to that of the codicil where the Savior is said to commission his disciples, as children of the light, to trample upon the powers and humble their Pronoia (BG 126.5-9). The allegory of the light-drop concludes:

82

Sophia of Jesus Christ BG 105.14-106.10

You yourselves have been sent by the son who
was sent in order that you should be enlightened and removed far from the oblivion of the
powers, so that on account of you no longer
should appear that defiled intercourse which
is something from the fearful fire, something
which came forth from the fleshly ones among
them. And you shall trample on his Pronoia.

The above passage, like that of the codicil, implies
that the disciples have a role to play in the salvation
of souls. Though the flesh is base, righteous souls
can be saved by gnosis-laden spirits, among whom are
the disciples. A similar passage in the *Apocryphon of
John* relates that the soul which is bound by the chain
of oblivion can be saved by connection with another
soul who possesses the spirit, and thus avoid being
cast again into the flesh (II.27.6-21).

The theme of the light-drop also occurs in *On the
Origin of the World* 113.21-115.3. Here it is presented
as the myth of the conception and birth of Eve, the
daughter of Sophia. The myth is said to apply to "the
souls who will come into the plasma", and is certified
as a revelation of "Sabaoth and his Christ" (II.114.16).
The version in *Origin of the World* is without sexist
imagery, and apart from the mention of Sabaoth's Christ,
bears no Christian traces. Here Sophia is not identified with the fallen and imprisoned souls. Rather, she
sends forth the light-drop "upon the water" (113.23),
and struggles against the "Archigenetor" (114.20,25),
the same title applied to Ialdabaoth in the allegory in
the *Sophia of Jesus Christ* (BG 119.14-16). As in the
Sophia of Jesus Christ, the souls are shut up in the
prisons of the flesh (plasma), Adam is vivified by the
breath, and the souls will not be perfected until the
"consummation of the age" (*Orig. World* 114.24), or
until "the number of chaos is complete" (BG 121.10).
In both accounts, the statement from Gen. 2:7, "And
Adam became a living soul" is essential. The version
in *On the Origin of the World*, however, makes almost no
use of the soul-spirit distinction, nor is there any
mention of a saving male spirit. There is nothing like
the statements in the *Sophia of Jesus Christ* that Sophia
must be justified from "the fault" (BG 107.24) or that
she is ultimately responsible for the imprisonment of
the light-drop - "bound in the Will of Sophia" (BG 107.
7).

One must conclude that the account in *On the Origin of the World* is the more primitive of the two. At this stage, the higher element in man is imparted by Sophia against the will of the Creator god. Of course, Sophia cannot be a fallen entity at this point. The Christianized stage in the *Sophia of Jesus Christ* both downgrades Sophia and introduces the Savior as circumventing the "Will of Sophia." Here the light-drop is depicted as withering and slumbering in "the oblivion of the soul" (BG 120.1) at the same time that Gen. 2:7 is cited: "by the breathing into a living soul." Thus we have the paradox of the Christianized version introducing "the hot breath of the great light of the male" (BG 120.5f) as a remedy for the (weak) breathing of Sophia, which itself was a gnostic interpretation of the *same* verse showing that the creator's breath was effective only because it secretly came from Sophia.[38]

In the light of this comparison, Professor MacRae's suggestion that the fallen Sophia figure might be traceable to rabbinic speculation about the fallen Eve, appears implausible.[39] The Nag Hammadi mythical accounts of Eve generally present her as a salvific figure, an agent and assistant to Sophia. The supernatural Eve is an important figure in some of the documents which have been described as the earliest in the Nag Hammadi collection. These include the *Apocalypse of Adam*, the *Apocryphon of John*, the *Hypostasis of the Archons*, and *On the Origin of the World*. In addition, the apparent identification of Christ with "the virgin" in II Apoc. James 58.18, - "He was the Holy Spirit, and the invisible One who did not descend to earth. He was the Virgin, and that which He wishes happens to him" - might stem from an identification of Christ with the salvific Eve. Gnostic speculation about the unfallen Eve, - "the virgin whom no power hath defiled," the helpmeet who says to the first man, "Rise up, Adam," the one who becomes the tree of knowledge - looks like an expansion of Wisdom's role by means of the first woman. Even if the *fallen* Eve motif should be taken as the source for the *fallen* Sophia theme, one still cannot avoid seeing Eve's salvific roles as ultimately derived from Wisdom speculation.

---

38. For the gnostic account of the breathing into Adam (Gen. 2:7), see *Apoc. John* II.19.21-34; *Orig. World* 115.4-15; and *Hyp. Arch.* 88.3-4, 13-16.
39. See G. W. MacRae, "The Jewish Background of the Gnostic Sophia Myth," *Novum Testamentum* 12 (1970), pp. 99-101.

*Soteriological Motifs in Eugnostos and
The Sophia of Jesus Christ*

In the letter of Eugnostos there are no evil powers
nor cosmic salvation drama. The document does not fit
Jonas' standards for a gnostic writing, since there is
no fallen god, redeemed redeemer, nor divine tragedy.
The view of the universe is, on the whole, optimistic.
Nevertheless, there is a theme of salvation, and mankind can go astray by a false understanding of the
universe's nature and functions. Salvation is achieved
by a correct understanding of the universe and by
keeping oneself in harmony with it.[40] Basically this
is a neo-Pythagorean approach, whereby the author
begins with the ultimate One and shows how this in turn
produces the duad and all of the fundamental and eternal
numerical elements of the universe.

Eugnostos III.78.15-23

As I have already said, the monad is the
first among those that have been begotten. The
duad follows it, and the triad, unto the decad.
And the decad rules over the hundreds, and the
hundreds rule over the thousands, and the
thousands rule over the ten-thousands. This is
the pattern among the immortals.

The number system also includes three divine men, the
Ogdoad, seventy-two powers, and is taken as far as the
"three hundred and sixty firmaments."[41]

There are only two passages in *Eugnostos* which could
possibly be thought of as reflecting a cosmic drama and
indicating the need for a supernatural salvation.
Interestingly, these both are concerned with Sophia.
The first passage decribes the creation of the immortal,
androgynous Man, consisting of the "Begetter of perfect
mind (NOYC)" and the "all-wise Sophia." Here Sophia is
said to be like unto her brother, "a truth against which
one is not wont to strive."

Eugnostos III.76.23-77.9

. . . an immortal, androgynous man. His masculine name is called 'the Begetter of Nous,'

---

40. Cf. *Eugnostos* III.71.5-13.
41. Cf. *Eugnostos* III.84.24-85.1.

while his feminine name is 'all-wise Sophia, 'Generatrix'. It is also said of her that she resembles her brother, her syzygy, a truth against which one is not wont to strive. However, the lower truth wages war with the error (ΠΛΑΝΗ) which is with it.

The last sentence seems to allude to the "lower Sophia," or the fallen Sophia. The sentence can be seen as a redactional attempt to alter an original equality into a relationship of subordination. The juxtaposition of Sophia with Planē, "error," has no significance within the framework of the Eugnostos document.[42] However, in Christian gnosticism Sophia can be identified or replaced by the hypostatized Planē, as in the *Gospel of Truth*.[43]

The second dark allusion to cosmic drama appears to be equally incongruous within its context. The passage concludes a long section on the production of androgynous aeons by the Savior-Sophia syzygy. Where we should expect to find this in the *Sophia of Jesus Christ*, in its place there is a soteriological passage dealing with the captivity of Sophia and her children. The "fault of Sophia" is mentioned, and it is "the Great Savior" who will justify her of that fault (BG 105.2-7). Within this context, the concluding words of the passage on "the weakness of womankind" are logical and in order. Within the *Eugnostos'* passage they stand out as a redactional gloss.

Eugnostos III.85.1-9

And three hundred and sixty powers appeared from out of the firmaments. When they were completed, they were named "the Three Hundred and Sixty Heavens," according to the names of the heavens which were before them. And all these are perfect and good. *And thus was made manifest the weakness of womankind.*[44]

---

42. Compare, however, the identical idea in the *Sophia of Jesus Christ* (BG 118.15-18): "so that the fault of the woman should < be made manifest > and that she should come into being while contesting with error."
43. Cf. the *Gospel of Truth*, I.17.10-18.24.
44. Cf. the parallel in the *Sophia of Jesus Christ*, BG 107.10-13, "Through these was made manifest the fault in the woman."

Outside of these two passages, there is no allusion in *Eugnostos* to the Christian plan of salvation. However, these two passages would be quite appropriate within the *Sophia of Jesus Christ*, where the plan of salvation is clearly worked out in male and female terms. Before we present the male-female relation in the soteriology of the *Sophia of Jesus Christ*, it is necesary to say a little more about the community and its salvation in *Eugnostos*. The designation employed for the community is "the people (lit. "generation") over whom there is no kingdom" (III.75.17-18). Whether this designation in any sense reflects a radical self-consciousness against earthly authority is open to question. There is also a heavenly aeon described as "the aeon over whom there is no kingdom" in *Eugnostos* III.85.15-16. A similar phrase occurs in the ending of the *Hypostasis of the Archons* with apparent reference to a heavenly power: "from the generation which has no king" (II.97.4-5). In the *Apocalypse of Adam*, at the conclusion of the account of the births of thirteen saviors, there occurs a Christian-sounding reply to the birth of all these saviors which perhaps includes a reference to the community.

Apocalypse of Adam V.82.19-25

But the generation which does not make kings over it says, 'God chose him among all the aeons.' He caused a pure gnosis of the truth to come into being from him.

In the letter of Eugnostos, the members of the community are identified with the mysterious "antopoi." These are thought of as a myriad of light-projections of the Forefather, and as such partake in his essential nature. The members of the community are also called "the children of the unbegotten father."

Eugnostos III.75.12-23

But after him (the Father), a multitude of "projections" (ΑΝΤΟΠΟΙ), were revealed, self-begotten, co-temporal and equal in power, being according to glory without number, which are called, '*the generation over whom there is no kingdom*," (set) down among kingdoms that are established. But the whole throng of the place over whom there is no kingdom is called "the children of the unbegotten Father."

87

Here the members of the community see themselves as projections (ΑΝΤΟΠΟΙ) of the Forefather, belonging to a "kingless" race, but set within an earthly order of established kingdoms.

A few lines before the above-quoted passage, the Father himself is defined as ΑΝΤΟΠΟC, "a projection" of the Forefather, and he is said to have been revealed "as in a mirror" (*Eug.* 75.4-8). Thus it is clear that the "antopoi" are consubstantial with the Father, and with him are equally reflections or projections of the transcendent Forefather. All of this is expressed in terms of light imagery, and there is no hint that the "antopoi" are male, nor is there in Eugnostos any doctrine that the "antopoi," or the community represented by this term, are spiritual elements destined to save imprisoned psychic elements. However, when we look at the development of the idea of the "antopoi" in the *Sophia of Jesus Christ*, that is the picture that emerges there.

The male-female dichotomy in the *Sophia of Jesus Christ* is expressed by the active, procreating aspects of spirit (ΠΝΕΥΜΑ) and the passive, imprisoned aspects of soul (ΨΥΧΗ). In a passage without parallel in *Eugnostos*, the Savior explains that the (masculine) spirit is the active element.

Sophia of Jesus Christ BG 87.12-19

The perfect savior said, "I have come forth from the infinite that I might teach you all things." The essential spirit was a type of begetter; there was with it a power of begetting substance (ΟΥCΙΑ) and of giving form (ΜΟΡΦΗ). . . .

Here there is an explicit correlation of the philosophical notions of substance and form with the religious concept of spirit. There is no direct affirmation that the spirit is to be conceived of as masculine but this is clearly stated on several occasions later in the document. The doctrine of "antopoi" is picked up from *Eugnostos*, and the believers are included in the designation.

Sophia of Jesus Christ BG 91.17-92.14

And after him (the Father), a multitude of "projections" (ΑΝΤΟΠΟΙ) was revealed, all of

88

them self-begotten, co-temporal and equal in
power, being according to glory without number,
whose people (ΓΕΝΟC) are called "*the generation
over whom there is no kingdom,*" the one in
which *you* have been made manifest. And by
those people of the place over whom there is no
kingdom, they are called, "the unbegotten God,
the savior of the children of God."

The last part of the passage in the Berlin codex may be
corrupt; the codex three version reads, "But that whole
throng over whom there is no kingdom is called 'the
children of the unbegotten Father'" (III.99.22-100.2).
This is more logical and closer to the reading of
Eugnostos the Blessed. The only important change in
the *Sophia of Jesus Christ* with respect to *Eugnostos*
is the affirmation that "*you* (pl.) have been made manifest," which again refers to the saving community. The
community is also identified with the Immortal Man –
"through this Immortal Man we made our first appearance"
(BG 95.4-6) and with the Son – "you yourselves have been
sent by the Son who was sent" (BG 105.14-17).

These passages show that the community understands
itself as of the same nature as the Father and Son,
that is, of light and spirit. That this also involves
masculinity becomes abundantly clear from other passages
of the *Sophia of Jesus Christ*. The role of the Savior
and the saving community are identical; it is to bring
the spiritual element to the lost and imprisoned feminine souls. Even supernatural beings are created not
only by light but also by the male spirit.

Sophia of Jesus Christ BG 95.17-96.5

He (the Ogdoad) created for himself gods and
angels and archangels, thousands without number
for his service out of that light and the
spirit of *the triple-male*, that is, the one
whose consort is Sophia.

Earlier we gave the passage from the Berlin codex
version of the *Sophia of Jesus Christ* in which the
Savior's rescue of Sophia is vividly portrayed in sexual
imagery. Here we give the complete passage from the
version in codex three where the most important varia-
tion is the addition at the end of the second paragraph
of the word *MNT2OOYT*, "masculinity."

Sophia of Jesus Christ III.106.24-108.7

Everyone who comes into the world was sent
forth by this one, like unto a drop from the
light into the world of the Pantocrator
(Ialdabaoth) that it (lit. "they") should be
guarded by his hand. And his chain of oblivion bound it in the will of Sophia so that by
him this thing should be <manifest> to the
whole world of misery on account of his vanity
and blindness and ignorance - for he
(Ialdabaoth) named himself.
But I, I came forth from the upper realms,
in the will of the great light. I came out
from that bond. I tore through the business
of the robbers. I raised it up, that is, that
drop that was sent forth by Sophia, so that it
should be complete and not suffer lack, but
that it should be fructified by me, the great
savior - in order that his glory (the father's)
should be revealed, that the other Sophia
might be justified from that fault, so that her
children might no longer suffer lack but attain
unto honor and glory, and that they might
ascend to their father and know the words of
the light of *masculinity* (MNT2OOYT).
You yourselves have been sent by the son who
was sent. . . .

The codicil of the *Sophia of Jesus Christ* also contains the word 2OOYT, "male," in two significant passages which unmistakenly relate the concept of
masculinity to that of the spiritual community. The
first instance has to do with the breathing in of the
breath of life as recounted in Gen. 2:7. In gnostic
exegesis the breath could stand for the spiritual element while the incomplete Adam was thought of as merely
psychic. The account of the *Sophia of Jesus Christ*
contrasts the incomplete Adam, that is the psychic man,
with the perfected Adam who shows his spiritualization
by his ability to name the animals. Nevertheless, in
a typically illogical fashion, Adam is subsequently
defined as "psychic," probably because the Adamic man
continues to function as a symbol of imperfect humanity
in contrast with the perfected saints of the community.

Sophia of Jesus Christ BG 119.17-121.13

That drop revealed their plasma by means of
'the breathing into a living soul.' It (the

90

soul) cooled and slept on account of the oblivion of the soul. When it (the soul) warmed
with the *breath of the great light of the Male*
(200YT), then he (Adam) thought the thoughts
of naming everything - that is, those in the
world of chaos and everything from it by means
of that immortal one - when the breath should
blow within him.
And these things came to pass in the will of
our Mother Sophia, so that the curtains of that
place would be co-ordinated by the immortal man,
as a judgment against those robbers. And *they*
(the pneumatics) responded to the puff (ΠΝΟΗ)
from that breath.
But because he (Adam) was psychic, he was not
able to take to himself that power until the
numbers of chaos be fulfilled. But when the
time calculated by the great angel is completed
. . . .

Here the indefinite "they" in the second paragraph must
refer to the members of the spiritual community. The
imagery is still in terms of the "breathing in of the
breath of life" related in Gen. 2:7, but is now broad-
ened to include the "pneumatics" as well as the
"psychics." The latter, like Adam, will not fully
receive that spirit until the eschaton. The "spiritual"
members of the community, unlike Adam, are pictured as
welcoming and embracing the life-giving breath of God.
The connection of "the breath of life" (Gen. 2:7) with
"the great light of the Male" is clearly a gnostic
interpretation and similar in tone to the account of
the creation of gods and angels from the "light and the
spirit of the triple-male" in BG 95.17-96.4

The continuation of the above-quoted passage follows
with an allusion to Gen. 3:24, "and the two of them
shall become one," where the masculine element is presumably identified with the spirit and the feminine
element with the soul: "I have come to this place so
that they should be united with that spirit, and the
breath, and that the two of them should become a single
one" (BG 122.6-11). Here the reconstitution of the
original androgyne becomes a symbol of salvation, as is
also the case in the *Gospel of Philip* 70.13-15: "Christ
came to remove the separation which came to pass at the
beginning, and again unite the two"; and in the *Exegesis
on the Soul* 133.3-4, "They will become a single flesh,
for they were united to each other in the beginning
with the father."

The last instance of 200YT, "male," in the *Sophia of Jesus Christ* is an explicit designation of the community as "the manly multitude." We should not expect that this designation would mean to exclude women from the community, and one might choose other translational variants to express the idea, such as "brave," "militant," or "mighty."

Sophia of Jesus Christ BG 124.9-16; 125.6-10

Behold, I have revealed to you the name of the perfect one, the universal will of the holy angels, and the Mother, so that in this place *the manly (200YT) multitude* should be perfected . . . so that they may all receive of his goodness and the riches of the place of rest over which there is no kingdom.

Within the context of the *Sophia of Jesus Christ* this designation is probably the equivalent of "the spiritual multitude," as contrasted with the rest of humanity. The passage stresses that perfection should be achieved "in this place," so that it should be understood to mean an earthly community. The conclusion again makes mention of the "kinglessness" of the community.

The pagan *Eugnostos the Blessed* knows the importance of the community's being one with the transcendent deity. The imagery is basically that of light and light-fragments without any pejorative allusions to the male and female principles. However, the Christianized document, the *Sophia of Jesus Christ*, expands this imagery in a mythological direction with the addition of explicit sexual categories in which the masculine is the dominant type. The approach is less intellectual in scope, more pessimistic, and very much more of a personal nature. One could use the term "remythologization" to describe the process, but without implying the exact extent to which mythological figures have replaced the earlier more abstract language of *Eugnostos the Blessed*. Our attempts to understand the sexist language of the *Sophia of Jesus Christ* can only be preliminary, because nothing very definite can be said about the sociological structure of the community which referred to itself in these terms.

CHAPTER FOUR

FEMININE MOTIFS IN ON THE ORIGIN OF THE WORLD

AND IN THE HYPOSTASIS OF THE ARCHONS

*Introduction to On the Origin of the World
(II.5 and XIII.2) and to The Hypostasis
of the Archons (II.4)*

Among the writings of codex two in the Nag Hammadi
collection stand two documents which relate in a general way to the subject of the origin of the universe.
One is now called *"The Hypostasis of the Archons" (Hyp.
Arch.)* in accord with a title written at the end of it
(II.97.22-23). If the title is understood as applying
to the preceding material, then the document following
it is left without title; it has been called *"The
Untitled Writing from Codex II."*[1] Its present English
title, *"On the Origin of the World,"* derives from Hans-
Martin Schenke who in 1959 published a partial trans-
lation, *"Vom Ursprung der Welt; eine titellose
gnostische Abhandlung aus dem Funde von Nag-Hammadi."*[2]
The English form of this, *"On the Origin of the World"
(Orig. World),* is used in *The Nag Hammadi Library.*[3]

The *Hypostasis of the Archons* and *On the Origin of
the World* contain much parallel material and appear to
stand in some sort of dependent literary relationship.
It is possible that the title, *"The Hypostasis of the
Archons,"* was really the name of the document now known

---

1. Alexander Böhlig and Pahor Labib, ed., *Die koptisch-gnostische
Schrift ohne Titel aus Codex II von Nag Hammadi im Koptischen
Museum zu Alt-Kairo* (Berlin: Akademie-Verlag, 1962).
2. Hans-Martin Schenke, "Vom Ursprung der Welt, Eine Titellose
gnostische Abhandlung aus dem Funde von Nag Hammadi, " *Theologische
Literaturzeitung* LXXXIV (1959), col. 243-56.
3. James M. Robinson, ed., *Nag Hammadi Library,* p. 161.

as "*On the Origin of the World.*" In the manuscript, the first document ends with a colon and then a series of diples. These are followed by a space, the Coptic title, "*The Hypostasis of the Archons*" and then another colon, a space and then directly the text of *On the Origin of the World*. It is a unique instance of the use of a colon after a title in codex two, and may suggest that the title belongs to either or to both documents. The first of the two documents may originally have been named according to its opening words, "*Concerning the Hypostasis of the Exousias.*"[4] The word "exousia," rather than "archōn" is the term used in the quotation from Ephesians which opens the document and may have suggested the change from "archōn" to "exousia." The writer appears to have rewritten a Sophia document (*Orig. World*) originally entitled "*The Hypostasis of the Archons*" so that the new writing proclaims the Christian Father to be the ultimate source of the forces of the universe.

The *Hypostasis of the Archons* and *On the Origin of the World* are integrally related both by reason of their contiguous position in codex two and by their apparent sharing of a common title. This has not been sufficiently discussed by the editors and commentators. The documents, for the most part, have been treated separately, although much of the material in the *Hypostasis of the Archons* is inexplicable without knowledge of *On the Origin of the World*. We shall try to show that the *Hypostasis of the Archons* is based upon some version of *On the Origin of the World*, and is a Christianized, patriarchalized, and defeminized summary.

On the Origin of the World, numbered as the fifth writing in the second codex of the Nag Hammadi collection, became accessible to the scholarly world through the German translation of Alexander Böhlig in 1962.[5] A long tractate of thirty pages (97.24-127.17) in comparison with the eleven pages of the *Hypostasis of the Archons* (86.20-97.23), *On the Origin of the World* is structurally divided by interpolated passages which break the flow of the narrative. The *Hypostasis of the Archons* is no less disjointed and its recapitulations of parts of *On the Origin of the World* make it difficult to understand.

---

4. But compare Roger Bullard, *The Hypostasis of the Archons* (Berlin: Walter de Gruyter and Co., 1970), p. 42 and references in n. 1.
5. Böhlig, *Die koptisch-gnostische Schrift ohne Titel.*

Although the documents may have been written originally in Greek,[6] the extant copies are in the Sahidic
dialect of Coptic. Ten lines of another Sahidic copy
of *On the Origin of the World* are preserved on the verso
of the last surviving folio of codex thirteen, and a
fragment in the Subachmimic dialect has been found
recently in the British museum.[7] The manuscripts are
from around 350 A.D., but the contents are certainly
much older. Of the sects described by the fathers of
the church, the Ophites and Sethians seem to have more
ties with the subject matter than do other groups. This
connection and the idea of Sophia's shadow being pro-
jected into matter, an idea present in the cosmology of
On the Origin of the World, suggest ancient traditions
and pre-Christian influences. Both documents contain
material which seems to have been known by Irenaeus when
he wrote Book I, Chapters 29 and 30 of *Against Heresies*
about 180 A.D., and both have relationships to the
earlier-discovered *Pistis Sophia* and the *Apocryphon of
John*.[8]

The *Hypostasis of the Archons* was first translated
into a modern language in 1958 by H.-M. Schenke.[9] In
1970 there went to press another edition in German, that[10]
of Peter Nagel, and an English version by Roger Bullard.
The Coptic text and another English translation, by
Bentley Layton, appeared in *The Harvard Theological Review*
in 1974-76.[11] Although there is some research on the

---

6. See pp. 143-51 for a fuller discussion.
7. Christian Oeyen, "Fragmente einer subachmimischen Version der
gnostischen 'Schrift ohne Titel,'" *Essays on the Nag Hammadi Texts*,
ed. Martin Krause (Leiden: E.J. Brill, 1975), pp. 125-44.
8. G. R. S. Mead, *Pistis Sophia* (London: John M. Watkins, first ed.
1896). The *Apocryphon of John* is known in four versions, found in
the Nag Hammadi codices II.1; III.1; IV.1; and in Berlin codex
8502.2.
9. H.-M. Schenke, trans., "Das Wesen der Archonten: eine gnostische
Originalschrift aus dem Funde von Nag-Hammadi," *Theologische
Literaturzeitung* LXXXIII (1958), col. 661-70.
10. Peter Nagel, *Das Wesen der Archonten aus Codex II der gnostischen Bibliothek von Hag Hammadi* (Halle: Saale, 1970). Bullard's
English translation has the Coptic text and translation and an
introductory article by Martin Krause "Die Sprache der Hypostase
der Archonten," pp. 4-17.
11. Bentley Layton, "The Hypostasis of the Archons," *Harvard Theological Review* 67:4 (1974), pp. 351-425 and 69:1-2 (1976), pp. 31-
101.

Hypostasis of the Archons,[12] there is no detailed comparison of it with *On the Origin of the World*, nor a specialized treatment of the feminine motifs in either document. We shall begin this study with a consideration of the literary structure of the documents and a tradition critique of the material common to both documents. We shall then detail the Christian and feminine motifs in the specific material of each document, and present some literary evidence for the priority of *On the Origin of the World*. Finally we examine some key motifs and their different treatment in the two documents before drawing conclusions centered around the four main characters of the documents: the Christian Father, Pistis Sophia, Ialdabaoth, and the Immortal Light-man.

Literary Structure of On the Origin of the World

On the Origin of the World is structurally complicated and addresses many themes from several literary sources. Basically, one can discern a quasi-philosophical beginning, a soteriological ending, and a narrative which is interrupted at least four times by non-integral excursi. The document may be divided in the following way:

Contents	*Page and Line*
Beginning	97.24 - 100.1
Narrative Section I	100.1 - 103.32
Sabaoth Intrusion	103.32 - 107.17
Narrative Section II	107.17 - 108.14
Pronoia Intrusion	108.14 - 111.28
Narrative Section III	111.29 - 113.10
Eve Intrusion	113.10 - 114.15
Narrative Section IV	114.15 - 121.35
Egyptian-Signs Intrusion	122.1 - 123.2
Narrative Section V	123.2 - 123.25
Ending	123.25 - 127.17

---

12. In particular see two important articles: Rudolphe Kasser, "L'Hypostase des Archontes," in *Essays on the Nag Hammadi Texts in Honour of Alexander Böhlig*, ed. Martin Krause (1972), pp. 22-35, and Bentley Layton, "Critical Prolegomena to an Edition of the Coptic 'Hypostasis of the Archons' (CG II.4)" in *Essays on the Nag Hammadi Texts in Honour of Pahor Labib*, ed. Martin Krause (1975), pp. 90-109.

The narrative sections of the documents are logically connected when the excursi are deleted, a fact which indicates that the editor made use of sources. Moreover, the use of source documents is established by the text itself. For three of the four intrusions, sources which are no longer extant are named: *"The Book of Solomon"* (107.3) and *"The Patterns of Divine Destiny Which are Under the Twelve"* (107.16), in the Sabaoth intrusion; and an unidentified *"Holy Book"* in both the Pronoia and Egyptian-Signs intrusions. Two other sources, *"The Annals of Moses the Prophet"* (102.8) and *"The First Book of Noraia"* (102.10), probably also referred to at 102.24 as *"The First Logos of Noraia,"* are named in the narrative sections. On the other hand, no sources are referred to in the beginning and the ending of the work.

The lack of acknowledgement of sources and the style and content of the opening and ending of *On the Origin of the World* suggest that these sections are the work of the compiler-author. In the ending, there are unmistakable signs of Christianization which for the most part are absent from the rest of the document. One notes the use of the terms "Savior" (124.33), "logos" (125.14), the New Testament echo "there is nothing hidden which is not revealed" (125.17-18), and Matthean appocalyptic motifs (126.10.12).

Despite some distracting intrusions and unevenness of style, there is a certain structural unity to *On the Origin of the World*. This is most clearly noticed when the author writes in the first person, as for example, "I shall begin the proof" (97.29), and "Let us now return . . . so that we should continue the proof" (123. 2-4). It is useful for understanding the literary structure of *On the Origin of the World* to note that the proposed subject matter, viz., the truth about "the constitution of Chaos and its origin" (97.28), is completed when the author writes: "This should suffice for you for now" (123.24). The concluding material is extrinsic to the original topic and may be looked upon as an editorial expansion pertaining to soteriology. The soteriological scheme has much in common with that of the Christian document, the *Sophia of Jesus Christ*. The Immortal Man sends into the plasma of the archons gnosisladen spirits from his heavenly abode. These spirits judge the archons, condemn them to utter darkness, and return to the dwellings of the kingless generation from which they came.[13]

_____

13. Compare the endings of Orig. World 123.25-127.17 and the

The literary structure of *On the Origin of the World*
may also be compared with that of the *Sophia of Jesus
Christ.* We have shown in the last chapter that the
editor of the *Sophia of Jesus Christ* went beyond his
source, the philosophical letter of Eugnostos, and wrote
a codicil in which he expounded Christian soteriology.
In the case of *On the Origin of the World,* the source
documents are not extant, and we are only able to note
the similarity of method by which the *Sophia of Jesus
Christ* and *On the Origin of the World* were Christianized. For ease in understanding the composition of *On
the Origin of the World,* we shall consider its contents
according to (1) source material which the author inserted into a mythological narrative, (2) the narrative
itself, and (3) the Christian beginning and ending.

The Sabaoth Intrusion (103.32-107.17). This intrusion is joined to the narrative by a clause that suggests that the archon Sabaoth has been eavesdropping on
a conversation between Pistis and Ialdabaoth concerning
the Immortal Light-man. When Sabaoth hears about the
glorious Man and his light, he rejects his father
Ialdabaoth and praises Pistis. Thereupon, Pistis pours
light upon Sabaoth, gives him her daughter to teach him
about the Eighth, and places him in charge of the twelve
gods of Chaos.

The archigenetor (Ialdabaoth) witnesses the glory
which has come to his son and envies him. Through this
envy he begets the androgyne, Death. Death begets
seven androgynous sons with pessimistic names as Envy,
Anger, and Groaning, each in turn begetting seven
androgynous sons. The names are said to have been
found in *"The Book of Solomon."* Opposed to these,
Sophia's daughter creates many beneficent androgynous
spirits with names such as Contentment, Happiness, and
Joy. Their names and efficacies are said to have been
found in *"The Patterns of Divine Destiny."*

Within the Sabaoth intrusion there are two lines
which disrupt the continuity. There occurs here a
reference to "Jesus, the Christ," apparently a gloss by
a Christian editor.

> . . . and a first-born one, who is called
> 'Israel', that is the man who sees God, *and
> another, 'Jesus, the Christ', who is like*

Sophia of Jesus Christ, BG 118.2-127.10.

unto the Savior who is above the Eighth, sitting on his right hand upon an exalted throne.
(105.25-27).

The Pronoia Intrusion (108.14-111.18). The second
intrusion follows upon the use of the term "Pronoia" at
108.11. "Pronoia" appears to be a feminine entity who
is with Ialdabaoth when he sees the light which shows
forth the human image of the Immortal Man. The material
about Pronoia does not seem to fit with the general
narrative, but is more akin to Hermetic literature. The
Poimandres tractate tells of a Light-man whose image is
so beautiful on the water that lower nature falls in
love with it.[14] Moreover, there is an odd phrase found
here that occurs also in *Poimandres*, "deprived of
rationality" (111.34).[15]

The Eve Intrusion (113.10-114.15) The Eve intrusion is also illustrative of an attempt to syncretize
other traditions with those of the author. The intrusion focuses on Eve and tells of the begetting of an
Instructor(ess) who is to save man from the evil
archons. According to this account, Sophia begets the
Instructoress as an androgyne and calls her "the Living-Eva," whom the Greeks are said to have called
"Hermaphrodite" (113.30-33). A syncretistic turn is
indicated in the dual name recorded for the *Instructoress*. The author then apparently refers to a traditional poem: "Therefore it is said of her that she said,
'I am a portion of my mother . . .'" (114.6-8), thus
beginning the *Song of the Woman*. Part of this aretalogy
is found in another Nag Hammadi document, *The Thunder,
Perfect Mind* (VI.2), and the same self-praise of the
woman in the name of Eve is referred to obliquely in
Hyp. Arch. 89.16-17.

After the *Song of the Woman,* the author makes a
reference to "Sabaoth and his Christ," apparently an
attempt to align the Eve intrusion with the Sabaoth
intrusion. He then returns the reader to his narrative
with the words, "And at that time the archigenetor made
a decision . . . concerning the Man" (114.24). This

---

14. For a new translation of *Poimandres*, see *Sourcebook of Texts
for the Comparative Study of the Gospels*, fourth ed., corrected,
by David L. Dungan (Missoula, Montana: Scholars Press, 1974),
pp. 87-94.
15. *Poimandres* 10, 14. Cf. also *Tripartite Tractate* I.78.34-35.
The *NHL* translation of *Orig. World* 111.34 "...darkness came upon
the whole world" is also plausible.

man is the plasmic man, the subject of Narrative Section III, which precedes the Eve intrusion.

The Egyptian-Signs Intrusion (122.1-123.2). The last intrusion concerns the Phoenix bird and the crocodile, signs uniquely Egyptian, according to our author. This material is also tied to "Sabaoth" by the suggestion that the Egyptian signs, like the sun and the moon, are witnesses of Sabaoth against the wicked angels. That this intrusion reflects a written source is suggested by a comment on the Phoenix: "It is written concerning it that 'the righteous shall sprout up like the Phoenix bird'" (122.28-29).[16]

What begins to emerge from a study of the intrusions is that Sabaoth is used as an integrating figure in them. His role as the repentant son of Ialdabaoth is extrinsic to the narrative of Sophia, Ialdabaoth, and the Immortal Light-man, but is useful for the purposes of an editor for whom repentance is the beginning of salvation. Let us now look at the narrative sections to note how they present a unified story when the above-mentioned intrusions are removed.

Narrative Section 1 (100.1-103.32). The first narrative section follows upon the introduction and makes use of traditional myth to substantiate religious beliefs. Summarily, this part of the narrative relates that Pistis Sophia willed the manifestation of the archon Ialdabaoth. He, in turn, made heaven, earth, and armies of divine powers as his servants. Ialdabaoth boasts of his uniqueness but is challenged by Pistis Sophia who tells him that there exists an immortal Light-man who will be revealed in the archontic plasma and will destroy it. Then Pistis shows forth *her image* upon the water and makes her way back to her light. This image seems to be distinguished from the subsequent manifestation of the image of the Immortal Light-man (108.7-9). The translation of A. Böhlig as well as that of *The Nag Hammadi Library* obscures this point by omitting "her" in the phrase "her image (likeness)" (103.30). That this is the image of Pistis is clearly stated in 107.18-19 as well as in the parallel in *Hyp. Arch.* 87.13-14.

---

16. Interpretation of Psalm 91:12 (LXX), "The just shall flourish like a date-palm tree." The meaning "like a Phoenix" was known by Tertullian (*De Resurr. Carn. 13*). Cf. Job 29:18, "I shall multiply years like the Phoenix."

Narrative Section II (107.17-108.14). The second
narrative section follows upon the Sabaoth intrusion
and relates that Ialdabaoth, upon seeing the image of
Pistis on the waters comes to understand that indeed
there is a pre-existent Light-man. Ialdabaoth fears
that the other gods might renounce him if they should
learn of the Light-man, but being a foolish god he
exclaims, "If there is one existing before me, let him
reveal himself so that we might see his light" (108.1-2).
In response, a light comes forth from the Eighth, pas-
sing through all the heavens. Within it there appears
a human image which is seen only by Ialdabaoth and the
Pronoia who is with him.[17]

Narrative Section III (111.29-113.10). This section
begins with the mention of an unidentified "he," probably the Light-man of the narrative before the Pronoia
intrusion. It relates that "when he was revealed on the
first day, he remained on the earth in this way for two
days." The narrative then recounts the arrogant archigenetor's struggle to prevent the Light-man's destruction of his work. The plan is to make a man from the
earth according to the likeness (ειχων) of the archon's
own androgynous body and according to the image (ΕΙΝΕ)
of the Light-man. Ialdabaoth supposes that when the
Light-man sees this image he will be enamored of it,
and all of the entities conceived through this union
will be his servants.

The author submits that the plan of the archigenetor
is an ignorant one, because Pistis is making use of the
plasma of the archons in the fulfillment of her plan.
The episode ends: "But all this came to pass according
to the Pronoia of Pistis in order that the Man should
be revealed opposite his image and condemn them in their
own plasma, and their plasma become a display of light"
(113.5-10).

Narrative Section IV (114.15-121.35). The fourth
narrative section relates the archigenetor's struggle
to take the Light-man hostage in the plasma. Ialdabaoth
creates a man of plasma, but fears that the true man may
come into it and fulfill the design of Pistis. Sophia
Zoe sends her breath into the plasmic man and makes him
move, although he does not yet stand erect. The breath
informs the seven archons that it has come for the
destruction of their work. Then Zoe (Eve), the

---

17. Cf. the similar account in *Apocryphon of John* II.14.24-34.

101

Instructoress, awakens "Adam in whom there was no soul, in order that those whom he would beget should become vessels of the light" (115.34-36). When Adam sees Eve, his co-image, he says to her, "Thou shalt be called 'the Mother of the Living,' because thou art the one who gave me life" (116.6-8).

The archons see Eve speaking with Adam, and they say to one another, "Who is this Light-man (fem.)? For truly she appears like unto that image which was manifest to us in the light" (116.13-15). They try to seize her, cast their seed upon her, and defile her, so that she might not be able to return to her light. They bring a forgetfulness over Adam and tell him that Eve came from his rib and that he is lord over her. Eve, however, leaves her image, the created Eve, by the side of Adam and magically enters into the tree of knowledge where she frightens away the evil archons.

Then the archons come to Adam, and upon seeing the lower Eve beside him, defile her. She brings forth Abel and some other children. The archons command the first couple not to eat from the tree of knowledge, but an *Instructor* inspires them to disobey the order. When Eve takes from the tree of knowledge and gives of it to her husband, the light of gnosis shines upon them. The archons curse the *Instructor* (the serpent), the woman, her husband, her children, the ground, and its fruit. Blinded by the *Instructor*, the archons are aware that there is one who is stronger than they. Great envy comes into the world "because of the immortal man" (120.16-17).

Lest Adam should eat from the tree of life as he had eaten of the tree of knowledge, the archons cast him out of Paradise and guard its gates with fiery cherubim. When Sophia Zoe perceives that the archons have cursed her co-image, she drives them down to the sinful cosmos where they "become like evil demons " (121.34-35).

Narrative Section V (123.2-123.25). This last narrative section relates that the fallen archons create hordes of demons who teach mankind innumerable errors, including the worship of idols, blood-offerings, and sacrifices. The demons take fate as their co-worker and cause the universe to turn to confusion and ignorance. The narrative of the origin of the world and the plight of mankind ends with these words: "All of them erred until the advent of the true man. This should suffice for you for now" (123.23-25).

Beginning (97.24-100.1). The third level of material in *On the Origin of the World* includes the opening and ending of the document and seems to represent the work of a Christian writer. We shall summarize his views and make some comparisons with the editorial rewrite of *Eugnostos the Blessed* as found in the *Sophia of Jesus Christ*.

The opening of *On the Origin of the World* is in the nature of a philosophical disputation, as is that of *Eugnostos the Blessed*. The authors of both, in their introductions, propose to correct false interpretations regarding the origin and ordering of the universe, and to proclaim the aeon of truth as the ultimate and indescribable light from which came forth all things.

The author of *On the Origin of the World* states that it is said that nothing existed before the Chaos, but argues from the contingent concept of Chaos as shadow to the fact of its derivation from light. He seems to distinguish between Pistis and Sophia, with the latter being perceived as the image of the former.

The concept of a supreme being with two aspects, one less powerful than the other, but mysteriously united, is also found in Eugnostos' description of God and his "antopos" or mirror image, also called "Father."[18] The philosophical tone of *Eugnostos the Blessed*, however, is markedly different from that of the opening of *On the Origin of the World*. Eugnostos reminds his readers that everything is created good, while the author of *On the Origin of the World* is quick to mention the concept of the ŠTA (ⲰⲦⲀ), the "lack" or "flaw" in the universe (99.30). The pessimistic attitude of the beginning of *On the Origin of the World* accords more closely with that of the author of the *Sophia of Jesus Christ* than it does with that of Eugnostos.

The imagery of light which gradually grows less bright the farther it passes from its source is widely used in philosophical and theological treatises. As regards the relation between a higher and lower soul, Plotinus explains that the devolution of the soul is nothing but the illumination of that which is beneath her. Through illumination a reflection originated, which is said to be the lower soul. However, the

---

18. Cf. *Eugnostos the Blessed*, III.75.2-14.

original soul can still be thought of as in the upper
spheres.[19]

A similar doctrine was held by the gnostics whom
Plotinus attacked. Plotinus reports their views about
the soul and about Sophia, but he is not certain whether
Sophia is considered by them to be different from the
soul or the same. He writes:

> The Soul, they say, and a certain Wisdom turned
> downward . . . and with her descended the other
> souls; these, as it were, "members" of the
> Wisdom, put on bodies. . . . But then again
> they say that she on whose account they
> descended did in another sense not descend her-
> self and somehow did not really turn downward,
> but only illumined the darkness, and from this
> an "image" (eidolon) originated in Matter.[20]

Jonas correctly explains that the main difference
between the doctrine of Plotinus and that of the gnostics he criticized concerning the descent of the light-
image is that Plotinus affirms it as the necessary and
positive self-expression of the first source, while the
gnostics deplore it as the cause of divine tragedy.[21]
Plotinus' own view seems more closely represented by
the _Letter of Eugnostos_. The pessimistic nature of the
preface of _On the Origin of the World_ is closely related
to the author's concept of the "lack" (ψTA) in the
universe and the specific soteriological plan called for
to remove this lack.

Ending (123.25-127.17). The ending of _On the Origin
of the World_ belongs to the same level of material as
the opening. This is established by the author's use
of first-person pronouns in both sections and also by
his concept of salvation, which is predicated upon the
idea of the "lack" in the universe disclosed in the
opening. The author again appears in the "we" and "I"
of the join between the main body of the document and
the "Father" material of the Christian ending. He
writes:

---

19. Plotinus, _Enn._ I.1.12, as referenced in Hans Jonas, _The Gnostic
Religion_, p. 163.
20. Plotinus, _Enn._ II.9.10 quoted in Jonas, _Gnostic Religion_, p.
163.
21. Jonas, _Gnostic Religion_, p. 164.

Now we shall come to our world so that we should
complete its analysis and organization more
exactly. Then it will be evident how Pistis of
the hidden things has been found ⟨in⟩ the visible things from the foundation unto the consummation of the age. And now I come to the main
point concerning the immortal man. I shall
speak concerning all those that belong to him
. . . (*Orig. World* 123.25-33).

The author then presents a soteriological plan which
closely resembles that found in the Christianized document, the *Sophia of Jesus Christ*. In that document,
the Father sends forth a host of "antopoi," mirror
images of his spiritual nature, who evidently are the
elect community.[22] In the codicil of the *Sophia of
Jesus Christ* these spirits are specifically male and
are sent to yoke up with the psychics "so that the two
should become a single one as it was from the beginning."[23] These seem to correspond in *On the Origin of
the World* to the "blessed spirits" who are to bring to
naught the archons and their plasma. One notes that
the plan for overcoming the archons is no longer that
of Pistis as expressly noted in the third narrative
section (113.5-10), but is that of "the immortal Father."
One notes further that the immortal Father and the "lack"
(ϢⲦⲀ) are introduced in the same sentence, as though
one were conditioned by the other.

A host of mankind came into being [from Adam] –
the one who had been molded. And because of
matter (ὕλη), as soon as the world was completed, the archons became masters over it, that is,
they held it in ignorance. What is the reason?
It is this. Since the immortal Father knows
that a fault (ϢⲦⲀ) came into being from the
truth within the aeons and their world; therefore, when he wished to dispossess the archons
of destruction through their own plasma, he
sent your images down into the world of destruction – these are the blessed, innocent,
little spirits (*Orig. World* 123.34-124.11).

The use of the term "Father" is remarkable; except in
reference to Ialdabaoth (101.14, 15, 18, 21, 22, 23;
103.35; 104.6, 10) and Adam (114.12; 115.2), the term
had not been used before in *On the Origin of the World*.

_____

22. Cf. the *Sophia of Jesus Christ*, BG 91.17-92.9; 110.5-111.16.
23. Cf. the *Sophia of Jesus Christ*, BG 122.7-12.

The last part of the ending is characteristically an apocalyptic passage heralding the triumph of light over darkness and the return of the light to its root. Like the Christian codicil of the *Sophia of Jesus Christ*, the ending records different levels of salvation: "For it is necessary that each one go to the place from which he came. For each one shall show forth by his actions and his knowledge (γνωσισ) his own nature" (127.14-17).

Literary Structure of The Hypostasis of the Archons

The *Hypostasis of the Archons* appears to be a composite document combining elements from at least three sources: Genesis, a revelatory discourse, and a cosmological tractate. The literary design of the composition is complex. Christian elements appear at the beginning (86.20-87.23) and at the ending (96.35-97.23). As with some other composite documents there appear to be at least two endings.[24] For most of the document, the author seems to be rewriting his sources. He retells the Genesis stories of Cain and Abel, and the building of Noah's ark in 91.12-92.18. The cosmogonic source, which appears in two segments, may be a version of *On the Origin of the World*. The revelatory discourse, the "Norea source," is not extant for comparison. The general outline of the *Hypostasis of the Archons*, together with parallel sections from *On the Origin of the World* may be seen in the following chart.

Hypostasis of the Archons		*Origin of the World*
Christian opening	86.20 - 87.23	
First cosmogonic narrative	87.23 - 91.7	112.33 - 120.22
Sermonic intrusion	91.7 - 91.11	
Genesis rewrite	91.12 - 92.18	
Norea transition	92.18 - 93.2(?)	
Eleleth epiphany scene	93.2 - 94.3	
Revelation (cosmogonic narrative)	94.4 - 96.17	98.13 - 106.29
Dialogue ending	96.17 - 96.34	
Christian ending	96.35 - 97.23	

---

24. The first ending of the *Sophia of Jesus Christ*, BG 117.8-12, follows the ending of *Eugnostos the Blessed*, III.90.4-11. The first ending of the codex two version of the *Apocryphon of John* begins at 31.26. Cf. the second ending which begins at 31.32.

After the Christian opening, there occurs a section which is parallel with *On the Origin of the World*. The material appears to be an answer to a request for information:

> . . . since you (masc.) ask about the hypostasis of the authorities (*Hyp. Arch.* 86.26-27).

This first block of parallel material ends with a phrase common to both documents: "there is no blessing with them." (*Hyp. Arch.* 91.5-6; *Orig. World* 120.10-11). Whereas *On the Origin of the World* then continues with the myth of the gnostic Light-man, the *Hypostasis of the Archons* adds a sermonic passage which serves as a transition to its own version of Genesis. This section, too, may be the work of the final author.

> But they cast mankind into great distractions and the troubles of life, so that their mankind should be preoccupied with making a living and not have leisure to attend to the Holy Spirit (*Hyp. Arch.* 91.7-11).

Although the passage consists of only five lines, there are eight Greek loanwords providing the basic content of the thought. Some of these are rare in Coptic documents - περισπασμοσ (distraction), σχολαζειν (have leisure), προσκαρτερειν (attend to). Certainly, the ideas for the passage were conceived in the Greek idiom, although the passage may have been written in Coptic by a Greek-speaking scribe.

The Genesis rewrite is basically the story of the birth of Cain, Abel, and two other children, probably Seth and Norea. There is also an account of the flood which relates that the ark was to have been set atop Mt. Seir, but a certain Orea (Noah's wife?) burned it. The mention of the name Orea seems to be used to lead into the epiphany scene of the Norea revelatory discourse.

A study of the Norea document presents serious difficulties because it is impossible to determine clearly where it begins or where it ends. Should it begin with the appearance of the angel Eleleth at 93.2 in a manner characteristic of revelatory dialogues, then the preceding section (92.18-93.2), related neither to Genesis nor the revelation, must be seen as a lengthy transition. We call it "the Norea transition" because it records Norea's name within a conflict story with the archons of darkness. It is in answer to her plea, "Help me against the archons of unrighteousness and rescue me from their hands immediately" (93.1-2) that the revealer Eleleth appears. More difficult is the question of the revelation proper. It appears that the author made use of a source with a revelatory discourse, an angelic epiphany and a dialogue ending. But he seems to have replaced the revelation proper with parallel material from *On the Origin of the World*, leaving only a skeleton consisting of the epiphany and the conclusion of the original Norea document.

If we count the ending of the parallel material from *On the Origin of the World*, then three endings can be seen in the *Hypostasis of the Archons*. (1) ". . . that the number of Chaos should be completed" (96.13-15). This seems to be parallel with the statement in *Orig. World* 106.26-27, "And thus was completed the number six of the powers of Chaos." This is a destiny motif familiar from other gnostic and Hermetic writings. (2) After this, Eleleth completes his revelation in these words:

> Lo, I have taught you (fem.) the type of the archons and the matter in which it was begotten, and their father and their world (*Hyp. Arch*. 96.15-17).

There follow two questions and answers which may have belonged to the original Norea document. The exact point of the ending of this source and the beginning of the Christian ending is obscured. Perhaps the second question has been added or modified to lead into the Christian ending. The first question has a typical gnostic ring: "Lord, do I perhaps also belong to their matter?" The second question seems Christian-oriented: "Lord, how long a time?" (3) Beginning with the answer to the second question we are definitely into a Christian ending: "When the true Man appears in their plasma, the Spirit of Truth whom the Father has sent . . ." (96.33-97.1)[25]

---

25. Bullard and Layton translate 2N NOYΠⲖⲀCMA in 96.34 as if ΠⲖⲀCMA were preceded by the indefinite article OY-. In fact, ΠⲖⲀCMA is never preceded by OY- in the *Hypostasis of the Archons* or *On the Origin of the World*, but is usually preceded by a possessive adjective. The plural is not uncommon: cf. *Orig. World* 103.21; 114.2; 117.25, 27-28; and 124.8-9.

The most intriguing question with regard to the composition of the *Hypostasis of the Archons* is the appearance of overlapping material on pages 86-87 and page 94.
The key scene of the arrogant archon's boast and the
rebuke from heaven is told in almost identical words in
these two places. A careful study of the two accounts
will convince the reader that the first is a simplifica-
tion of the later account. Since an almost identical
passage appears in *Orig. World* 103.11-18, the number of
possible relationships becomes multiple. One theory
that could account for the facts is this: an author
of the *Hypostasis of the Archons* writing in Coptic
began his work with a Coptic quotation from Ephesians
(page 86) and then summarized a source (pages 86-87) to
which he would later return (page 94).[26] This source
had some direct Coptic relationship with *On the Origin
of the World*. The two passages from the *Hypostasis of
the Archons* are given below.

Hyp. Arch. 86.30-87.4

'I am God, there is
no one [apart from me.]'
When he said this he
sinned against
[the All.] And this word
reached up to Imperisha-
bility. But lo!
A voice came forth
from Imperishability,
saying
'You are wrong, Samael,'
which is, the god
of the blind ones.
His thoughts were blind.

Hyp. Arch. 94.21-26

'I am God, and there is
no other apart from me.'
When he said this, he
committed sin against
the All.

But a voice came forth
from the height of
Authenticity, saying
'You are wrong, Samael,'
that is, the god of
the blind ones.

The first passage in the *Hypostasis of the Archons* omits
"and" in the first line. It avoids the odd Greek term
AYΘENTEIA in 94.24, making use in its stead of the key
word MNTATTAKO, "Imperishability." It tries to explain
the corrupt phrase, "the god of the blind ones," by the

---

26. The quotation from Eph. 6:12 in *Hyp. Arch.* 86.23-25 agrees
with the Coptic text of the New Testament in omitting NAN, "to us."
The Coptic omission is undoubtedly due to the juxtaposition of NAN
AN, "not to us" which could cause the haplography. Textually, this
is a very rare reading. Cf. the same quotation in *Ex. Soul* II.131.
9-13 where NAN AN correctly occurs. The implication is that the

addition: "His thoughts were blind."[27] None of these
deviations can be found in the parallel in *Orig. World*
103.11-18. On the other hand, all of the differences
of *Hyp. Arch.* 94.21-26, about eight in number, with
respect to *Orig. World* 103.11-18, also appear in *Hyp.
Arch.* 86.30-87.4. This pattern of minor literary
changes strongly indicates that *Hyp. Arch.* 86.30-87.4
is a direct reconstruction of *Hyp. Arch.* 94.21-26,
with no use made of *On the Origin of the World.* The
Coptic of the two passages in the *Hypostasis of the
Archons* is so close that one is led to believe that
the literary identity occurs on the *Coptic level*, and
this in turn suggests a *Coptic origin* for the first
page of the *Hypostasis of the Archons.* Certainly, the
words, "His thoughts were blind" (87.4) did not occur
as an explanatory note in a Greek vorlage; they must
have been written *in Coptic* to explain the corruption
in the Coptic text, i.e., the addition of the letter
N- to the phonetically rendered ΒΒΛΛΕ standing in
place of proper Sahidic ΝΒΛΛΕ, "blind" (sing.). This
additional letter yielded the incorrect plural,
ΝΒΒΛΛΕ, "of the blind ones," which called for the
comment, 'his thoughts (pl.) were blind."

The sources for the *Hypostasis of the Archons* are
rich in feminine imagery. They include the woman Norea,
the recipient of the revelation from Eleleth; Sophia who
made "the images of heaven"; her daughter Zoe who rebukes the arrogant archon; as well as the "pneumatic
woman" Eve who awakens Adam with the words, "Rise up,
Adam." However, the Christian beginning and ending are
significantly devoid of any of this imagery. There is
the shadowy abstraction "Imperishability" and a single
reference to Pistis Sophia identifying her with the
Abyss (87.7-8), and this is all the feminine imagery of
the Christian portions of the *Hypostasis of the Archons.*

---

author of the *Hypostasis of the Archons* quoted from a *Coptic* text
while the author of *On the Exegesis of the Soul* used the *Greek*
Testament.
27. The original reading was probably "the blind god," ΠΝΟΥΤΕ
ΒΒΛΛΕ, as it occurs in the parallel passage in *Orig. World* 103.18.
The incorrect addition of *N-* made this into a plural, "god of the
blind ones." It seems highly improbable that the author of 87.4
both added the incorrect *N-* and then the explanatory phrase, "his
thoughts were blind." It seems more likely that he was rewriting
the source that occurs in 94.26, with the corruption already
there, rather than following the correct parallel in *Orig. World*
103.18.

Critique of the Material Common to
On the Origin of the World and
The Hypostasis of the Archons

What is the nature of the material which is common
to both *On the Origin of the World* and the *Hypostasis
of the Archons?* Is it gnostic, Jewish? Does it derive
from a pagan or Christian milieu? Does it contain apocalyptic material? These questions must be answered in
the context of the larger issues surrounding the definition of gnosticism and its origins.

Is the common material gnostic? From a strictly
literary point of view, the inclusion of the documents
within the Nag Hammadi collection may be a priori
grounds for calling their contents gnostic, but one must
also consider whether the material is "gnostic" as
modern scholarship has defined the term. Most scholars
agree that a radical ontological dualism between the
supreme god and created things is constitutive of
gnostic thought. Daniélou, for example, wrote:

> It is this radical dualism, therefore, which is
> the properly Gnostic element, not the various
> images through which it is expressed.[28]

Hans Jonas, too, considers dualism as fundamental to
any description of gnosticism:

> A Gnosticism without a fallen god, without be-
> nighted creator and sinister creation, without
> alien soul, cosmic captivity and acosmic sal-
> vation, without the self-redeeming of the
> Deity - in short: a Gnosis without divine
> tragedy will not meet specifications.[29]

Noting that gnosticism is neither an acute Helleniza-
tion of the Christian religion nor a fossilized survival
of Iranian religious concepts, G. Quispel also considers
dualism and divine tragedy as basic to gnosticism:

---

28. Jean Daniélou, *The Theology of Jewish Christianity*, vol. 1, tr.
and ed., John A. Baker (Chicago: H. Regnery Co., 1964), p. 73.
For a discussion of the problems concerning a definition of gnosticism see Yamauchi, pp. 13-21.
29. Hans Jonas, "Response to G. Quispel's 'Gnosticism and the New
Testament'" in *The Bible in Modern Scholarship*, ed. J. P. Hyaat,
p. 293.

It is rather a religion of its own, with its own
phenomenological structure, characterized by the
mythical expression of self-experience through
the revelation of the 'Word,' or, in other
words, by an awareness of a tragic split within
the Deity itself.[30]

Does the common material of *On the Origin of the
World* and the *Hypostasis of the Archons* portray a divine
tragedy? Indeed, *On the Origin of the World* has quite
an extensive myth of a fallen deity, the Light-man.
The same myth is repeated in an abbreviated form in the
Hypostasis of the Archons. Let us first consider the
presentation in *On the Origin of the World*. The characters in the myth are Pistis Sophia, the Light-man,
and Ialdabaoth, the benighted creator. The constitutive
features are Ialdabaoth's boast of being the unique
deity, - "I am God, and there is no other" - the rebuke
from Pistis Sophia, the flash of the Light-man's image
upon the waters, and Ialdabaoth's use of the image as
the model for his own plasmic man. The benighted creator
challenges,

If there is one existing before me, let him reveal himself so that we might see his light"
(107.36-108.2).

Ialdabaoth's first boast is rebuked by Pistis' words,
"'You are wrong, Samael,' that is, the blind god" (103.
17-18). His second boast is repudiated by a penetrating
light from the Eighth, the sphere of the feminine, and
within it there is revealed a human image which Ialdabaoth forthwith uses as his model man (108.3-9; 112.33-
113.1). When the Light-man wishes to return to his
light in the eighth sphere, he is unable to on account
of the "poverty (MNT2HKE) which was mixed with his light"
(112.10-13).

In the *Hypostasis of the Archons*, the tragedy of the
Light-man is less clearly presented, but the main
features are there, namely, the boast of the archigenetor
(86.30-31; 94.21-22; 95.5); the feminine rebuke (87.3-4;
94.25-26; 95.7-8); the flash of light from above (94.28-
31); and the archons' creation of Adam "according to
their body and [according to the image] of God which
appeared [to them] on the waters" (87.31-33). Although
the *Hypostasis of the Archons* does not explicitly name

---

30. Gilles Quispel, "Gnosticism and the New Testament" in the *Bible
in Modern Scholarship*, pp. 259-60.

112

the Light-man, his existence is implied in the passage above as well as in the continuation:

> Come, let us catch him (the Light-man) in our plasma . . . so that he will see his co-image (masc.) (*Hyp. Arch.* 87.33-35).

There shows up here the strange anomaly that the *Hypostasis of the Archons* knows the mythological figure of the Light-man but not once explicitly mentions him. The "co-image" cannot be Eve, because it is of masculine gender and, therefore, must signify Adam. The co-image of Adam, then, must be the immortal Light-man, as is clearly expressed in the parallel account in *On the Origin of the World*.

> And he said, 'I am God, and there is none other existing beside me.' Now when he said these things, he committed sin against all of the immortal ones who took notice and watched him. Indeed, when Pistis saw the impiety of the great archon, she was very upset. Without anyone seeing her, she spoke, 'You are wrong, Samael,' that is, the blind god, 'there is an immortal Light-man who exists before you who shall be revealed in your plasma.' (*Orig. World* 103.11-21).

The use of the Light-man's image as the model for the archontic creation of Adam is presented in detail in another passage in *On the Origin of the World*:

> They mocked the archigenetor because he had lied when he said, 'I am God; there is none other before me.' When they came to him they said, 'Is this the god who has destroyed our work?' He answered and said, 'Verily, if you wish that he should not be able to destroy our work, then come, let us make a man from the earth according to the likeness of our body and according to the image of that one, and it will serve us; so that if that one should see his image he will fall in love with it and no longer destroy our work (*Orig. World* 112.27-113.3).

No study of gnostic myth would be complete without reference to the redeemed redeemer concept which Bultmann distilled from the works of Bousset, Lidzbarski, and Reitzenstein. His reconstruction supposes the existence of a primitive gnostic myth in which a primal Light-man

113

falls and is divided by the demonic powers. The particles become sparks of light imprisoned as spiritual human beings. The demons attempt to make these humans forget their divine origin, but a transcendent deity sends another Light-being who descends through the demonic spheres in deceptive bodily garments, reminds those humans of their heavenly origin, and gives them the passwords necessary for their return. Having defeated the demons, the redeemer reascends and makes a way for the redeemed spirits. When the spirits of all men are thus collected, cosmic redemption is achieved. The redeemer is himself redeemed in that the Light-man who fell in the beginning is reconstituted.[31]

The gnostic myth as found in the common material of *On the Origin of the World* and the *Hypostasis of the Archons* supports the basic hypothesis of Bultmann but indicates the need for some important changes in the reconstruction. At Nag Hammadi, the primal Light-man appears in connection with Sophia, and he is sent from the Eighth, the feminine sphere. Bultmann's reconstruction lacked the essential feminine deity, the personified Pistis Sophia. Bultmann's proto-Mandaean gnostic source is of dubious value here; it is more likely that Old Testament speculation about personified Sophia provided the background for the myth. Moreover, Bultmann supposed the Light-man motif to have been integrated directly into Christianity, but in the common material of *On the Origin of the World* and the *Hypostasis of the Archons* the Light-man is connected with a Jewish Sophialogy and Genesis midrash in which Christian elements do not appear.

Having noticed in the reconstructed myth of the immortal Light-man the heavy dependence upon the Genesis story, one can hardly dispute the Jewish background of the material common to *On the Origin of the World* and the *Hypostasis of the Archons*. But inquiry is still necessary with regard to the exact nature of the Jewish influence. In the continuing debate concerning the origins of gnosticism, certain scholars, particularly Hans Jonas, consider that gnosticism always reacted against Judaism when the traditions met. In his observations on the Coptic gnostic library, Jonas affirms

31. R. Bultmann, *Primitive Christianity* tr. R. H. Fuller (New York: The World Publishing Co., 1956), pp. 163-64. Cf. Yamauchi, pp. 29-55 for a discussion of the gnostic redeemer myth in relation to New Testament exegesis.

that the identification of Ialdabaoth with the Judaic god is an element "one has to consider in forming any hypothesis on the origins of Gnosticism."[32] He claims that the assertion by Ialdabaoth that he is the only god, in a style reminiscent of Isaiah 45:5 and 46:9, is employed as a deliberate mockery of Judaism. Analysis of the common material of *On the Origin of the World* and the *Hypostasis of the Archons* lends little weight to this proposal.

To be sure, identification of the gnostic creator god and the God of the Jews was made by certain Christian gnostics. According to Irenaeus, a certain Saturninus of Antioch taught early in the second century that the God of the Jews is one of the angels who created man, and that because the powers wished to annihilate Christ's father, Christ came to destroy the God of the Jews.[33] The identification of Ialdabaoth with Jehovah, however, is not necessary for understanding the myth of the overthrow of Ialdabaoth and Sophia's plan to overcome personified folly by means of the Immortal Light-man. The Nag Hammadi myth does not necessarily represent an anti-Semitic stance. The boast of the archigenetor need not be construed as that of the Jewish god, even if it sounds similar to the words of *Isaiah*. In Is. 47:8-10 a comparable expression is used for the boast of a Chaldean sorceress flaunting her abilities in magic: "I am, and there is none other." The author of Isaiah records the downfall of fools even as the gnostic myth common to *On the Origin of the World* and the *Hypostasis of the Archons* foretells the ultimate destruction of the foolish Ialdabaoth, "Saklas," by the wise goddess, "Sophia." The context is that of personified Wisdom versus personified Folly. Neither Isaiah nor the common material of our two documents should be called anti-Jewish because they are pro-Sophia.

There is nothing anti-Jewish in the material common to *On the Origin of the World* and the *Hypostasis of the Archons* with regard to the Old Testament figures, Adam, Eve, and Sabaoth. The book of Genesis is used extensively, and although the hermeneutic is non-normative, it is not anti-Semitic. Moreover, titles of source documents mentioned in *On the Origin of the World* include the Jewish names, Moses, Hieralias, Noraia, and Solomon.

---

32. Jonas, *Gnostic Religion*, p. 296.
33. Irenaeus, *A.H.* I.xxiv.2.

Only the mention of the "Book of Solomon" (107.3) could be considered to be within a pejorative context.

There are a number of significant pagan ideas in the common material of *On the Origin of the World* and the *Hypostasis of the Archons*. The more prominent ones seem to derive from Greek and Egyptian mythology. In the next chapter we shall discuss some of the similarities of *The Song of the Woman* (*Orig. World* 114.7-15), alluded to in the *Hypostasis of the Archons* (89.16-17), with the Isis inscriptions. The assimilation of Isis material within an account of Eve is a remarkable instance of the interweaving of Egyptian and Jewish motifs.

"Tartaron," the lowest part of the Greek underworld, appears in *Orig. World* 102.34 and *Hyp. Arch.* 95.12. In both instances it is the place into which the archontic power is cast. It is linked with "*NOYN*," the underworld of Egyptian mythology, in *Hyp. Arch.*95.13. The Greek "Chaos" appears frequently in both documents. The *Hypostasis of the Archons* links Chaos with both the Egyptian *NOYN* and Pistis in 87.6-7, "down to Chaos and *NOYN*, his mother by Pistis Sophia."

Motifs from the pagan myth of the androgyne are found in the common material of *On the Origin of the World* and the *Hypostasis of the Archons*. In *Orig. World* 100.7 and *Hyp. Arch.* 94.18, the word "androgynous" is used to refer to an arrogant, lion-faced beast, who presumably is Ialdabaoth. In *Orig. World* 101.11-12 and *Hyp. Arch.* 95.3, the word is also used to describe Ialdabaoth's offspring.

Significantly, in *On the Origin of the World*, the Hellenistic myth serves to present the primeval unity of mankind basic for the interpretation of Genesis. The story of the birth of the androgyne Eve is placed just before the creation of Adam in *Orig. World* 113.21-34. The purpose is obviously to show that the androgyne Eve existed before the creation of Adam. The translation of Bethge-Wintermute in *The Nag Hammadi Library* obscures the main point of this passage by taking this to be the account of the birth of Seth rather than Eve. This interpretation leads to several incongruencies.

. . . and it (Eve) fulfilled itself in twelve months. An androgynous man (Seth) was begotten, one whom the Greeks call "Hermaphrodites.' But the Hebrews call his mother 'Eve

116

of Life,' i.e. 'the instructor of life.' But her son is the begotten one who is lord (*Orig. World* 113.29-35, *NHL*).

We have provided the words in parentheses to clarify the meaning of *their* translation, which must be that the passage tells of the begetting of two personages, both Eve and her son Seth. In fact, "the androgynous man" should be *Eve*, now born an androgyne after twelve months' gestation. The following sentence should mean that *her* name in Hebrew is "Eve," contrasting with *her* Greek name "Hermaphrodites." The translation obscures the main point of the syncretistic motif, that is, that the same person can be called "Hermaphrodites" or "Eve." A problem with the Coptic text in this passage is that the androgyne is grammatically masculine, resulting in some mixed genders that make either Seth or Eve possible equivalents of "Hermaphrodites." A more consistent translation with the personages in parentheses appears below.

Now the begetting of the Instructor (the serpent) came to pass in this way. When Sophia had cast forth a light-drop, it floated upon the water. Immediately, the Man was made manifest, being androgynous. That drop took its first form as a feminine body. Afterwards, she (Eve) took her bodily form in the image of the Mother (Sophia) which had been revealed. She (Eve) was completed in twelve months. An androgyne (Eve) was born, whom the Greeks call 'Hermaphrodites.' But its mother (Sophia) in Hebrew[34] called her (Eve) 'the Living Eva,' that is, 'the Instructoress of Life.' And her (Eve's) son is the begotten one (Seth), who is the lord. Afterwards, the authorities called him 'the Beast' in order to deceive their creatures. The interpretation of 'the Beast' is 'the Instructor.' For they found that he (the serpent) was wiser than all of them. (*Orig. World* 113.21-114.4)

The motif of the androgynous first man also seems to occur in the *Hypostasis of the Archons*. Here we should

---

34. ⲦⲈⲨⲘⲀⲀⲨ, "its mother," the first word of the sentence is not likely to be the object of the verb. A literal translation of the sentence is: "But its Hebrew mother called her the Living-Eva, that is, the Instructoress of Life."

expect that it is Adam who was created androgynous. In
Hyp. Arch. 89.10, the phrase ΕΠΕϹΜΑ, "in her place," is
interpreted by Bullard to refer to the female half of
Adam which has been removed from the original androgyne.[35]

> And he slept. They opened his side like a liv-
> ing woman and they built up his side with flesh
> in her place (ΕΠΕϹΜΑ), and Adam became wholly
> psychic (*Hyp. Arch.* 89.7-11).

The meaning of the passage is obscure, but a reference
to the Adamic androgyne seems likely.

Both *Orig. World* 108.24-25 and *Hyp. Arch.* 88.13-14
make use of the Greek loanword ΑΔΑΜΑΝΤΙΝΗ in the expression "adamantine earth." According to Bullard, a
chthonic spirit, "from the adamantine earth," is responsible for Adam's pneumatic character.[36]

> After these things the Spirit saw the psychic
> man on the earth, and the spirit came forth
> from the adamantine earth. It came down and
> settled within him. That man 'became a living
> soul' (Gen. 2.7). It called his name Adam
> (*Hyp. Arch.* 88.11-16).

The Genesis reference, however, is to God's blowing
the breath of life, πνοη ζωησ, into Adam's nostrils, an
inflatus which in gnostic exegesis was interpreted to be
the impartation of spirit through the personified Zoe,
the daughter of Sophia. Bullard's view that a chthonic
spirit performs this function does not completely satisfy. The ending of the passage, "that man became a
living soul (ΨΥΧΗ ΕϹΟΝϪ)" seems to imply that the
chthonic spirit made Adam psychic rather than pneumatic.[37]

A comparison with the similar passage in *Orig. World*
108.19-25 helps explain the background for the phrase,
"the spirit . . . from the adamantine earth." In the
parallel in *On the Origin of the World*, the Semitic
name Adam is provided with a Hellenistic etymology:
"adamantine earth."

---

35. Cf. Bullard, pp. 78-80.
36. Ibid., p. 70.
37. Cf. R. Horsley's search for exegetical treatment of Gen. 2:7
in the gnostic tradition in "Pneumatikos vs. Psychikos Distinctions
of Spiritual Status Among the Corinthians," *Harvard Theological
Review* 69:3-4 (1976) pp. 269-88.

From that day forth that angel was called 'the light-Adam,' the interpretation of which is 'the blood-man of light.' And the earth spread out upon him, 'the holy Adaman,' the interpretation of which is 'the holy adamantine earth' (*Orig. World* 108.19-25).

In *On the Origin of the World*, this angel is not Adam, but an angelic power with whom Pronoia fell in love. Nevertheless, the fanciful etymological connection may have provided the stimulus for the idea in *Hyp. Arch.* 88.13-16 that a spirit "from the adamantine earth" entered Adam and made him psychic. The downgrading of the gnostic spiritual infusion delivered by the personified Zoe to the work of an earth-spirit would not be out of place in a post-gnostic document. The more usual gnostic exegesis is found in *Apoc. John* 19.21-20.24 as well as in *On the Origin of the World*.

On the fortieth day, Sophia Zoe sent her breath into Adam, in whom there was so soul. He began to move upon the earth. (*Orig. World* 115.11-14).

The theme of an inviolate virgin attacked by supernatural powers is a common one in pagan art and mythology. In the *Harvard Theological Review* (1976), B. Pearson describes a mosaic from Pompeii in which the god Pan is trying to grasp a beautiful maiden, but she is pictured as turning into a tree.[38] Pearson also notes the myth of the virgin Daphne, who was assaulted by Apollo and miraculously replaced by a laurel tree. This pagan theme, modified by incorporation into the narrative of Genesis events, occurs in *Orig. World* 116.11-33 and *Hyp. Arch.* 89.17-27.

Orig. World 116.11-33	*Hyp. Arch. 89.17-27*
They came to Adam, and when they saw Eva speaking with him, they said to one another, 'Who is this Light-man (fem.)? For truly she appears like unto that image which was manifest to us in the light. Come now, let us seize her and cast our	And the authorities came to their Adam. And when they saw his co-image (fem.) speaking with him, they were exceedingly terrified. And they fell in love with her. They said to one another, 'Come, let us cast our seed upon her.'

---

38. Cf. Birger Pearson, "'She Became a Tree' - A Note to CG II, 4:89, 25-26," *Harvard Theological Review* 69:3-4 (1976) pp. 413-15.

seed on her so that she
shall be defiled and no
longer be able to return
to her light, and those
whom she shall beget will
be subordinate to us.
And let us not tell Adam
that *she* is also (AN) one
of us, but let us bring
a forgetfulness over him
and teach him during his
sleep that she came forth
from his rib, in order
that the woman should be
subordinate and he should
be lord over her.'

Then Eva, because she
was powerful, laughed at
their decision. She cast
mist upon their eyes, and
she left her image secretly there with Adam and
entered into the tree of
knowledge and remained
there. But they followed
after her, and she
revealed to them that she
had entered into the tree,
and she had become a tree.
And when they became
exceedingly terrified,
they fled away <blind>.

They followed after her,
and she laughed at them
because of their stupidity
and their blindness.

And in their hands she
became a tree. She left
a shadow like unto herself
with them.

The two accounts agree closely in describing Eve's
escape from the archons, even to the unusual phrase,
ACP (OY)ⲰϨⲚ, literally, "She did a tree." As is the
case with most of these parallels, the version in the
Hypostasis of the Archons is considerably shorter.
Nothing is said of Eve being a supernatural light-being,
or of the archons' falsehood in saying that she came
forth from Adam's rib. Indeed, no explanation is given
of the archons' terror before her, except that they
fell in love with her (89.21). Instead of leaving her
light-image with Adam, she leaves her "shadow" with the
archons, and this subsequently is defiled by them.

In *Hyp. Arch.* 92.2-3, the daughter of Eve is described
as "the virgin whom no power hath defiled." The daughter's name is not given, but she is said to be a "saving

120

virgin (ΠΑΡΘΕΝΟC NBOHΘΕΙΑ) for generations of generations of mankind." One suspects that the daughter's
name is Norea. The interesting point is that her epithet seems to set up a spiritual line of "the daughters
of Eve" which can extend even to the New testament era.
In *Goꞩp. Philip* 55.27-28, Mary, the mother of Jesus, is
described in the same words: "Mary is the virgin whom
no power hath defiled." Apparently the pagan motif of
the inviolate virgin had entered gnostic Christianity
and was capable of being applied to a number of feminine
salvific figures.

The feminine salvific figure Norea occurs in both *On
the Origin of the World* and in the *Hypoꞩtaꞩiꞩ of the
Archonꞩ*. Bullard compiled some impressive evidence to
show that an Egyptian prototype, whose name variously
occurs as Orea and Oraia, may be here compounded with
Norea, the legendary wife of Noah.[39] In fact, both
forms, Orea, and Norea, occur in the *Hypoꞩtaꞩiꞩ of the
Archonꞩ*, while Oraias and Noraias occur in *On the Origin
of the World*.[40] This coincidence of alternate forms in
the two tractates is remarkable. Although it may be
true that independent traditions can be explored for
both of these figures, one must also consider direct
borrowing as an explanation. The name "Norea" also
occurs twice in another Nag Hammadi tractate, which has
been titled "*The Thought of Norea*."[41] However, it seems
unlikely that another instance of alternate forms such
as Norea and Orea would show up in the gnostic literature. One cannot help but suspect that a direct literary dependence is the cause of the alternate spellings.[42]

The sum of common pagan motifs behind the gnostic
myth of *On the Origin of the World* and the *Hypoꞩtaꞩiꞩ of
the Archonꞩ* is impressive. The sharing of specific common themes such as the androgyne and the inviolate vir-

---

39. Cf. Bullard, pp. 95-98.
40. In the *Hypoꞩtaꞩiꞩ of the Archonꞩ* there is ŌREA 92.14,32 (?);
NŌREA 92.21,32 (?); 93.6. In *On the Origin of the World* there is
NŌRAIA 102.11; ŌRAIAS 102.25.
41. Tractate IX.2 has been assigned its modern title "*The Thought
of Norea*" on the basis of its contents. Like the *Hypoꞩtaꞩiꞩ of
the Archonꞩ* it presents Norea as crying to heaven for help and
being delivered.
42. For an explanation of the origin of the misspelling of Norea
see the linguistic evidence for the priority of *On the Origin of
the World* at the end of this chapter, pp. 146-47.

gin, some specific terminology in the *Song of the Woman,* as well as "Tartaron," "*NOYN,*" and the figure "(N)orea," all indicate a rich pagan background for these documents. However, one must also consider the view that the two documents may be in a state of literary dependence, and this would considerably limit the significance of the pagan motifs here.

We now need to inquire concerning the nature of the apocalyptic material of *On the Origin of the World* and the *Hypostasis of the Archons.* In gnostic documents one may expect to find not only theories of the beginnings of the universe but also speculation about its end. Rather conventional apocalyptic material is found in the endings of both documents. Within this apocalyptic material there are Christian motifs. *On the Origin of the World* gives a clear allusion to Matt. 24: 29, while the *Hypostasis of the Archons* alludes to John 14:17,26, I John 2:20,27, and to Eph. 4:6. There are, however, no common traits which are recognizably Christian; the two documents seem to have incorporated their Christian elements in an independent fashion.

Important for us in our study of feminine motifs is the "mindless fury" presented in the apocalyptic ending of *On the Origin of the World.* The power is not named, but several of her characteristics seem to identify her with the Sophia of Christian gnosticism.

> Then the sun will be darkened, and the moon shall lose her light. The stars of heaven will be displaced from their courses, and great thunder shall come forth from a great power, which is above all the powers of Chaos, from the place of the feminine firmament.
> After that one (fem.) has created the first force, she will take off the wise flame of Epinoia and she will clothe herself with mindless fury. Then she will drive out the gods of Chaos whom she created with the archigenetor. She shall cast them down to the abyss (*NOYN*). . . . the force (*EPΓON*) which the darkness followed after will be dissolved, and the fault (*ϢTA*) shall be torn out by its roots in darkness. And the light shall make its way back to its root. (*Orig. World* 126.10-22; 127.1-5).

Having taken off "the wise flame of Epinoia," she will put on "mindless fury" (*OPΓH MMNTAΘHT*). As an hysterical Fury, she thunders forth from "the place of the feminine firmament." She will cast down to the abyss "the gods of Chaos whom she created with the archigenetor." Sophia as mistress of the universe and goddess over creation is familiar from both Christian and non-Christian cosmogony, but Sophia at fault because of the creation seems to be unique to Christian gnostic documents. Significantly, the *ŴTA*, "the lack" or "the fault" (of Sophia), appears only at the beginning and ending of *On the Origin of the World*. After the archigenetor will have been destroyed, then "the fault shall be torn out by its roots."

One may speculate concerning the omission of Sophia's name in a passage which quite clearly refers to her. If, as we suppose, the impersonal view concerning the origin of the universe found at the beginning of *On the Origin of the World* represents the ideas of the Christian author, then this impersonal view of the universe will dominate the ending also. His one use of the term "Sophia" in the opening cosmogony is only partly personal: " . . . then from Pistis an image flowed forth which is called 'Sophia'" (98.13-14). The older myth is employed only to make the metaphysical reality more familiar.[43] To admit the personified Sophia here in the ending would perhaps undermine the author's initial impersonal presentation.

Feminine imagery in Christian presentations of apocalyptic material is unusual. One needs to go all the way to the Book of Revelation in the New Testament before one comes upon any extensive use of feminine motifs in this much-used type of material. For an instance of the use of feminine imagery in non-Christian apocalyptic, one can compare the figure of the virgin Tabitha in the *Apocalypse of Elijah.*[44]

A summary statement regarding the question of the nature of the common material of *On the Origin of the World* and the *Hypostasis of the Archons* is in order. We have found the common material to be gnostic: it contains the basic myth of Sophia, Ialdabaoth, and the Light-man. We have found the common material syncretistic; it reconciles Jewish, Greek, and Egyptian mythologies. We have

43. Cf. Goodenough, pp. 1-4 on the function of myth in the Hellenistic world.
44. For a new translation, see Jean-Marc Rosenstiehl, *L'Apocalypse d'Élie*, (Paris: Librarie Orientaliste Paul Geuthner, 1972).

found the endings to be apocalyptic and Christian; they are concerned with the presentation of the end of the aeons and the beginning of the new age. In the following sections we shall consider some feminine motifs which are not common to *On the Origin of the World* and the *Hypostasis of the Archons*.

Feminine Motifs in the Unique Material
of On the Origin of the World

The beginning of *On the Origin of the World* may be understood as directly related to the Christian soteriology found in the ending. The opening concern is with the origin of the universe, and it is suggested that all things derive from a primal light. Then the author posits a kind of chaos "without bounds" (98.31) following upon the shadow of the light. That shadow he calls Sophia, and from her "lack," "fault," or "diminution" (ϢΤΑ) proceeds the archigenetor and his creations.

> Then the shadow perceived that there was that which was stronger than herself. She became envious and when she had conceived by herself, immediately she brought forth envy. From that day forth the rule of envy was manifest in all of the aeons and their worlds. And that envy was found to be as an abortion in which there was no spirit. (*Orig. World* 99.2-10)

By assigning to Sophia a lack (ϢΤΑ) comparable to the poverty (ΜΝΤϨΗΚΕ) of the Light-man in the gnostic myth (112.10-13), the author paves the way for the soteriological solution which he propounds in the ending. Apparently the author has transferred the temporary victory of the powers of darkness over the Light-man in an earlier myth into the fundamental "lack" of the woman. In the latter case the fault of the universe is basically the diminution of the original light of Pistis Sophia. The more primitive-sounding narrative in 112.10-13 relates that some taint accrued to the Light-man when he was seen and used by the archons as the model for their creation of Adam.

> But when the light-Adam wished to return to his light, that is, to the Eighth, he was not able to on account of the poverty (ΜΝΤϨΗΚΕ) which was mixed with his light (*Orig. World* 112.10-13).

The "fault" of Sophia appears to be related to parthenogenic conception, which is condemned for producing
the abortion known as Ialdabaoth. The author relates
that when the shadow (Sophia) had conceived by herself
she brought forth envy and wrath (99.3-7), and that
when Pistis saw that which had come into being through
her "fault" (ϢΤΑ), she was disturbed.

> And the disturbance was manifest as a fearful
> force. It fled [down into] Chaos. And she
> turned to it and [breathed] into its face in
> the Abyss which is underneath all the heavens
> (*Orig. World* 99.31-100.1).

This basic flaw of the universe, the "fault" of
Sophia, is mentioned on three other occasions in *On the
Origin of the World*. Two of these are in the Christian
ending; the third occurs in that important passage in
which Pistis rebukes the arrogant archon's boast: "I am
God, and there is none other existing beside me."

> You are wrong, Samael, that is, "the blind
> god." There is an immortal Light-man who
> exists before you, who shall be revealed in
> your plasma. He will trample upon you as
> upon a clay vessel which is stepped on, and
> you will go with those who belong to you down
> to your mother, the Abyss. For in the con-
> summation of your works the universal fault
> (ϢΤΑ) which was revealed from the truth shall
> be done away with, and it shall pass away and
> be as that which never came into being (*Orig.
> World* 103.17-28).

In the soteriological ending of *On the Origin of the
World* a plan is presented for the eradication of the
fault, which must be presumed to be that of the parthenogenetic Sophia, for the cure is an infusion of
"blessed spirits" possessing gnosis which will appear
in "the visible church."

> Since the immortal Father knows that a fault
> (ϢΤΑ) came into being from the truth within
> the aeons and their world; therefore, when
> he wished to dispossess the archons of
> destruction through their own plasma, he
> sent your images down into the world of
> destruction - these are the blessed, inno-
> cent, little spirits. They are no strangers
> to gnosis, for the complete gnosis is as an

angel who is manifest before them. This one is not powerless before the Father to give them gnosis . . . Now the blessed ones, when they became manifest in light, manifested themselves in different ways, and each one of them from his own land showed forth his gnosis to the visible church in the plasma of destruction (*Orig. World* 124.5-15; 25-30).

The final reference to the "fault" occurs almost at the end of the document and affirms that "the fault (ϢΤΑ) shall be torn out by its roots in darkness, and the light shall make its way back to its root" (127.3-5).

We have said that the ending of *On the Origin of the World* resembles the codicil of the *Sophia of Jesus Christ*. Both are concerned with a particular type of soteriology which claims that spiritual gnostics from the Father shall help do away with the psychic "fault" associated with Sophia. In the *Sophia of Jesus Christ* these are the "antopoi," mirror-images of the Father, "the kingless generation among whom you have been made manifest."[45] These are the pneumatic ones, and they accomplish a kind of yoking with the psychic generation that brings about the end of the "fault." The basic pattern includes the concept of the superiority of the Father and the masculine spirits together with a hierarchy of gnostic persons each receiving his own reward. A similar pattern occurs in the concluding words of *On the Origin of the World*:

> And those who have not been made perfect within the unbegotten Father shall receive a glory in an eon and in an immortal kingdom. But they shall not ever enter kinglessness. For it is necessary that each one go to the place from which he came. For each one shall show forth by his actions and his gnosis his own nature (*Orig. World* 127.10-17).[46]

What is the status of Pistis in the ending of *On the Origin of the World*? The word occurs only once, and is translated "belief" by Bethge-Wintermute in *The Nag Hammadi Library* volume. The passage is important because it begins the final section of *On the Origin of*

---

45. Cf. the *Sophia of Jesus Christ*, BG 92.1-9.
46. Cf. the *Sophia of Jesus Christ*, BG 123.2-124.9.

the World, and was apparently meant by the author to
sum up his argument. Because the translation seems
faulty in *The Nag Hammadi Library*, it may be helpful
first to give a very similar statement from the *Sophia
of Jesus Christ*:

Sophia of Jesus Christ III.98.15-20

And she, the emanation of the Ennoia, will reveal to you how (πωσ) Pistis of the invisible
things has been found in the visible things
[of the unbegotten Father.]

The final phrase appears in brackets because it lacks
in the parallel in *Eugnostos* 74.16-19. Otherwise the
Eugnostos' parallel is almost identical. The Berlin
codex version of the *Sophia of Jesus Christ* also contains the passage in an almost identical form. In all
three of these documents the key phrase is introduced
by the Greek loanword ΠWC, "how." The usual Coptic
equivalent for this is NT2E, literally "in this way,"
or "just as." The Bethge-Wintermute translation makes
use of the second alternative and comes up with a translation of entirely different meaning:

*Origin of the World 123.28-31 (Bethge-Winter-
mute)*

Then he (?) will appear just as the belief was
found in the hidden things, which appear from
the foundation to the consummation of the aeon.

The pronoun "he," better translated "it," could refer
to the previous sentence where the antecedent "organization" occurs. The Bethge-Wintermute translation
seems to make the passage into a prophetic announcement
of the coming of Christ, which is completely alien to
the context of the discussion. The following translation takes the parallel from the *Sophia of Jesus Christ*
as a model and translates NT2E as "how." And, of
course, Pistis is taken to refer to the personified
gnostic deity. The preceding sentence is also given to
help show the context.

Origin of the World 123.28-31 (Arthur)

Now we shall come to our world so that we should
complete its analysis and organization more
exactly. Then it will be evident *how* (NT2E)
Pistis of the hidden things has been found (in)

the visible things from the foundation unto the consummation of the age.

Apparently, the personified Pistis could stand for a hidden rationale found in the visible things of creation. This idea should not be overlooked in the ending of *On the Origin of the World.*

The distinctive material within the intrusions in *On the Origin of the World* includes a number of feminine motifs which are not found in the Christian beginning and ending. The motifs probably belong to the source documents and should not be attributed to the Christian compiler, although some of the interpretations may be his.

In the Sabaoth intrusion (103.32-107.17), the main feminine figures are Pistis Sophia and her daughter Zoe. The name "Sophia" does not occur without the correlative "Pistis," and Pistis Sophia does not appear as a fallen being. Zoe (Life), the daughter of Pistis Sophia, is characterized as Sabaoth's teacher and as a creator of good powers which oppose those created by the androgyne, death. From the good powers emanate "many beneficent and innocent spirits" (107.13-14). In a later passage these spirits seem to be related to "the souls of Sabaoth and his Christ which are to come into the plasma of the authorities" (114.16-18).

There is another passage within the Sabaoth intrusion which suggests a Christian update. This is the mention of "Jesus the Christ, who is like unto the Savior." The passage is interesting because it reports on a sphere higher than the feminine eighth sphere.

> Afterwards, he (Sabaoth) created an angelic church, thousands upon ten-thousands without number, which is like unto the church which is in the Eighth, and a first-born one, who is called "Israel," that is the man who sees God, and another, "Jesus the Christ," who is like unto the Savior who is *above the Eighth*, sitting on his right hand upon an exalted throne (105.20-29).

It is twice reported that Sophia dominates the eighth sphere (104.28-31; 106.5-8), and in the ending of the document it is the eighth sphere which is called "the feminine firmament" (126.16). One can only suppose that the Christian Savior must be above the feminine sphere. For a ninth sphere which seems to be identified with Sophia's son, one may compare the account in *Apoc. John* II.14.9-13. The ninth sphere also occurs in the ending of the *Poimandres* tractate, and of course, there is a Hermetic tractate in codex six now entitled "*The Discourse on the Eighth and Ninth*" (VI.6).

The Pronoia intrusion (108.14-111.28) is concerned with the cleansing creative power of the "blood of the virgin." The word "pronoia" is generally used to refer to a plan either that of Pistis or of the evil archons. Immediately before the section begins, a strange juxtaposition occurs: "no one saw it (the light-image) except the archigenetor himself, and the Pronoia who was with him" (108.10-12). Perhaps the mention of the Pronoia has been added at this point to make less awkward the transition to unrelated Pronoia material. In the intrusion, Pronoia represents a feminine power whose efforts to embrace the Light-man are rejected "because she was in darkness." She pours forth her blood upon him and upon the earth, and the earth is purified.

> From that day forth, all of the authorities honored the blood of the virgin (108.25-27).

From the sequel it becomes apparent that it is this blood which causes the earth to sprout forth and grow plants and flowers. The androgyne motif reappears; here the feminine element is said to be "a blood-soul; she is from the substance (ουσια) of the Pronoia" (109. 5-6). This is the androgyne Eros, a pagan theme which is treated with sympathy. Within the discourse upon the purifying effects of Pronoia's blood there is also praise for Pistis Sophia:

> And even more was the water purified through the image of Pistis Sophia, she who was re- vealed to the archigenetor in the waters. Indeed, it is correctly said, 'through the waters,' since the holy water makes all things alive. It purifies (108.28-109.1).

The account of the origins of the various flowers is lyrical; each one is attributed to a virgin daughter of Pronoia. However, along with the blood motif there also occurs the theme of the authorities creating in the waters. Perhaps the mixture of the water and the blood motifs represents the weaving of separate tradi- tions into an etiological account.

129

After this also sprang up the beautiful, sweet-
smelling flowers upon the earth, according to
their kind, each from a virgin of the daughters of Pronoia. When these fell in love with
Eros, they poured forth their blood on him and
upon the earth. After these things, all the
vegetation sprang up on the earth, according
to its kind, each possessing seed from the
authorities and their angels. After these
things, the authorities created from the waters
every beast, according to its kind, and every
reptile and bird, according to its kind, each
possessing seed from the authorities and their
angels (111.14-28).

At one point in the intrusion, the Bethge-Wintermute
translation in *The Nag Hammadi Library* unaccountably
introduces the presence of the male gender.

<The man followed>the earth,
the woman followed<the man>,
And marriage followed the woman,
And reproduction followed marriage,
And death followed reproduction.
(109.22-25 *NHL*)

It hardly seems correct for modern scholars to introduce
the primacy of the male where there is no textual argument for it. The "earth" occurs in the previous sentence, and the sequence is perfectly intelligible
without the uncalled for additions of the phrases "the
man followed" and "the man." The correct translation
follows:

The first pleasure (2HΔONH) sprang up on the
earth.
The woman followed after the earth.
And marriage followed after the woman.
Generation followed after marriage.
Dissolution followed after generation.
(109.21-25)

The Eve intrusion (113.10-114.15) is remarkable for
the inclusion of the *Song of the Woman*. In fact, the
whole purpose of this section seems to be to build up
to this song. The beginning of the intrusion relates
the birth of Eve, an androgyne who was created before
Adam:

Then the authorities took knowledge that they
should make the man. (But) Sophia Zoe, she
who is by the side of Sabaoth, anticipated
them, and she mocked their decision. (113.10-
14)

The Eve intrusion comes directly after the announcement
by the powers: "Come, let us make a man from the earth
. . ." (112.33-34), and after the intrusion the account
continues with the molding of the man by the assembled
archons (114.29-30). The meaning seems obvious: the
author intended to show that the first *woman* began the
reproduction of the human race "without a man." This
is explicitly said in the introduction to the *Song*,
where the woman of the *Song*, probably originally Isis,
is identified with Eve. Again, *The Nag Hammadi Library*
translation is incorrect, ending a sentence in the
middle of a relative clause. The words TAEI AXN 200YT,
literally, "this one (fem.) without a man" cannot end a
sentence. The demonstratives ΠAEI, TAEI, NAEI are
never used this way in *On the Origin of the World*. The
important idea that Eve is the first virgin who gave
birth without a man is replaced by the absurd-sounding
sentence: "Moreover Eve is the first virgin, *not having
a husband*" (114.4-5, NHL). The correct translation
must take the TAEI AXN 200YT as the beginning of a
relative clause, "the one who without a man gave birth."
This yields the sense of the passage and is in accord
with the theme of the whole section.

The following parallel gives the *Song of the Woman*
in *On the Origin of the World* and the abbreviated elements of it found in the *Hypostasis of the Archons*.
In the latter document, the words are presented as
praise from Adam to Eve introduced by a reference to
Gen. 3:20.

Origin of the World 114.4-15   *Hyp. Arch. 89.13-17*

Now Eva is the first virgin   And when he (Adam) saw
who gave birth without a man.   her he said: "Thou art
She is the one who played her   the one who gave me
own doctor. Therefore, it is   life. Thou shalt be
said of her that she said: called the 'Mother of
I am a portion of my mother;   the living'" (Gen. 3:
    and I am the Mother.   20), for (XE):
I am the woman; and   She is my mother
I am the maiden.   She is the doctor,
I am the one who is with   and the
    child; (and)   woman,
I am the doctor.

131

I am the consoler of the
    labor pains.

The one who begat me is my
    husband; and
I am his mother; and
    he is my father and
    my lord. He is my
    power. That which he
    wishes he speaks. With
    propriety I exist, but
I have begotten a child   and she who
    with the lord.   has given
                                       birth.

Both documents clearly indicate that the *Song* is a
traditional piece inserted in the respective texts. In
the *Hypostasis of the Archons* this shows up in the introductory XE, customarily employed to introduce a quotation. The unexpected "*She* is my mother" also is a good
indication that the author is at this point moving his
attention from one source (Gen. 3:20) to another (*Orig.
World?*). The author alludes to traditional poetry,
asserts it is the words of Adam, and rephrases the
material in the third person.

On the other hand, in *On the Origin of the World*, the
words are said to be those of Eve spoken at the time she
gave birth. The aretalogy is reminiscent of those of
Isis, and has some close parallels with the opening
lines of *The Thunder* (VI.2).[47] The meaning of the ending of the *Song* is not entirely clear. The last line
reads literally: "I have *begotten* a lordly human."
Within the context, this could refer to Seth and also
hark back to the beginning of the intrusion in which
the son of Eve is said to be "the *begotten* one, who is
the lord" (113.34-35). Of course, this could indicate
that the ending of the *Song of the Woman* has been adapted
to the context of the narrative in *On the Origin of the
World*. The ending might also be seen as a reference to
Gen. 4:1, "I have *begotten* (acquired) a man with the
Lord," words said by Eve when she brought forth Cain.
The phrase, "the one who *begat* me" (114.11) must not be
construed as "caused me to give birth" but "caused me
to be born." The meaning is: "The One who caused me to
be born is (also) my husband," thus implying a kind of

---

47. See the comparison of the *Song of the Woman* in *The Thunder* and
On the Origin of the World in chapter five, pp. 158-64.

132

"hieros gamos" motif. The same idea recurs in the
words, "He (God) is my father and my lord (husband)"
(114.12-13).

The Egyptian-signs intrusion is of interest because
of the syncretistic linking of Sophia with the two
sacred bulls of Egypt, Apis and Mnevis. There is no
hint of the fallen Sophia, although the section contains
some Christian elements. Three baptisms are spoken of;
even the crocodiles are said to be witnesses to the
baptism "of a true man" (122.20). One reference to the
Phoenix bird implies that the eschaton has arrived:

> The Phoenix appears first of all alive and then
> dies, and then again rises up, being a sign of
> him who has been revealed at the consummation
> of the age (122.30-32).

The reference to Sophia in connection with the sacred
bulls of Egypt is not without difficulty. The Bethge-
Wintermute translation is unsatisfying:

> The two bulls in Egypt, in so far as they pos-
> sess the sun and the moon as a mystery, exist
> for a witness to Sabaoth because ⟨he exists⟩
> above them. Sophia (of Astaphaios) received
> the universe, since the day when she created
> the sun and the moon and sealed her heaven
> until ⟨the consummation of⟩ the aeon (122.21-
> 26, NHL).

This is probably not correct. The sun and the moon are
witnesses (watchers) for Sabaoth, since these two
heavenly bodies, represented in Egypt by the two sacred
bulls, can be depicted as *observers* of "the cosmos."
The text seems to say that the higher heaven, that of
Sophia, has been sealed off from observation. Sabaoth
is presented as the ruler of the lower spheres, including "the cosmos." This is in agreement with 103.32-104.
31, where in payment for his repentance Sabaoth is
rescued from the lower heavens and installed over the
seventh heaven by Pistis Sophia. With this picture in
mind we can take the passage to mean that Sophia has
taken "the cosmos" down to the realms of personified
sun and moon so that they may watch over it as agents
of Sabaoth. By maintaining a single sentence until the
word "since" in the above translation, and by translating ЄⲀⲢⲀⲒ "down to" instead of "above" (in Sahidic the
word has both of these meanings), we can translate the
Coptic text without any emendations.

The two bulls of Egypt possess the mystery of
the sun and the moon, which exist as *witnesses*
of Sabaoth, because Sophia took the cosmos down
to them (sun and moon). From the day that she
created the sun and the moon, she sealed off
her heaven until the aeon (122.21-26).

The difficult phrase, "she took the cosmos down to them"
can be interpreted as meaning "she placed the world in
their (sun and moon) charge." The picture is consistent
with other imagery from *On the Origin of the World* in
which Sophia rules over all the other spheres from a
transcendental sphere known as "the Eighth." In the
original cosmology this must have been identical with
the sphere of the immovable stars known from ancient
Egyptian religion as the realm of the imperishable
spirits.

Important feminine motifs occur in all sections of
On the Origin of the World, within the narratives and
within the intrusions. But only in the Christian beginning and ending do we find mention of the fallen Sophia,
her envy of "that which was stronger than herself" (99.
3-4), and "the lack" which "shall be torn out by its
root" (127.3). The single reference to a lower Sophia
in the main body of the text indeed contrasts her with
a higher power, but that power is Pistis.

Now Sophia, who was in the lower heaven, when
she wished, received authority from Pistis.
She created great luminaries and all of the
stars and placed them in the heaven so that
they should shine upon the earth (112.1-5).

Distinctive Feminine Motifs in The
Hypostasis of the Archons

Three main sections of the *Hypostasis of the Archons*
present material independent of that of *On the Origin
of the World*: the beginning (86.20-87.23), the ending
(96.35-97.23), and portions of the Norea narrative (92.
9-94.3; 96.11-96.35). We shall consider these sections
with regard to their feminine and Christian nature. In
general, the feminine figures in the *Hypostasis of the
Archons* are treated with less sympathy and occur relatively less often than the corresponding figures in *On
the Origin of the World*.

The opening of the *Hypostasis of the Archons* contains
the phrase "Father of Truth." This appellation is used

frequently in gnostic documents to distinguish the
supreme deity from the archigenetor who also begets
offspring and is also called "father." In the *Hypostasis of the Archons*, the "Father of Truth" is certainly higher than the creator deity Ialdabaoth, but he
also seems to be presented as superior to the goddess,
Pistis Sophia. The *Hypostasis of the Archons* is written
by its own acknowledgement "in the spirit of the Father
of truth" (86.21), that is in the spirit of the Father
God of Christianity.

Pistis Sophia occurs in the opening section at 87.
7-8, where she is connected with the Egyptian *NOYN*, the
abyss, the mother of the arrogant archon. In addition
to this, she is probably to be understood as the figure
behind the codeword "imperishability" which occurs in
87.1, 2, 11, 20; 88.18 and 93.29. This "imperishability" rebukes the archon's blasphemy; her image appears
"upon the waters"; and the powers of darkness fall in
love with her. In fact, "imperishability" is explicitly
said to be Sophia in 94.5-6: "Imperishability, the
Sophia who is called Pistis . . ." It is noteworthy
that the Christian opening of the *Hypostasis of the
Archons* seems to avoid any direct mention of Pistis
Sophia except in the one passage in which "Chaos" and
the "Abyss" (*NOYN*) occur.

The ending of the *Hypostasis of the Archons*, too, is
basically Christian and patriarchal. It contains the
trinitarian terms "Father" (97.18), "Son" (97.18), and
"Holy Spirit" (97.16), as well as the phrase "the Father
of the All" (97.15-16). The latter phrase occurs elsewhere twice in the *Hypostasis of the Archons* (88.11; 96.
12) but never in *On the Origin of the World*. We have
noted before that whereas the *Hypostasis of the Archons*
extols "the will of the Father of the All" (88.11; 96.
12), *On the Origin of the World* praises "the plan
(προνοια) of Pistis" (113.6-7).

Patriarchal imagery for the Christian God in the ending is also to be found in a passage reminiscent of John
14:26:

> [The Spirit] of truth whom the Father has sent
> . . . he will teach them about everything, and
> will anoint them with the anointing of eternal
> life (96.35-97.3).

The phrase "true man" is found in the ending of the
Hypostasis of the Archons. Since it is surrounded by
so many Christian motifs, it is quite certain that the

135

phrase refers to Christ. Sophia does not occur in the
ending, nor does any other feminine motif except perhaps in the disguise of Planē, "error" in 96.31: "After
three generations he will appear, rescuing them from
the bond of the error (πλανη) of the powers" (96.29-31).

Within the unique material of the *Hypostasis of the
Archons*, there is an important section devoted to Norea,
a feminine being who is presented in a three-fold manner. She is Eve's daughter "whom no power hath defiled"
(92.2-3), the destroyer of Noah's ark (92.17), and the
recipient of a revelation upon her cry for help to the
God of the All (92.18-93.2). Concerning the first
Norea, Eve is reported as saying:

> He (God) has begotten for me a saving virgin
> (ΠΑΡΘΕΝΟC ΝΒΟΗΘΕΙΑ) for generations and gener-
> ations of mankind. This is *the virgin whom no
> power hath defiled*" (91.35-92.3).

From a literary point of view, the second Norea
serves to join the Genesis midrash with the revelatory
discourse. But why should this Norea burn Noah's ark?
In gnostic speculation, Noah is sometimes the favorite
of the archigenetor, as in the *Apocalypse of Adam*.[48]
If Noah could represent the lackey of Ialdabaoth, and
Norea be the gnostic spirit, then the burning of the
ark in gnostic tradition may have implied a victory of
feminine spiritual forces over the male powers of darkness. On the other hand, the present context (of the
story) seems to make this Norea a demonic individual
who interrupts the working out of God's plan for Noah.

The third Norea is presented as crying out to the
God of the All for help against the archons of darkness.
The angel Eleleth is sent to speak with her, to rescue
her from the lawless archons, and to teach her about
the powers. Perhaps this third Norea is a type of the
psychic person who receives a gnostic revelation upon
her call for help.

Generally speaking, there are very few feminine
motifs in the specific material of the *Hypostasis of
the Archons*. Most of the feminine themes of this document can be found in the material parallel with *On the
Origin of the World*, and as a rule the feminine themes
are reduced in scope and emphasis in comparison with

---

48. Cf. the *Apocalypse of Adam* V.70.16-74.21.

that document. This is particularly true of Sophia who
is regularly replaced by the term "imperishability" in
the *Hypostasis of the Archons*. In *Hyp. Arch.* 93.29-32,
Sophia, i.e., Imperishability, is clearly described as
a place rather than a person, although the underlying
Sophia traits may still be seen:

> For your abode is in Imperishability, the *place*
> where the virginal spirit is, the one who is
> over the powers of chaos and their world (93.
> 29-32).

The daughter of Eve, whom we may take to be Norea,
is an exception. She seems to be portrayed as a salvific figure initiating a righteous line that will be "a
help (βοηθεια) for generations and generations of mankind" (92.1-2). The daughter of Pistis Sophia, called
Zoë, is also important in the *Hypostasis of the Archons*.
It is she, rather than Pistis (*Orig. World* 103.15), who
rebukes the boast of the arrogant archon with the words,
"You are wrong, Saklas!" (*Hyp. Arch.* 95.7). In all this
one may see a certain limitation of the extra-worldly
authority of Sophia in the account of the *Hypostasis of
the Archons*. She becomes the equivalent of an abstraction, "imperishability" (94.4-5), a place (93.29-30),
an earth-spirit (88.13-14), or the abyss (87.7-8), and
her functions seem to be given over to her daughter Zoë,
or to Eve and her daughter Norea.

The description in *Hyp. Arch.* 90.11 of the serpent
as a feminine instructor may seem to be an exception to
this tendency. The serpent of the Garden of Eden story
is not described as a feminine being in the account in
Orig. World 118.17-120.11. Rather, the serpent is
called "the Beast," "the Instructor," who in an earlier
passage was said to be the Son of Eve (113.34-114.4).
This is apparently Seth, and the Instructor, "the
Beast," may be taken as the primitive totem of the
Sethian community. However, the important feminine
term, "*Instructoress*" does occur in *Orig. World* 113.33-
34, where it is said that Eva-Zoë is "*the Instructoress
of Life*." Also in *Orig. World* 115.32-33, Zoë is described as "Instructor." The basic difference in the
two accounts seems to be that in *On the Origin of the
World* the Instructor(ess) is Seth or Eve, while in the
Hypostasis of the Archons the serpent, as in Genesis,
takes on this role. Indeed, the serpent in the *Hypostasis of the Archons* speaks as an agent of "the pneumatic woman" (89.11, 31), but as serpent he is punished
and not honored as in the account in *On the Origin of
the World*. In the parallels below, Genesis allusions

137

are given only for the *Hypostasis of the Archons*. It will be seen that this account follows Genesis more closely than that of *On the Origin of the World*. Italicized portions show identical material which is *not* taken from Genesis.

Orig. World 118.17-120.11	*Hyp. Arch. 88.25-89.3; 89.31-91.6*
They went up to Adam and Eve and said to him in terror: 'Every tree which is in Paradise was created for you to eat of the fruit thereof, but keep yourselves from the tree of knowledge. Do not eat from it. If you eat, you will die.' . . .	They placed him in the garden to work it and guard it (Gen. 2:15). And the archons commanded him saying: 'From every tree which is in Paradise thou shalt eat, but from the tree of the knowledge of good and evil, do not eat, neither touch it, because the day you shall eat from it, you will surely die' (Gen. 2:16-17) . . . in the will of the Father they said this in this way so that he would eat, and Adam would be regarded by them as wholly hylic. . . .
Then along came he who was wiser than all of them, whom they called 'the Beast,' and when he saw the image of their mother, Eva, he said to her: 'What is it that God said to you (pl.), 'Do not eat from the tree of knowledge?' She answered: 'He said *not only* 'Do not eat from it' *but also* 'Do not touch it, lest you die.'	But along came the pneumatic one (fem.) in the serpent, the Instructor, and it [instructed them], saying: 'What is it that [he said to you], 'From every tree [which is in the] garden thou shalt eat, [but from the tree] of knowledge of evil and good do not eat?' The fleshly woman said: '*Not only* did he say, 'Do not eat' *but also* 'Do not touch it, because on the day you eat from it, you will surely die' (Gen. 3: 3).
He said to her: 'Do not be afraid. Certainly you will not die. For [he knows] that if you eat	And the serpent, the Instructor, said, 'Certainly you will not die (Gen. 3:4). *For he said this to you*

138

from it your mind will be enlightened, and you will become like the gods knowing the difference which exists between evil and good men. *For he said this to you because he is envious* lest you eat from it.'

And Eva trusted herself to the words of the Instructor. She gazed upon the tree. She saw it was beautiful and very tall. She fell in love with it.

She took from its fruit and she ate. She gave to her husband and he also ate. Then their mind was opened. For when they had eaten, the light of Gnosis shone upon them. And when they had clothed their shame, they knew that they had been naked of Gnosis. And when they reflected, they saw that they were naked, and they fell in love with each other. And when they saw that their makers were in the forms of beasts, they loathed them and became more understanding.

Then the archons, when they learned that they had transgressed their commandment, came with quaking of the earth and great threatening into Paradise and approached Adam and Eve to see the outcome of this assistance.

because he is envious. Rather your eyes will be opened, and you will become like the gods knowing evil and good' (Gen. 3:5). And the Instructoress was taken away from the serpent, and she left it alone as an earthly being.

And the fleshly woman took from the tree and she ate (Gen. 3:6). And she gave to her husband with her, and the psychic ones ate. And their evil arose from their ignorance. And they knew that they had been naked of the spiritual. They took some fig leaves and bound them around their loins (Gen. 3:7).

Then the Great Archon came and said:

139

Then Adam and Eve were sorely distressed and hid themselves under the trees which are in Paradise. And since the archons knew not where they were, they said, 'Adam, where are thou?' He said, 'I am over here. And I hid myself from fear of you when I was ashamed.' But they spoke to him out of their ignorance: 'Who is it that told thee of the shame which thou hast clothed, unless thou hast eaten of the tree?'

He said, 'The woman whom thou (sic) gavest me, she is the one who gave to me and I ate.' And then [they said to her,] 'What is it that thou hast done?' She answered and said, 'The Instructor is the one who provoked me, and I ate.'

Then the archons went up to the Instructor. Their eyes were blinded by him. They were not able to do anything to him. They cursed him because they were powerless. Afterwards, they went up to the woman and cursed her and her children.

After the woman, they cursed Adam and the ground for his sake, together with the fruit. And all things which they made were accursed. *There is no blessing with them.*

'Adam, where art thou?' (Gen. 3:9). For he did not know what had happened. And Adam said, 'I heard your voice, and I was afraid because I was naked, and I hid' (Gen. 3:10). The Archon said, 'Why did you hide, unless you have eaten of the tree that I commanded you, 'Do not eat of it alone,'and you have eaten' (Gen. 3:11). Adam said, 'The woman whom you gave me, gave to me, and I ate' (Gen. 3:12). And the arrogant archon cursed the woman. The woman said, ['It was the serpent] that deceived me, and I ate' (Gen. 3:13).

. . . the serpent. They cursed his shadow . . . powerless, not knowing that . . . plasma. From that day forth, the serpent has been under the curse of the authorities, until the perfect man should come. That curse came down on the serpent (Gen. 3:14,15). They turned to their Adam, they seized him, they cast him out of Paradise (Gen. 3:23) with his wife, because *there is no blessing with them.*

140

Most of the verbal parallels in the above passages can be directly traced to the Septuagint and in some instances perhaps to the Coptic version of Genesis.[49] The whole account in the *Hypostasis of the Archons* is very much in agreement with the Genesis story except for the use of the archons (pl.) and the Great Archon as substitutes for Jehovah, and the description of the serpent as "the pneumatic one (fem.)," and "the *Instructor(ess)*." This latter term occurs just once with the feminine article (90.11) and twice with the masculine article (89.32; 90.6). On the other hand, the account in *On the Origin of the World* is embellished with a number of *gnostic* motifs: "your mind will be enlightened" (119.1); "then their mind was opened" (119.11-12); "the light of *Gnosis* shone upon them" (119.12-13); "they cursed him (the serpent) because they were powerless" (120.5-6).

The apparently unique emphasis on the serpent as a feminine spiritual instructor in the *Hypostasis of the Archons* disappears when one considers that the *Instructor(ess)* is the mother of "the Beast" in On the Origin of the World.

> . . . the living Eva, that is 'the *Instructoress* of Life.' And her son is the begotten one (Seth), who is the lord. Afterwards, the powers called him 'the Beast,' in order to deceive their creatures. The interpretation of 'the Beast' is 'the Instructor.' For they found that 'he was wiser than all of them' (*Orig. World* 113.33-114.4).

The presentation of the extended parallels of the temptation story in Gen. 3 also helps lead us to the next topic of discussion: the possibility of literary dependence between the documents. We mentioned the number of gnostic comments and expansions in the account given in *Orig. World* 118.17-120.11. While it is true that there are also a number of independent comments in the account of *Hyp. Arch.* 88.25-91.6, the natural question arises who is responsible for their *shared* comments? Three of these are italicized in the presentation. While any one of them might be fortuitous, the impact of all three of them seems to imply some sort of literary relationship, especially when one considers that the Coptic in each case is identical.

---

49. Cf. Bullard, p. 72 for the Sahidic version of Gen. 2:15-17.

The Coptic of the three identities is given below together with an English translation.

On the Origin of the World   *Hypostasis of the Archons*

(1)

AYϪOOC ϪE OY MONON ϪE   OY MONON ΠEϪAY ϪE
MΠPOYWM EBOΛ N2HTY AΛΛA   MN OYWM AΛΛA
MΠPϪW2 EPOY (118.30-32)   MΠPϪW2 EPOY (90.3-4)

"He said *not only*   "*Not only* did he say
'Do not eat from it' *but*   'Do not eat' *but*
also 'Do not touch it."   *also* 'Do not touch it.'"

(2)

NTAYϪE ΠAEⲒ ΓAP NHTN   NTAYϪE ΠAEⲒ ΓAP NHTN
EYPØθONEⲒ (119.4-5)   EYPØθONEⲒ (90.7-8)

For he said this to you be-   For he said this to you
cause he is envious.   because he is envious.

(3)

MN ΛAAY NCMOY NTOOTOY   ϪE MN ΛAAY NCMOY NTOOTOY
(120.10-11)   (91.5-6)

There is no blessing with   . . . because there is no
them.   blessing with them.

The first of these identities is the coincidence of
the three Greek words: ου μονον and αλλα, "not only"
and "but also." The Septuagint of Gen. 3:3 does not
contain these three Greek words, but what is more unusual
is that they should show up in this exact manner in a
Coptic text. Of course, it may be argued that the shared
reading originated in a Coptic version of the bible known
to both documents. The Septuagint text may be compared
to show how far both *On the Origin of the World* and the
Hypostasis of the Archons are removed from the biblical
text: "God said, 'Do not (ου) eat from it, neither
(ουδε) touch it.'"

Interestingly enough, the first expression of God's
prohibition (Gen. 2:17) as presented in *Hyp. Arch.* 88.
30-32 adds the phrase "neither (ουδε) touch it." This
injunction, however, does not appear in the biblical
account in this verse, nor in that particular passage in
On the Origin of the World. Apparently the author of
the *Hypostasis of the Archons* wished to justify the
correctness of Eve's response to the serpent in Gen. 3:4

142

(LXX) by adding the phrase, "neither touch it," to the prohibition in Gen. 2:17!

The second agreement, "For he said this to you because he is envious," is in the form of a redactional comment.[50] It can hardly be thought of as having originated in a Coptic text of Genesis, as it appears in different positions in the two documents. In *Orig. World* 119.4-5 this comment occurs at the end of the Instructor's advice to Eve, while in *Hyp. Arch.* 90.7-8 it occurs towards the beginning. The Coptic parallel is particularly striking here, because among a large number of possibilities for translating "he said" the two documents agree in using the II Perfect tense. In fact, this is the *only* use of ⲚⲦⲀⲨⲬⲈ for "he said" in the *Hypostasis of the Archons*.[51]

The third identity, "There is no blessing with them," also appears to be a redactional comment. Again, one could consider a number of different ways in Coptic to express the idea, but the expressions are exactly the same in both documents.

The close Coptic agreement in these three identities strongly suggests a relationship between the two documents on the Coptic level. From these examples one would not be able to show convincingly which document has literary priority. We shall go into this subject in greater detail in the next section and try to show that *On the Origin of the World* is the earlier document and that the author of the *Hypostasis of the Archons* made use of a Coptic version of this document in writing the *Hypostasis of the Archons*.

Linguistic Evidence for the Priority of
On the Origin of the World over
The Hypostasis of the Archons

In this section we shall try to show that the *Hypostasis of the Archons* and *On the Origin of the World* show signs of literary dependence on the Coptic level, and that this dependence is best explained in terms of the priority of *On the Origin of the World* and its use

---

50. "For he said this to you because he is jealous," (90.7-8) is described by Bullard, p. 88, as "surely a gnosticizing gloss."
51. There is one instance of "they said," ⲚⲦⲀⲨⲬⲈ-, II Perfect, in 89.1. Usually "he said" is translated ⲠⲈⲬⲀⲨ or ⲀⲨⲬⲞⲞⲤ.

as a source by the author of the *Hypostasis of the Archons*. The issue is complicated by the assumed existence of another document, the Norea source, which also seems to have made use of *On the Origin of the World* as a source.[52] Here we shall confine ourselves to the evidence of close Coptic parallels that exist in both the *Hypostasis of the Archons* and in *On the Origin of the World*.

The linguistic argument includes two identities with Greek loanwords in which Greek case and gender, contrary to general Coptic practice, have been preserved: AΔAMANTINH (fem.), "adamantine," and TAPTAPON (acc.), "to Tartarus." There is also the occurrence in both documents of alternate forms for the names (N)WPEA and (N)WPAIA, and the shared error COEIN, "doctor," instead of correct CAEIN. The erroneous ANAEI, "become better (?)" occurs in both documents within the Genesis quotation, "Increase and multiply" (AEIAEI). Finally, an aporia in the *Hypostasis of the Archons* involving the Greek loanword CIXANE, "loathe," seems only explicable on the basis of the parallel text in *On the Origin of the World*. Some other identities, redactional in nature were discussed in the previous section.[53] Some of these identities give no indication of which document is prior; the more important ones also point to the origins of the peculiar or erroneous readings and supply evidence for answering the question of priority.

The Adamantine Earth.

Orig. World 108.19-25

From that day forth, that angel was called 'the light-Adam,' the interpretation of which is 'the blood-man of light.' And the earth spread out upon him, 'the holy Adaman,' the interpretation of which is 'the holy adamantine earth' (ΠΚA2 NAΔAMANTINH ETOYAAB).

Hyp. Arch. 88.13-17

And the spirit came forth from the adamantine earth (ΠΚA2 NAΔAMANTINH). It came down. It dwelt within him. That man 'became a living soul' (Gen. 2:7). It called his name Adam, because he was found moving upon the earth.

---

52. See pages 107-08 for a discussion of the Norea source and its relationship to *On the Origin of the World*.
53. See pages 141-43.

In *On the Origin of the World* the play on the words "adamantine" and "Adaman" is direct and obvious: Adam's name is interpreted as meaning "of steel-like earth." Since the Greek language lacked a word for "earth" phonetically akin to "Adam," another word only remotely related to "earth" but similar in sound to "Adam" was used for the etymology of his name. In Greek, the accusative case ending "n-" added to the similarity. The usual form for this name in the Nag Hammadi documents is AΔAMAC, although AΔAMAN also occurs in *Zostrianos* VIII.30.10. A translator rendering the passage from the Greek of *On the Origin of the World* into Coptic would need to keep the Greek word in his text to make the play on words intelligible for his readers. Thus the appearance of ΠΚΑ2 NAΔAMANTINH is not surprising, although the Coptic word for earth is masculine, and thus the phrase is syntactically *incorrect*. Usually in Coptic, inanimate objects take neuter Greek adjectives; thus in this case ΠΚΑ2 NAΔAMANTINON would be the correct translation of the Greek.

In the *Hypostasis of the Archons* the situation is not so clear. There, the derivation of Adam's name is not based on AΔAMANTINH, but apparently on the Hebrew word for "earth." It would seem that a Coptic translator here could have rendered his Greek original into Coptic without using the rare word AΔAMANTINH, nor would there be any constraint on him to mirror the syntactical error ΠΚΑ2 NAΔAMANTINH. B. Layton's suggestion that AΔAMANTINH "probably belongs to the esoteric vocabulary of gnostic myth" and should be translated as a proper noun does little to explain the identical phrase in *On the Origin of the World*.[54] It seems more likely that the odd phrase was legitimately called forth by etymological considerations in the passage in *On the Origin of the World*, and that its occurrence in the *Hypostasis of the Archons* is derivative.

Tartarus. The word TAPTAPON occurs in what is apparently the accusative case in an identical phrase in both our documents: AYNOXY EΠITN EΠTAPTAPON, "he cast him down to Tartarus" (95.12; 102.34).[55] The word occurs as TAPTAPOC in *Thomas the Contender* II.142.36, so that

----

54. Layton, *HTR* p. 52. Layton gives the following translation: "And the spirit came forth from the Adamantine Land."
55. Böhlig's restored text in *Orig. World* 102.34 reads [AC]NOXY EΠITN EΠTAPTAPON.

145

the agreement in ending is unusual. The fragment of *On the Origin of the World* published by C. Oeyen is inconclusive in this instance. Oeyen gives ΑΩΝ[ΟΥΧΕ ΜΜΑΥ ΑΠΤΑΡΤΑ]ΡΟΝ as the reading of the Subachmimic text. On the other hand, the *Paraphrase of Shem* VII.15.30-31 contains a similar sentence making use of the form ΤΑΡΤΑΡΟΝ: ΕΤΡΑΒΩΚ ΕΠΙΤΝ ΕΠΤΑΡΤΑΡΟΝ, "that I should go down to Tartarus."

The identical phrasing of the two documents is not likely to be fortuitous, but there is no indication in this case of which is the prior document.

The Names [N]orea and [N]oraia. The occurrence of the variant names Norea and Orea in the *Hypostasis of the Archons* has been the source of much discussion.[56] Less has been said of the two variants Noraia and Oraia found in *On the Origin of the World*.

Origin of the World 102.10-11; 24-25

. . . 2Ν ΤΩΟΡΠ ΝΒΙΒΛΟC ΝΝΩΡΑΙΑC.

. . . 2Μ ΠΩΟΡΠ ΝΛΟΓΟC ΝΩΡΑΙΑC.

. . . in the First Book of Noraia.

. . . in the First Treatise of Oraia (?).

One notices in both of these instances the final s-signifying the genitive case in Greek. In fact, the first occurrence seems to make use of both the Greek genitive and the Coptic genitive in Ν-, as if one were to translate the phrase into English as "the book of Noraia's." With this in mind, the second instance is probably to be understood as direct syntactic borrowing from the Greek without making use of the Coptic genitive in Ν-, i.e., "Noraia's book." In this way the variants in *On the Origin of the World* can be explained as translational variants for the title of what is probably one and the same book.

No such facile explanation is available for the variant names in the *Hypostasis of the Archons*. The short tractate in codex nine, now entitled *The Thought of Norea*, does not include the variant "Orea." It is possible that a literal, but incorrect, reading of the

---

56. Cf. Bullard, pp. 95-98 and Layton, *HTR* pp. 365-71.

Coptic words in *On the Origin of the World* was respo
ible for the short spelling ⲰⲢⲈⲀ in the *Hypostasis o*
the Archons. The situation is somewhat analogous to
the corruption ⲠⲚⲞⲨⲦⲈ ⲚⲂⲂⲀⲀⲈ (87.4; 94.26), "the god o
the blind ones" in the text of the *Hypostasis of the*
Archons, where the parallel in *Orig. World* 103.18 has
ⲠⲚⲞⲨⲦⲈ ⲂⲂⲀⲀⲈ, "the blind god." In this case the erroneous addition of the genitival *N-* produces an unwanted
plural. A too-literal perception of the Coptic genitive by the author(s) of the *Hypostasis of the Archons*
can account for both these errors.

TCOEIN *(The Doctoress)*. In the *Hypostasis of the*
Archons the first words of Adam to his wife are in the
form of a four-line paean of praise, the first portion
of which reflects *Orig. World* 116.6-8 and the latter
portion *Orig. World* 114.8-10, 5. In this latter por·
tion there occurs the identical misspelling TCOEIⲚ,
where we should have expected TCAEIN, "the doctor"
(fem.).[57]

Orig. World 116.6-8; 114.8-10; 114.5	*Hyp. Arch.* 89.14-17
'Thou shalt be called 'the Mother of the Living,' because thou art the one who gave me life.'. . .	'Thou art the one who gave me life. Thou shalt be called the 'Mother of the living'' (Gen. 3:20),
'I am the mother. I am the woman; and I am the maiden. I am the one who is with child; (and) I am the doctor (TCOEIN).'	for (ⲬⲈ) 'she is my mother.'
. . . who gave birth without a man.	She is the doctor (TCOEIN), and the woman, and she who has given birth.'

The misspelled COEIN is apparently an instance of "overcorrection," that is, the characteristic Sahidic vowel
O- has mistakenly replaced the Achmimic vowel *A-*. The
ⲬⲈ in line 16 is to be understood as the introductory
particle rather than as "because." It marks the beginning of an allusion to a quotation. This is also indicated by the incongruous phrasing, "she is my mother,"

---

57. CAEIN occurs regularly in the Nag Hammadi Codices. In *Gosp.*
Thomas 39.6 the anomalous COEIN also occurs.

e the original context of Adam speaking is mixed
n a third-person presentation of the aretalogy. Thus
appears that the passage in the *Hypoáataáiá o{ the
ʋchoná* is made up of two separate allusions, the first
ɔne being to Gen. 3:20, and the second to an aretalogical piece very much like the *Song o{ the Woman* in *Oʋig.
Woʋɫd* 114.7-15. The reference to Gen. 3:20 does not
seem to be independent of the context given it in *On
the Oʋigin o{ the Woʋɫd*, because both documents share
the *non-Geneáiá explanatoʋy áentence*, "Thou art the one
who gave me life."

From a form-critical point of view, the united passage in the *Hypoátaáiá o{ the Aʋchoná* shows itself to
be constructed from two source units. The second part
is clearly elliptic and secondary in form. The *Song o{
the Woman* in *Oʋig. Woʋɫd* 114.7-15 meets the require-
ments for the second source even down to the misspelled
COEIN. The fact that the passages are widely separated
in *On the Oʋigin o{ the Woʋɫd* and imperfectly yoked
together in the *Hypoátaáiá o{ the Aʋchoná* also indicates
the dependence of the latter document. From the point
of view of the history of traditions, the originally
independent I-am proclamation of Isis (Barbelo?) which
was first brought into the Judaic-Christian tradition
as the words of Eve, is now presented as words of Adam
in praise of his wife.

Incʋeaáe and Muɫtipɫy (AEIAEI). Both documents
share a corrupt reading in an allusion to the command
of Gen. 1:22, "Increase and multiply." Instead of the
expected word for "multiply," *AIAI,* they make use of a
hitherto undocumented verb *ANAEI.* This word has been
translated as "become better" (Bullard), "improve"
(Layton), and "flourish" (Bethge-Wintermute), although
the context in both passages clearly calls for the
meaning "multiply." The mistake probably goes back to
a misreading of the plene form of the verb, viz., *AEIAEI,*
"multiply." In a poorly-preserved manuscript the initial *EI-* could be read as an *N-,* thus giving the present
reading *ANAEI.* Quite obviously, this mistake should be
thought of as a single error which somehow entered the
text of both documents.

Oʋig. Woʋɫd 114.18-19   *Hyp. Aʋch. 92.3-4*

ETBE NAEI ATECMH   *TOTE ANPⲰME PAPXEI*
ETOYAAB XOOC XE AⲰAEI   *NNPAY3ANE*
AYⲰ NTETNANAEI (áic)   *AYⲰ NCEANAEI (áic)*

On account of these,	Then mankind began
the holy voice spoke, 'In-	to increase,
crease and multiply.'	and they multiplied.

The passage is not extant in the Sahidic version of
the Old Testament, but Bullard quotes a Sahidic fragment of Gen. 1:22, which gives AⲰAI NTETNAIAI, "Increase and multiply," making use of the Conjunctive
to continue the imperative AⲰAI.[58] Thus the error in
On the Origin of the World can be accounted for as a
misreading of a poorly preserved biblical text. However, the passage in the *Hypostasis of the Archons* contains an additional error which marks it as dependent
on the text of *On the Origin of the World*. This is the
improper use of the Conjunctive NCEANAEI to continue
the First Perfect ANPⲰME PAPXEI.[59] How did this error
come about? It can be understood as an incorrect
rendering of the text of *Orig. World* 114.19. The author
of the *Hypostasis of the Archons* seems to have taken
the *imperative* of *On the Origin of the World* and trans-
posed it into a *third-person* narrative, without regard
to syntactic niceties. The author seems to have found
the erroneous root form (ANAEI) of the verb in a copy
of *On the Origin of the World* and simply changed the
second-person plural Conjunctive NTETN·ANAEI to the
third-person plural Conjunctive NCE·ANAEI. In so doing
he created an unusual and *improper sequence* of Coptic
verbal forms. The continuation of the imperative by
the Conjunctive, as in the parallel in *On the Origin of
the World*, is proper and common, but the continuation
of the narrative First Perfect by the Conjunctive is
improper. Thus, both of the errors in NCEANAEI in the
text of the *Hypostasis of the Archons* can be explained
as a result of dependence on the Coptic text of *On the
Origin of the World*.

The Daughter of the Archigenetor.

Orig. World 104.10-13   *Hyp. Arch. 95.15-17*

He hated his father, the	He condemned his father,
darkness, and his mother, the	and his mother, Matter.
Abyss. He loathed (CIXANE)	He loathed (CIXANE) *her.*

---

58. Bullard, p. 94.
59. Cf. W. Till, *Koptische Grammatik* (Leipzig, 1961) paragraph
322. See, also P. Nagel, "Grammatische Untersuchungen zu Nag
Hammadi Codex II" in Franz Altheim and Ruth Stiehl, *Die Araber in
der Alten Welt* (Berlin: Walter de Gruyter, 1969), Bd.5.2, p. 455.

his sister, the thought of the
Archigenetor, who moved to and
fro over the waters.

The account in the *Hypostasis of the Archons* appears
to be elliptic. Who is the antecedent of "her"? Apparently this is Sabaoth's mother, but why she alone should
be the object of loathing (*CIXANE*) is hard to understand. A glance at the parallel in *On the Origin of the
World* gives the proper antecedent. She is *another*
member of the family, the sister of Sabaoth and the
daughter of the Archigenetor. The Greek loanword *CIXANE*,
"loathe" is rare in Coptic. The word occurs three times
in *On the Origin of the World*, but outside of this passage in the *Hypostasis of the Archons* there are no other
instances of its use in codex two.[60] The word might
reasonably be said to be more at home in *On the Origin
of the World* than in the *Hypostasis of the Archons*. The
occurrence of this rare word in the *Hypostasis of the
Archons* and the elliptic nature of the sentence indicate
that the text here is dependent on that of *On the Origin
of the World*.

The idea that the Coptic text of the *Hypostasis of
the Archons* stands in some sort of literary dependence
upon the Coptic of *On the Origin of the World* receives
further support from a study of the beginning section
of the *Hypostasis of the Archons*. We mentioned before
two important indications of a prior Coptic text behind
the beginning of the *Hypostasis of the Archons*.[61] These
are the witness to the Sahidic biblical text of Eph. 6:
12, <*NAN*>*AN*, in 86.23, and the editorial remark that
must have been composed in Coptic, *ANEYMEEYE PBΛΛE*, "His
thoughts were blind" (87.4). This remark reflects some
perplexity over the preceding Coptic text. But this
text appears in almost identical Coptic in a later section of the *Hypostasis of the Archons*, and therefore it
seems right to conclude that the comment was made upon
an already established Coptic text. B. Layton noticed
this when he wrote of the passage, *ΠNOYTE NBBΛΛE*, "the
god of the blind" (87.3-4):

---

60. *CIXANE* also occurs in *Orig. World* 111.1; 119.18. See also the
three occurrences of *CIXANE* in codex seven; 2.24, 23.4, 45.3.
61. Cf. pp. 109-10 for a discussion of the Coptic textual variant
of Eph. 6:12 reflected in *Hyp. Arch.* 86.23, <*NAN*>*AN*, and the
Coptic comment in 87.4, "His thoughts were blind."

However, exactly the same expression occurs
again at 94.26, suggesting that we have here
a traditional gnostic misunderstanding of the
etymology (as Scholem suggests) rather than a
mere textual corruption.[62]

Layton is correct in saying that the misunderstanding
is prior to the composition of the opening of the
Hypostasis of the Archons. But a thorough examination
of the latter passage (94.21-28) would indicate that
it in turn is dependent upon the Coptic of *On the
Origin of the World* (103.17-18) and that the misunderstanding he refers to is ultimately only one of Coptic
orthography.[63] Such an analysis would be beyond the
scope of our purpose here. Our discussion has tried
to show that feminine motifs are more pronounced in
On the Origin of the World and that from a literary-
critical point of view there is some evidence that the
Hypostasis of the Archons is a later and dependent
document.

*A Comparison of Key Figures in On the Origin of
the World and in the Hypostasis of the Archons*

By way of summary, let us compare the key figures
in *On the Origin of the World* and the *Hypostasis of
the Archons*: the Christian Father; Pistis Sophia;
Ialdabaoth; and the Immortal Light-man.

The Christian Father. In the analysis of the
material common to both *On the Origin of the World* and
the *Hypostasis of the Archons*, we found motifs which

---

62. Cf. Layton, *HTR*, p. 47.
63. Cf. *Hyp. Arch.* 94.25-26: ΚΡΠΛΛΑΝΑϹΘΕ ϹΑΜΑΗΛ ΕΤΕ ΠΑΕΙ ΠΕ ΠΝΟΥΤΕ
ΝΒΒΛΛΕ with *Orig. World* 103.17-18: ΚΡΠΛΛΑΝΑ ϹΑΜΑΗΛ ΕΤΕ ΠΑΕΙ ΠΕ
ΠΝΟΥΤΕ ΒΒΛΛΕ," 'You are wrong, Samael, 'that is, the blind god."
The passage in *On the Origin of the World* makes use of archaic
orthography, phonetically based, for the adjectival form, ΒΒΛΛΕ,
"blind," which in proper Sahidic is ΝΒΛΛΕ. The form in *Hyp.
Arch.* 94.26, ΝΒΒΛΛΕ, seems to be an erroneous improvement of the
phonetic form in *Orig. World* 103.18. The additional Ν- turned
the form into a plural and gives the meaning "of the blind ones."
It is this plural meaning which calls for the Coptic comment in
the other occurence of the passage, *Hyp. Arch.* 87.3-4: ΚΡΠΛΛΑΝΑϹΘΕ
ϹΑΜΑΗΛ ΕΤΕ ΠΝΟΥΤΕ ΠΕ ΝΒΒΛΛΕ ΑΝΕΥΜΕΕΥΕ ΡΒΛΛΕ, "'you are wrong,
Samael', which is, the god of the blind ones. *His thoughts were
blind.*" See pp. 109-10 for further discussion of these passages.

151

are non-Christian, Jewish, and gnostic. We tried to
show that the author of the *Hypostasis of the Archons*
patriarchalized the common traditions at the same time
that he was Christianizing them. The process shows up
in the usage of the term "Father," an important term in
the *Hypostasis of the Archons* for the transcendent
deity, but one that is only used in this way in the
ending of *On the Origin of the World*. The Christian
Father appears in the *Hypostasis of the Archons* under
the title "Father of Truth" (86.21), "Father of the
All" (88.11; 97.15-16), as well as simply "Father" (87.
22; 88.34; 96.20,35; 97.18). The frequency of the term
in this short document underscores the fact that the
Father is the primary character in the *Hypostasis of
the Archons*. In stressing the Father's will as supreme,
the author subordinates all other divine beings of the
common tradition, and sets them under the influence and
control of his will. Even the concept of a semi-inde-
pendent Pronoia as a type of divine providence is missing from the *Hypostasis of the Archons*.

Orig. World 113.5-6 *Hyp. Arch. 88.10-11*
114.15-17

But all this came to pass But all these things came
according to the Pronoia to pass in the Will
(forethought) of Pistis. of the Father of the All.

Now these things were
revealed in the Will to
the souls of Sabaoth and
his Christ.

Pistis Sophia. The term "Pistis" is frequently used
in *On the Origin of the World* without the addition of
"Sophia," but this usage does not occur in the *Hypostasis
of the Archons*. As synonyms for "Pistis," the author of
the *Hypostasis of the Archons* employs "Imperishability"
regularly and "Authenticity" once.[64] The process of
reinterpreting the hypostatized Pistis as an abstraction
can be seen in the critical doublet of *Hyp. Arch.* 86.
30-87.4 = 94.21-27 compared with the parallel in *On the
Origin of the World*.

---

64. "Imperishability" occurs in *Hyp. Arch.* in 87.1,2, 11-12, 20-21;
88.18; 93.29-30; 94.5. "Authenticity" occurs at 94.24.

Orig. World 103.11-20	*Hyp. Arch.* 86.30-87.4
He said, 'I am God, and there is none other existing beside me.' Now when he said these things, he committed sin against all of the immortal ones who took notice and watched him. Indeed, when Pistis saw the impiety of the great archon, she was very upset. Without anyone seeing her, she spoke, 'You are wrong, Samael' that is, the blind god, 'there is an immortal Light-man who exists before you . . .'	. . . 'I am God. There is no one [apart from me.]' When he said this, he committed sin against [the All.] And this word reached up to Imperishability. But lo! A voice came forth from Imperishability, saying, 'You are wrong, Samael,' which is, the god of the blind ones. His thoughts were blind.

Hyp. Arch. 94.21-27

. . . 'I am God, and there is no other apart from me.' When he said this, he committed sin against the All. But a voice came forth from the height of Authenticity, saying, 'You are wrong, Samael,' that is, the god of the blind ones. And he said, 'If there is another. . .'

On the third occasion (95.7-10) of the rebuke of the archigenetor in the *Hypostasis of the Archons*, it is "Zoē, the daughter of Pistis Sophia" who utters the words, "You are wrong, Saklas." The contrast in interpretation of Pistis Sophia in the two documents shows up clearly in the continuation of the first passage quoted above. Whereas in *Orig. World* 103.23-24 Pistis warns the archigenetor that he and his kind will do down to "your mother the Abyss (NOYN)," in the *Hypostasis of the Archons* the archigenetor goes down to the abyss (NOYN), "his mother by Pistis Sophia." The last three words are ambiguous but seem to imply a close relation of Pistis Sophia and the abyss.

Orig. World 103.21-24	Hyp. Arch. 87.4-8
He will trample upon you as upon a clay vessel which is stepped on, and you will go with those who belong to you down to your mother, the Abyss.	He sent forth his might, which was the blasphemy that he had spoken. He followed it down to Chaos and the Abyss, his mother by Pistis Sophia.

We must recognize that the two mythological personages, Sophia and Samael (=Ialdabaoth) derive from different traditions, and that their being joined
together here as mother and son represents a later
syncretistic development. In all of the Sophia passages
in the Hypostasis of the Archons, the author employs
typical methods of reinterpreting a once-powerful deity.
She can be represented as an abstraction; she can be
replaced by her daughter; and finally she can be related
to a figure in the underworld.

Ialdabaoth. A variety of names are used for the
arrogant archon of the gnostic myth in our two documents.
He is referred to as Saklas, Samael, and "the great
archon."[65] The account of his birth is much abbreviated
in the Hypostasis of the Archons.[66] In this document -
in contrast with On the Origin of the World, where his
ultimate destruction is assured - there are some indications of a process of rehabilitation. The important
event of the impartation of breath into Adam is not
described as the activity of Sophia or Zoē, instead the
biblical words are used "And he breathed into his face"
(Gen. 2:7). The context seems to imply that the antecedent of "he" is the "God" of the previous sentence.

. . . not realizing the power of God in their
weakness. And he breathed into his face; the
man became psychic upon the earth. For many
days, however, they were not able to raise him
up on account of their weakness (Hyp. Arch. 88.
1-6).

It cannot be argued that the passage is early and does
not know the gnostic myth, for in the narrative the

---

65. For the ruler of the archons as an equivalent for Saklas,
Samael, cf. Hyp. Arch. 90.19 "the Great Archon"; 90.24 "the
archon"; 92.8 "the archon of the powers"; 92.27 "the arrogant
archon."
66. Hyp. Arch. 94.8-18. Cf. the account in Orig. World 98.28-
100.14.

breathing-in is pictured as ineffective. Another passage also employs proper biblical language in the midst of the gnostic myth.

They molded their man according to their body and [according to the image] o𝔣 God which had appeared [to them] in the waters (87.30-33).

The image on the waters is variously described in *On the Origin o𝔣 the World* as Pistis' image (103.30; 107.18-19) and that of the Light-man (108.7-10; 112.35-113.1), but never as the "image of God."

In one episode in the *Hypostasis o𝔣 the Archons*, "the archon of the powers" seems to be pitted against "the archons." This is the story of the building of the ark, and it is "the archon of the powers" who warns Noah of the plan of the archons to destroy mankind by the flood. Significantly, this story does not appear in *On the Origin o𝔣 the World*. It seems that the picture of the chief archon given in the *Hypostasis o𝔣 the Archons* is not without redeeming features. Perhaps the author is aware of the developed gnostic tradition in which the God of the Old Testament is pictured as a necessary sovereign for that dispensation. This view is found in some of the documents of codex one, particularly in the *Tripartite Tractate*.[67]

The Immortal Light-man. The existence of an immortal Light-man is necessary for the myth common to *On the Origin o𝔣 the World* and the *Hypostasis o𝔣 the Archons*. Otherwise there is no substance to the rebuke from above: "You are wrong, Samael." The strange thing is that the Light-man is *completely omitted* from the account of the myth in the *Hypostasis o𝔣 the Archons*.

Orig. World 107.36-108.12	*Hyp. Arch.* 94.27-33
. . . and he dared to say, 'If there is one existing before me, let him reveal himself so that we might see his light.' And immediately, behold, a light came forth from the Eighth which is above, penetrating all of the heavens earth-	. . . and he said, 'If there is another existing before me, let him reveal himself to me.' And immediately, Sophia stretched forth her finger.

---

67. Cf. the *Tripartite Tractate*, (I.5), 100.19-36.

ward. When the Archigene-
tor saw the light, that it
was beautiful and dazzling,
he was astonished and he was
greatly ashamed. When that
light was revealed, a human   She brought light into the
image showed forth within   matter, and she followed
it, which was exceedingly   it down to the regions of
wondrous, and no one saw it   Chaos. And she made her
except the Archigenetor   way [. . .] her light.
himself and the Pronoia who
was with him.

The immortal Light-man is nowhere specifically mentioned
in the *Hypostasis of the Archons*.[68] It seems incredible
that the Christian author was not aware of this personage or of his importance in the gnostic myth. We must
conclude that after being identified with the Savior
Jesus, this figure was doomed to vanish. On the other
hand, the Christian teaching of the "true" or "perfect"
man is clearly presented in the *Hypostasis of the
Archons*.

> From that day forth, the serpent has been under
> the curse of the authorities - until the *per-
> fect man* should come (90.34-91.2).

> He said to me, "When the *true man* is revealed
> in their plasma, [the spirit of] truth, whom
> the Father has sent . . . that one will teach
> them about everything." (96.32-97.2).

The mystical figure of the immortal Light-man was
probably an important model for early christological
speculation. In the *Hypostasis of the Archons* it would
seem that this figure has been completely subsumed under
the Christian savior.

---

68. The Light-man's existence, however, is presumed in *Hyp. Arch.*
87.35, "He (Light-man) will see his co-image (Adam)." Cf. pp.
134-35.

CHAPTER FIVE

FEMININE MOTIFS IN THE THUNDER

AND IN THE GOSPEL OF TRUTH

The documents brought together in this chapter are
related more by way of contrast than similarity. *The
Thunder, Perfect Mind,* is the self-proclamation of an
unnamed feminine deity, while the *Gospel of Truth* is a
meditation upon a deity described as "the Father of
Truth." These two documents may represent beginning
and end points of Nag Hammadi literature as regards a
development in the history of religions, or they may
be considered as logical complements in the gnostic
tradition. We shall attempt to show that the general
tone of *The Thunder* is feminine and non-Christian while
that of the *Gospel of Truth* is masculine and Christian.

The Thunder, the second tractate in codex six of the
Nag Hammadi collection is a well-preserved document.
The dialect is Sahidic, although there is a great number
of Subachmimicisms and Greek loanwords. It appears that
the present text is based on a Subachmimic version of a
document once written in Greek. The extant copy is
dated, as nearly as possible, to the latter part of the
fourth century, but its vorlage is earlier and perhaps
even pre-Christian.[1]

Structurally, the tractate may be divided into three
sections of quite unequal length. Part one comprises
an introduction and the *Song of the Woman* on pp. 13-14;
part two is roughly pp. 14-20; part three takes up p.
21, the final page. The *Song of the Woman* appears to
be an independent piece of poetry embedded in the document and may have been the occasion for the long poetic

---

1. See Gilles Quispel, "Jewish Gnosis and Mandaean Gnosticism:
Some Reflections on the Writing Brontē, *Les Textes de Nag Hammadi,*
ed. Jacques-É. Ménard, (Leiden: E.J. Brill, 1975), pp. 82-94.
Quispel thinks the formulae in *Brontē* are survivals of very old
views that were suppressed and help us to recover "unknown and
forgotten aspects of Judaism" (p. 94).

discourse presented by a feminine personage whose self-proclamations usually begin with "I am." The goddess describes herself in antithetical or paradoxical predicates such as "life" and "death," "shameless" and "ashamed," "compassionate" and "heartless." Hortatory phrases, bids for attention, and reproaches for failure to heed the deity break the recital of "I am" pronouncements.

The last page of the document differs in style and contradicts the content of the earlier sections. Its style is more didactic and its message no longer paradoxical. It lacks the feminine grammatical forms used almost universally in the first sections and seems to be a critique or contradiction of the feminine aretalogy. The Christian allusions on the last page make it apparent that the deity being referred to by the masculine pronouns is the Christian Father-God.

The Form of The Thunder

The most striking characteristic of *The Thunder* is the repetitious "I am" with paradoxical predicates uttered by an unnamed goddess.

Should one look behind the paradoxes to find an "I am" statement with a positive declaration that might give a clue to the identity of the speaker, one comes upon "I am she whose images are many in Egypt" (16.6). Of all the Egyptian goddesses, it was Isis who was said to have embraced within herself all of the ancient deities, and it was she who after centuries of folklore, some of which is retained in the Isis aretalogies, became almost completely assimilated into Greek culture and into Jewish mysticism.[2] Her all-embracing character and her true name were revealed by her to Lucius:

> The Mother of all things, master and governor
> of the universe, chief of the powers divine,
> queen of all that dwell in heaven and in hell;
> at my will the planets of the sky and the winds
> of the seas are disposed. My divinity is
> adored throughout the world by many names. For
> the Phrygians call me Mother of the Gods; the
> Athenians, Athene; the Cyprians, Venus; the

---

2. See Bullard, p. 81 for a bibliography of Isis aretalogies.

158

Cretans, Diana; the Sicilians, Perserpine; the
Eleusinians, their ancient Goddess Ceres; some
Juno, some Minerva, some Hera, others Bellona,
others Hecate, others Rhamnusia. But the
Egyptians, which are excellent in all kinds of
ancient knowledge, do call me by my true name,
Queen Isis.[3]

Not only the universal character of Isis coincides
with descriptions of the deity in *The Thunder*, but also
this type of aretalogy was previously known from several
Isis inscriptions.[4] We can compare the "I am" utterances in the inscriptions from Cyme and Ios, and in the
citation from "Nyssa in Arabia" preserved by Diodorus
Siculus. In these three inscriptions, which fairly
represent the form, eighty-one of the ninety-one clauses
begin with "I," and the formula "I am" occurs twenty-
four times.

The similarity in style between the positive statements in *The Thunder* and those of Isis may be noted in
the following inscription from Ios. The numbers are
supplied for identification of the sayings.

(1)   Isis am I,
(2)   the ruler of all land,
(3)   and have been taught by Hermes, and with
      Hermes invented letters, both the sacred
      and the popular ones so that all would
      not be written in the same.
(4)   I gave laws to mankind, and ordained what
      nobody can alter.
(5)   I am the eldest daughter of Kronos.
(6)   I am the wife and sister of King Osiris.
(7)   I am the one who discovered crops for
      mankind.
(8)   I am the mother of King Horus.
(9)   I am the one who rises in the dogstar.
(10) I am the one called god with women.
(11) For me Boubastos city was built.
(12) I separated earth from heaven.
(13) I directed the orbits of the stars.
(14) I devised the journey of sun and moon.
(15) I invented the marine trades.
(16) I made what is right strong.

---

3. See Apuleius, *The Golden Ass*, tr. W. Adlington (London:
Heinemann, 1915), pp. 545–47.
4. See Werner Peek, *Der Isishymnus von Andros und verwandte Texte*
(Berlin, 1930).

(17)   I brought woman and man together.
(18)   I imposed on woman to bring forth the
       baby in the tenth month.
(19)   I ordained parents to be loved by the
       child.
(20)   I imposed punishment on those kindlessly
       disposed toward parents.
(21)   I with my brother Osiris put an end to
       cannibalism.
(22)   I showed initiations to mankind.
(23)   I taught to venerate the images of gods.
(24)   I established the shrines of gods.
(25)   I abolished the tyrants' rules.
(26)   I put an end to killings.
(27)   I forced women to be loved by men.
(28)   I made what is right stronger than gold
       and silver.
(29)   I ordained that truth should be considered
       good.
(30)   I invented the marriage contract.
(31)   I assigned languages to Greeks and bar-
       barians.
(32)   I made good and bad distinguished through
       nature.
(33)   I did not create anything more formidable
       than the oath.
(34)   I gave the one who unjustly persecutes
       others into the hands of the persecuted.
(35)   I imposed punishment upon those who do
       wrong.
(36)   I ordained to show mercy to supplicants.
(37)   I honor those rightly defending themselves.
(38)   What is right is strong before me.
(39)   I am mistress of rivers and wind and sea.
(40)   Nobody is glorified without my consent.
(41)   I am the mistress of war.
(42)   I am the mistress of thunder.
(43)   I rouse and calm the sea.
(44)   I am in the rays of the sun.
(45)   I attend the journey of the sun.
(46)   What I decide, that is also fulfilled.
(47)   To me all yields.
(48)   I free those in chains.
(49)   I am the mistress of shipping.
(50)   I make the navigable unnavigable whenever
       I decide.
(51)   I founded the city walls.
(52)   I am the one called Law-giving.
(53)   I brought islands to light out of the
       depth.

(54) I am mistress of rains.
(55) I conquer fate.
(56) To me fate obeys. Hail, Egypt who has raised me.[5]

Many of the statements within the Ios inscription are sufficiently close to warrant comparison. Some of the ideas in *The Thunder* are so typically Egyptian that an Egyptian background seems assured. Only in Egypt could the goddess claim to be both sister and mother of her husband. There Isis was revered as wife and sister of King Osiris and mother of King Horus, the reincarnation of Osiris. Although there does not appear to be any literary connection between the Isis inscriptions and *The Thunder*, the contextual similarities are too numerous to dismiss the possibility of shared traditions. Here are some parallels of the Ios inscription with *The Thunder*.

Isis Inscription from Ios	*The Thunder, Perfect Mind*
(42) I am the mistress of thunder.	(Title) The Thunder
(6) I am the wife and sister of King Osiris. (8) I am the mother of King Horus.	(13.30-32) I am the mother of my father, and the sister of my husband, and he is my offspring.
(1) Isis am I.	(14.14-15) I am the saying of my name.
(31) I assigned languages to Greek and barbarians.	(16.3-5) For I am the "Sophia" of the Greeks and the "Gnosis" of the barbarians.
(56) Hail, Egypt who has raised me.	(16.6-7) I am she whose images are many in Egypt.

---

5. For the translation and a critique of the Isis background of the ancient "I am" predications, see Dieter Mueller, "I am Isis," *Orientalische Literaturzeitung* 67 (1972), pp. 118-30. See also, Friedrich Solmsen, *Isis Among the Greeks and Romans* (Cambridge: Harvard University Press, 1979), pp. 42-51.

(4) I gave laws to man- kind.	(16.13-14)	I am she who is called "Law."
(29) I ordained that truth should be con- sidered good.	(20.7-8)	I am the one called "Truth."

In an important article on *The Thunder*, G. Quispel, while acknowledging that the tractate is inspired by the Isis aretalogical literature, suggests that it is a pre-Christian, Jewish writing indebted to ancient Jewish traditions which were combined with Isis motifs in Alexandria.

> Nevertheless, it may be a Jewish writing about Wisdom, like *Siracides* and *The Wisdom of Solomon.* It might have been written in the third century B.C., like *Siracides*, when Palestine was a part of Ptolemaic, Hellenistic Egypt and the national reaction of the Maccabees had not yet begun. On the other hand, the writing is so sophisticated that a later date, the first century B.C., and a Hellenistic milieu, Alexandria, all seem preferable. But there are, as far as I can see, no indications which lead us to suppose that the text, in its original form, is not Jewish and is not pre-Christian.[6]

In the last chapter we discussed the *Song of the Woman* in *On the Origin of the World* (II.114.7-15), and a shorter form of this which appears in the *Hypostasis of the Archons* (II.89.14-17). We noted that the author of *On the Origin of the World* indicates that he borrowed the Song by the introductory words: "Therefore it is said of her that she said, 'I am . . .'" Then the *Song of the Woman* is used to praise Eve's parthenogenic conception, illustrating a certain juxtaposition of Egyptian and Judaistic traditions. In *The Thunder*, the *Song of the Woman* is given in fuller form without the Judaistic connection, and we should conclude that this is the more original form of the poem. The final lines of the version in *On the Origin of the World*, "I have begotten a child with the lord" (Gen. 4:1) do not appear in *The Thunder*, and this indicates that these words in the *Origin of the World* are an addition that helps incorporate the poem into the context of the narrative of Eve.

---

6. Quispel, "Jewish Gnosis and Mandaean Gnosticism," p. 86.

Another important addition to the Song in *On the Origin of the World* is the phrase "and my lord" (*Orig. World* 114.13). In full, this statement reads, "I am his mother, and he is my father and my lord." The final words violate the symmetry of the poetic utterance, and since nothing like this statement occurs in the version of *The Thunder*, we can conclude that this is an anti-feminist addition subordinating the goddess of *The Thunder* to some male figure.

The Thunder (VI.13.15-14.9)	*Orig. World* (II.114.7-15)
For I am the first and the last.	
I am she who is honored and she who is disgraced.	
I am the harlot and the holy one.	I am a portion of my mother, and I am the Mother.
I am the woman and the maiden.	I am the woman, and I am the maiden.
I am ⟨the mother⟩ and the daughter.	I am the one who is with child.
I am the members of my mother.	
I am the barren one and many are her children.	
I am she whose weddings are many, and I have not married.	
I am the midwife and she who does not deliver.	I am the doctor.
I am the solace of my labor pains.	I am the consoler of the labor pains.
I am the bride and the bridegroom.	
The one who begat me is my husband, and	The one who begat me is my husband, and
I am the mother of my father, and the sister of my husband, and he is my offspring.	I am his mother, and he is my father, *and my lord.*
I am the slave of him who prepared me, and	
I am the mistress over my offspring, and	
It is he who [begat me] before all time in a kind of conception, and	

He is my offspring in due
time.
My power comes forth from
him.
I am the rod of his power in   He is my power.
his youth, and
He is my staff in my old age.
And whatever he wishes comes   That which he wishes he
to pass from me.   speaks.
                                   With propriety I exist, but
                                   I have begotten a child
                                   with the lord.

In *The Thunder*, the first three lines of the Song
seem to be introductory. They have no parallel with the
version in *On the Origin of the World*, and perhaps include an allusion to Rev. 1:8, "I am the alpha and the
omega." A comparison of *The Thunder* and *On the Origin
of the World* gives no indication that there is any relationship on the Coptic level. Both versions of the
Song of the Woman seem to be independently translated
from different Greek versions of a traditional piece.
The ultimate origin of the Song seems to have been in
an Egyptian aretalogy praising some Egyptian goddess who
is hardly anything less than the universal woman personified.

The Content and Feminine Motifs of The Thunder

Although the "I am" style may suggest Isis as the
goddess behind *The Thunder*, the total content of the
document argues against such an identification. Isis
always stamps her name on her inscriptions - "I am
Isis" - but the goddess of *The Thunder* has left us no
name. Further, the content of the Isis proclamations
is strictly of a praiseworthy nature, while that of *The
Thunder* presents the goddess as both good and evil.
Isis lauds herself as the one who initiates and preserves order in the universe, and her formulae are almost always positive. Only occasionally do the Isis
inscriptions present both sides of the coin, as it were,
as in saying (50): "I make the navigable unnavigable
whenever I decide." The same double-edged kind of
statement is also found in (43): "I rouse and calm the
sea." The Isis inscriptions represent a particular type
of religious propaganda which probably originated when
Isis cults were being established in competition with
other religions. The Sitz im Leben of *The Thunder*, whose
goddess presents herself in a pantheistic way, hardly
suggests propaganda of the Isis variety.

Efforts have been made, chiefly on the basis of a reconstructed title "(N)EBPONTH" to identify the goddess of *The Thunder* as Nebront, a deity equated with the Manichaean Nebroel or the Mandaean Namrūs.[7] M. Tardieu has rejected this identification on good grounds.[8] Nebront is not mentioned in other Nag Hammadi documents, and efforts to fit gods foreign to Nag Hammadi literature into it remain less than convincing.

The literature praising Barbelo may give us a clue to the identity of the goddess behind *The Thunder*. Of particular note are five documents: the *Apocryphon of John* (II.1; III.1; IV.1; and BG 8502.2); the *Gospel of the Egyptians* (III.2; IV.2); the *Three Steles of Seth* (VII. 5) *Allogenes* (XI.3); and the *Trimorphic Protennoia* (XIII.1). In all of these documents, there are "I am" statements comparable to those of *The Thunder*. Paradoxical elements such as "the male virginal spirit" also occur. In *Allogenes*, there is also an introductory horatatory "Hear!", not unlike the admonitions of *The Thunder*. The object of attention is the feminine deity (Barbelo) who can be described as "the triple male" (45. 37-38). The name "Barbelo" occurs six times in this tractate. The following passage is obscure but is noteworthy both because Barbelo is here described as "the first Archē" and "full of divinity" and because of her close relationship to the Savior, who is described as "perfect mind" (ΤΕΛΙΟC ΝΝΟΥC). The latter words, it will be remembered, appear in the title after "*The Thunder*," perhaps as an alternate epithet.

Allogenes XI.58.12-26

I saw the good divine Autogenes, and the Savior, that is, the youthful, perfect Triple Male; and the goodness of this one, the Protophanes-Harmedon of *perfect mind*; and the blessedness of the Hidden One; and the First Archē of blessedness, the Aeon of *Barbelo*, full of divinity, and the first Archē of that one without Archē, the spiritual invisible Triple Power, the All that is higher than perfect.

Barbelo is also an important figure in the *Gospel of the Egyptians*. According to this document, the invisi-

---

7. H.-G Bethge, "Nebront," *Theologische Literaturzeitung*, (1973), pp. 97-100.
8. M. Tardieu, "Le Titre du Deuxième Écrit du Codex VI," *Le Muséon*,

ble spirit dwells in solitary splendor, and from him
emanates a series of heavenly beings, beginning with the
trinity of Father, Mother Barbelo, and Son. These three
belong to the Ogdoad, a sphere which can be associated
with the woman. Of Barbelo the document records that
she originated from herself (III.42.17-18). This motif
may be compared with the affirmation in *The Thunder* 13.
30-31: "I am the mother of my father."

Another document with Barbelo affinities is the *Three
Steles of Seth* (VII.5). The second of the three "steles"
is completely devoted to Barbelo, and in it one finds
many of the terms which are used to describe the goddess
of *The Thunder*.

Three Steles of Seth VII.121.20-122.4; 123.16-28

Great is the first of aeons, the male virginal *Barbelo*, the first glory of the invisible
Father, she who is called "perfect" (*TEΛIOC*).
Thou (fem.) hast seen first the truly real one,
which first existed, because thou art non-
substantial; and from him and by him thou hast
come into being eternally. Thou art non-sub-
stantial, from the one indivisible, triple
power. Thou art a triple power. Thou art a
great monad from a pure monad (fem.). Thou art
an elect monad, the first shadow of the holy
Father, light from light.

Thou art a Sophia. Thou art a Gnosis. Thou
art truth. Because of thee, there is life.
Life is from thee. Because of thee, there is
mind (*NOYC*). Mind (*NOYC*) is from thee. Thou
art a mind (*NOYC*). Thou art a cosmos of truth.
Thou art a triple power. Thou art thrice
multiplied. Truly thou art multiplied three
times, the aeon of aeons. It is thou only who
seest in purity the first eternal ones and
those unborn ones.

In the above passages, Barbelo is called both "perfect" (*TEΛIOC*), and "mind" (*NOYC*), the words which make
up the second part of the title of *The Thunder*. She is
also called "wisdom," "gnosis," "truth," and "the source
of life," all epithets of the goddess of *The Thunder*.

LXXXVII, 3-4 (1974), pp. 523-30.

In the codex two version of the *Apocryphon of John*, the name Barbelo is found thirteen times. Towards the end of this document, there is an "I am" proclamation by what seems to be a feminine revealer in a vein very similar to that of *The Thunder*. The passage is greatly abbreviated in the Berlin codex - codex three version.

The Apocryphon of John II.30.11-31.1; 31.10-14

But I am the perfect Pronoia of the universe. I changed myself in my seed, because I was the first. I walk all paths, because I am the richness of the light. I am the remembrance of the pleroma.

I wandered in the great darkness, and I endured until I came into the midst of the prison. And the foundations of chaos were shaken, but I, I hid myself from them because of their wickedness, and they did not know me.

Again I returned for the second time, and I wandered about. I came out from those who are of the light, that is myself, the remembrance of the Pronoia. I went into the midst of the darkness and the inner part of Emente, and I sought after my task. And the foundations of chaos were shaken that they should fall down upon those who were in chaos and destroy them. But again I withdrew to my root of light lest they be destroyed before the time.

Again I went for the third time - I who am the light which exists in light - I am the remembrance of the Pronoia - that I should go into the midst of the darkness and the inner part of Emente. . . .

And I said, 'I am the Pronoia of the pure light. I am the thought of the virginal spirit, who raises you up to the place of honor.'

The Nag Hammadi document which most nearly approximates *The Thunder* in both style and content is the *Trimorphic Protennoia* in codex thirteen. Like the *Apocryphon of John* and the *Three Steles of Seth*, it proclaims three descents of the heavenly redeemer, Protennoia, who is called "Barbelo, the perfect glory" (XIII.38.9-10). Although the "I am" expressions are not so systematically arranged as in *The Thunder*, they are, nonetheless, quite striking. In the first section (35.1-42.3), the following "I am" statements occur.

I am the sight of those who dwell in sleep (35. 22-23).
I am the invisible one within the all (35.24).
I am numberless beyond every one (35.27).
I am immeasurable, ineffable, yet whenever I wish, I shall reveal myself (35.27-30).
I am the one hidden within [radiant] waters (36.6-7).
I am the one who dawned upon the All (36.7-8).
I am perception and knowledge, uttering a voice by means of thought (36.12-14).
I am the voice which exists (36.14).
I am the thought of the Father (36.17).
I am the one joined with everyone within the hidden thought (36.23-25).
I am the image of the invisible spirit (38.11).
(I am) the Mother and the light which she appointed as Virgin (38.13-14).
I am their Father and I shall tell you an ineffable mystery (41.1-3).
I am the first one who descended on account of my portion (41.20-21).

The goddess of the *Trimorphic Protennoia* truly belongs to a high order of pantheism. She partakes of opposites as does the goddess of *The Thunder.* She is frequently called "the voice," but is "silence" as well.[9] Although apparently the Mother of the universe, she also says that she is "the Father" as well as "the Son."[10] She is something above and beyond the trinitarian formula, and the author suggests that she is some kind of mathematical unity behind "masculinities," "powers," and "names."

Trimorphic Protennoia XIII.37.20-38.10

And the Voice that originated from my thought exists as three permanences (*MONH*): the Father, the Mother, the Son. A sound that is perceptive, it has within it a Logos endowed with every glory, and it has three masculinities, three powers, and three names. They exist in the manner of the triad ⬜ ⬜ ⬜ , which are quadrangles, secretly within the silence of the ineffable one.

---

9. *Trimorphic Protennoia*, XIII.37.29.
10. *Trimorphic Protennoia*, XIII.38.7-8; 41.1-2; 49.19-20.

. . . It was I who anointed him . . . that
is, the eye of the light, which gloriously
enlightens me. He gave aeons to the Father of
all the aeons, which is I, the thought (Mother?)
of the Father of the Protennoia, that is,
Barbelo, the perfect glory, and the invisible
hidden infinite one.[11]

The *Thunder* and the *Trimorphic Protennoia* are the
high points of feminism among the Nag Hammadi documents.
They seem to stem from a pre-Christian Barbelo cult
featuring a lofty pantheistic vitalism which could
easily adapt itself to Christianity. Neither of these
documents, however, has come down to us without traces
of Christianity, and the name "Barbelo" itself does not
even appear in *The Thunder*.

The Title of The Thunder

The title of the second tractate of codex six is
found only at the beginning of the document where it
occurs as TEBPONTH: NOYC NTEΛEIOC "*The Thunder, Perfect Mind.*" Since neither designation, "thunder" or
"perfect mind," occurs within the text itself, one needs
to look elsewhere for the significance of this title.

The association of thunder with heavenly voices is
widespread in ancient literature and in mythology in
general. Examples include the famous "Jupiter tonans,"
Greek magical formulae, Job. 26:14, John 12:29, and
Rev. 6:1. Epiphanius preserves an account of an epiphany
in which the sound of thunder figures within a "*Gospel of
Eve*" used by certain gnostics.

---

11. The phrase "the thought of the Father of the Protennoia" might
once have read "the Mother of the Father of the Protennoia," or
even "the Mother-Father of the Protennoia," if, as we suspect, some
of the readings MEEYE, "thought" in the *Trimorphic Protennoia* have
resulted from an earlier confusion with MEEY, Subachmimic for
"mother," and also a variant spelling for "thought." Cf. particularly the strange-sounding "sons of the Thought" in 44.30, which
reads more logically "sons of the Mother." In *The Thunder* 13.20,
MEEYE, "thought," wrongly occurs for "mother." Cf. K. Grobel, *The
Gospel of Truth* (Nashville: Abingdon Press, 1960), pp. 91-93, who
comments on the similarity in the *Manichaean Psalmbook* (in
Subachmimic) of the two Coptic words. In the passage of his commentary (*Gospel of Truth* 24.7), however, Grobel opted for an
original MEEYE, "thought" against the text's MEEY, "mother."

They begin from foolish visions and testimonies
in that (book) which they profess to be a gospel. For thus they allege: 'I stood upon a
high mountain and saw a tall man and another
one, short. And I heard, as it were, the sound
of *thunder*, and I drew near to hear, and he
spoke to me and said, 'I am thou, and thou art
I, and wherever thou art there am I, and I am
sown in all. And whenever thou wilt thou
gatherest me, and gathering me, thou gatherest
thyself.''[12]

Two typical instances of the use of thunder occur in
Nag Hammadi documents. The first has already been discussed in connection with the feminine apocalyptic deity
of *On the Origin of the World*.[13] There thunder is personified as a deity who comes from "the firmament of
the woman" to drive the gods of chaos down to the
abyss." She will take off "the wise flame of Epinoia"
and clothe herself "with mindless fury." It is possible
that this deity could be related in some way with the
goddess of *The Thunder* who says of herself, "I am . . .
the Epinoia who provokes many thoughts. I am the voice
of her whose sounds are many" (14.10-13).

In the *Trimorphic Protennoia* the sound of thunder is
represented as a voice from heaven, which is indeed the
etymology of the word "thunder" in Coptic - ҀΡΟΥ·ΜΠΕ,
"voice of heaven."[14]

Trimorphic Protennoia XIII.43.13-26

And the lots of Fate and those who measure the
domiciles were greatly disturbed over a great
thunder. And the thrones of the powers were
disturbed since they were overthrown, and their
king was afraid. And those who follow fate made
up their number of orbits along the path. They
spake to the powers: 'What is this disturbance,
and this shaking which has come upon us through
a voice〈belonging〉to the exalted sound? And
our entire habitation has been shaken and the
entire circuit of our upward way was met with
destruction, and the path on which we travel,
which takes us up to the Archigenetor of our
birth has ceased to be established for us.'

---

12. Epiphanius, *Pan.* XXVI.iii.1.
13. Cf. pp. 122-23 for a discussion of *Orig. World* 126.10-22.
14. For another instance of "thunder" see *Paraph. Shem* VII.36.19.

The context in which the term "thunder" occurs here is
that of the archons' asking their king about a heavenly
voice, the voice of thunder. The archons then accuse
their king of lying when he proclaimed that he alone was
God and that there was no other beside him. The tractate also records that the Archigenetor himself did not
know whence the voice had come. Sophia is not named,
but the revealer counsels:

O sons of the Thought (MEEYE, the Mother?), listen to me, to the sound of the Mother of your
mercy (Barbelo?) (Tnim. Pnot. XIII.44.30-31).

After this, she identifies herself in "I am" predications similar to those reported in The Thunden.[15]

We have seen that the words "NOYC" and "TEΛEIOC" are
closely linked with "the male virginal Barbelo" in the
Three Steles of Seth.[16] There are also references to
"perfect mind" in another Nag Hammadi document with
affiliations to Barbelo. This is Zostnianos, the first
tractate of codex eight.

Zostnianos VIII.18.5-9; 30.4-8

The great male invisible perfect mind (TEΛIOC
NNOYC), the first appearing one, has his own
water, as you will see when you arrive at his
place.

Adamas is the perfect (TEΛIOC) man because he
is the eye of the self-begotten, an ascending
knowledge (ΓNWCIC) of his, because the self-
begotten God is a word of the perfect mind
(NOYC NTEΛIOC).

Most of the pages of Zostnianos are very poorly preserved so that, although the name "Barbelo" occurs at
least fifteen times, her character and role remain un-
clear. Towards the end of the document, however, the
terms "Barbelo" and "perfect mind" occur linked together in a section which is well-preserved. The
passage relates that the visionary Zostrianos made
inquiry about "the triple powerful invisible perfect
spirit." Thereupon:

---

15. Tnimonphic Pnotennoia XIII.45.2-10.
16. See p. 166.

Zostrianos VIII.129.2-13

> The virgin light came before me and brought me
> to the first-appearing, great, male, perfect
> mind (ΤΕΛΙΟC ΝΝΟΥC), and I saw how all these
> who were there dwell within one. I joined with
> all of them and blessed the hidden aeon, the
> virgin *Barbelo*, the invisible spirit. And I
> became all-perfect (ΠΑΝΤΕΛΙΟC).

In this passage, as in the *Apocryphon of John*,
Barbelo seems to be a name for a three-fold spirit who
can be attained by the mind in a mystical vision. Probably Barbelo is to be identified with the mind that has
reached a certain level of mystic perfection, a ΝΟΥC
ΝΤΕΛΙΟC, "perfect mind." In these documents Barbelo
seems to have been linked up with the indwelling νουσ
of Hermetic literature.

The Hermetic tractate of codex six, the *Discourse on
the Eighth and the Ninth*, makes use of the words "I am
the Nous" in a context which implies they are a kind of
mantra to induce a higher level of consciousness.

Discourse on the Eighth and Ninth VI.58.5-27

> I see another mind (ΝΟΥC) which moves the soul.
> I see the one that moves me from pure forget-
> fulness. Thou givest me power. I see myself!
> I wish to speak (but) there is a fear which
> constrains me. I have found the archē (ΑΡΧΗ)
> of the power which is over every power, she
> who is without archē. I see a spring which is
> bubbling over (ΒΡΒΡ) with life. I said it, O
> my son, 'I am the Nous (ΝΟΥC).' I have seen!
> Language is not able to reveal this. For
> the entire Eighth, O my son, and the souls
> that are in it, and the angels, sing a hymn in
> silence. And I (am) the Nous; I understand
> . . . .
> I am silent. O my father. I wish to sing
> a hymn to you while I am silent.
> Then sing it, for 'I am the Nous.'

In this rather extraordinary scene the mystagogue speaks
of his vision as a "nous," an "archē," and as a "bubbling spring," apparently combining Greek, Semitic, and
Egyptian motifs, if we should see ΒΡΒΡ, "bubbling over"

172

in the same vein as ΒΛΒΙΛΕ, "seed," both evocative of
the name "Barbelo."[17]

The style and the content of *The Thunder* call one's
attention to Barbelo, but it is also possible that the
title itself identifies the goddess of the "I am" pronouncements. Consider the title to be divided in the
following way: TE B̄P̄Ō NTH, where B̄P̄Ō could be an abbreviation for Barbelo. Usually proper names, whether in
full or abbreviated, are distinguished in the Nag
Hammadi manuscripts by superlinear strokes, so that a
scribe might have mistaken the line above the abbreviation as part of the title's decoration.

What of the NTH after B̄P̄Ō? Obviously, what is needed
for the meaning here is an adjectival form corresponding
to "divine," so that the whole phrase would mean "the
divine Barbelo." Till noted in his edition of the Berlin codex that NTI could be used as an abbreviation for
NOYTE, "God," or for the adjectival form NNOYTE,
"divine."[18] The abbreviation TI for NOYTE, "God" also
occurs in the codex three *Apocryphon of John* (11.16;
12.19,25) as well as in the codex three *Gospel of the
Egyptians* (68.17).[19] In all of these passages the sign
✝ is probably not so much an abbreviation as a symbol
of divinity. The correspondence of this abbreviation
or symbol with the NTH of the title is not exact, but
the proposed coupling of these two shortened forms,
i.e., BPO NTI, could have suggested the Greek word
βροντη, "thunder" for the title of the document. The
final H of the present title BRONTH might have stood
originally as the connecting Greek particle "or" between

---

17. Cf. F.C. Burkitt, *Church and Gnosis* (Cambridge, 1932), pp. 54-
55; 58-60, for a derivation of "Barbelo" from the Coptic ΒΛΒΙΛΕ,
"seed." For a discussion of other derivations of the name Barbelo,
cf. S. Giversen, *Apocryphon Johannis* (Copenhagen: Prostant apud
Munksgaard, 1963), pp. 165-66.
18. Till, *Papyrus Berolinensis* 8502, pp. 300-301.
19. Cf. also *Gos. Eg.* III.63.1-2, 2ITM ΠΝΟΥΤΕ MN TEYΔΟΚΙΑ, which
Böhlig and Wisse in *Nag Hammadi Studies* (vol. 4) translate as
"through the⟨gift⟩ and the good pleasure," taking their lead from
what appears to be a very corrupt reading in the parallel passage
in codex four. Rather than relying on this, the editors should
have considered the almost identical phrasing in III.12.19, 21, 25,
2ITM ΠΤΙ (sic) MN TEYΔΟΚΙΑ, "by God and by grace." The correctness
of this translation can be verified by the other versions of the
Apocryphon of John, viz. BG 34.12-13; 34.20-35.1.

173

the two phrases, so that we could propose an earlier
title for the document as *TIBPO NTI H NOYC NTEΔEIOC*,
"*The Divine Barbelo or Perfect Mind.*"

The Ending of The Thunder

The ending of *The Thunder* presents a marked difference from the main portion of the document in style,
tone, and gender. These distinctions seem to support
the hypothesis that a Christian ending has been appended
to an older writing. When one reads the final page of
The Thunder, one perceives a change from the lyrical
and paradoxical "I am" poetry of the aretalogy to a
didactic presentation of a well-ordered mind. Exactly
where the modification of style begins is difficult to
determine because of the deterioration of the top of
page twenty-one. Beginning with line eleven, the writer
proclaims a deity quite different from the original
feminine one of the aretalogy.

> And I shall tell you *his* name. Look, then, at
> *his* sayings and (at) all the scriptures which
> have been fulfilled. Therefore, give heed,
> listeners, and ye angels also, and those who
> have been sent, and ye spirits who have risen
> from the dead: "I am *he* who alone exists, and
> there is no one who shall judge me" (*Thund.*
> 21.11-20).

The antecedents of the possessive pronouns here cannot
refer to the goddess of the aretalogy, for they are all
masculine. Since they are found within a call for
attention in which Christian signs predominate we suggest that they refer to the Christian God. The expressions "his name," "scriptures which have been fulfilled,"
and "spirits who have risen from the dead" belong to a
Christian milieu. Were these Christian allusions lacking, one might posit the gnostic Ialdabaoth as the "I"
of the pronouncement, "I am he who alone exists."
Surely this statement shows only an apparent agreement
of form, without belonging to the genre of the universal
statements of the preceding aretalogy.

The tone of the last page of *The Thunder* is pessimistic, encratitic, and exclusivistic in contrast to the
universalism of the "I am" statements of the earlier
portions of the tractate. There is denouncement of
sins, passions, and fleeting pleasures as causes of a
kind of drunken sleep, and there is hope for a sober
awakening into life eternal.

For there are many pleasant modes which exist in
innumerable sins, and some uncontrollable things,
and some damnable passions, and temporal pleasures, which are controlled until they cool and
flee down to their graves. And I shall be found
there, and they will live and not die again
(Thund. 21.20-32).

The poetry of the aretalogy has given way to solemn
prose. There is not a single feminine reference on the
last page. One can consider this ending to be a
Christian critique of all the myriad manifestations of
the feminine deity which were presented earlier. The
pantheistic tone of the preceding material is censured
by the monotheistic affirmation, and all of the poetic
descriptions of the goddess are lumped together as
"temporal pleasures" (ⲎⲆⲞⲚⲎ ⲠⲢⲞⲤ ⲠⲈⲞⲨⲞⲈⲒ).

    Most probably the document now entitled "The Thun-
der," known once as "The Divine Barbelo," was preserved
for its literary value rather than for its theological
content. At that, it seems to have been made accepta-
ble only by the inclusion of an ending which denounced
its teaching and affirmed a patriarchal deity.

The Gospel of Truth (I.3 and XII.2)

    The Gospel of Truth, the second tractate of codex one
in the Nag Hammadi collection, is a well-preserved document written in a type of Subachmimic. It bears indications of being translated from a Greek original.20 A
few fragments of a somewhat different version in the
Sahidic dialect are found in Codex XII.53-60. Comparison of the two copies shows that these are definitely
independent translations from a Greek original. The
Greek vorlage of the Gospel of Truth probably originated
in the period between 140-170 A.D.21 There is no reason
to suspect that it is a composite document preserving
earlier sources as is the case with some other documents

---

20. See Gos. Truth 22.35-38 and the note on p. 54 of Evangelium
Veritatis, ed. by Michel Malinine, Henri-Charles Puech, and Gilles
Quispel (Zürich: Rascher Verlag, 1956), which explains the disa-
greement in the gender of the Coptic endings on the basis of a
Greek original.
21. Cf. Jonas, The Gnostic Religion, pp. 309-10, who is inclined
to an early date for this document and states that "the author-
ship of Valentinus himself must not be ruled out."

from Nag Hammadi. There is a unity of form, Christian ideas, and imagery throughout the long tractate.

The *Gospel of Truth* is homiletic and meditative in style. The author illustrates his teaching from many points of view, and poses questions only to answer them himself as he eulogizes the Father of Truth and proclaims his fellowship with true Christian brothers. The tone of the tractate is joyous, for the author knows that the grace of gnosis has overcome ignorance, which he identifies with error and death. Such good news is correctly called a gospel even if the *Gospel of Truth* does not resemble the canonical gospels nor even the other gospels in the Nag Hammadi collection. The *Gospel of Truth* does not contain the story of Jesus' life, death, and resurrection, nor a revelation to favored disciples, but it does set forth the person and work of Christ, the revelation of the Father.

The document actually bears no title but receives its modern appellation from the opening words:

> The *Gospel of Truth* is a joy for those who have received from the Father of Truth the grace of knowing him, through the power of the word that came forth from the pleroma - the one who is in the thought and the mind of the Father, that is, the one who is addressed as the Savior, for that is the name of the work he is to accomplish for the salvation of those who were ignorant of the Father, since the name of the gospel is the revelation of hope, being a discovery for those who seek after him (*Gos. Truth* 16.31-17.4).

The main theme of the *Gospel of Truth* is "the salvation of those who were ignorant of the Father." With considerable skill, the author weaves biblical imagery and philosophical ideas of being and non-being into a theology of salvation by a knowledge of the cosmos and its correlation with the human condition. To undergird his elaborate presentations, he makes use of a gnostic mythological background which he must have expected his readers to understand. How else should they be able to appreciate such a passage as:

> All the spaces were shaken and disturbed because they had no order nor stability. Error (ΠΛΑΝΗ) was upset, not knowing what to do; she was grieved, in mourning, afflicting herself because she knew nothing. When knowledge drew

near her - this is the downfall of her (error)
and of all her emanations - error became empty
having nothing within her. Truth came into the
midst. All its emanations recognized it. They
greeted the Father in truth with a perfect
power that joins them with the Father (*Gos.
Truth* 26.15-32).

Cryptic sentences and unidentified pronouns make the
tractate difficult for the modern reader. Not until the
ninth page of the text does one learn that it is the
aeons who are searching for the Father, who lack knowledge of him, and finally attain such knowledge.

. . . in order that through the mercies of the
Father the *aeons* should know him and cease their
strivings in search of the Father, reposing
there in him, knowing that this is the repose
which filled up (EAYMOY2) the lack (ɰTA). *It*
abolished the system (CXHMA); his system is the
cosmos, that in which he served. For the place
where there is envy and strife, there is a lack;
but the place where there is unity, there is a
completion. Since the lack came into being because the Father was not known, therefore when
the Father is known, from that moment on the
lack will no longer exist. Just as with the
ignorance of a person, when he comes to have
knowledge, his ignorance vanishes of itself,
just as the darkness vanishes when light
appears, so also the lack vanishes in the completion (*Gos. Truth* 24.14-25.3).

Here we find "the fault (ɰTA) of the woman" under the
guise of a mathematical "lack" which when completed
abolishes the tension of envy and strife which exists in
an incomplete sum. MacRae's translation in *The Nag
Hammadi Library* repeats the erroneous picture given by
earlier translators - that it is *the Father* who supplies
"the lack."

Gospel of Truth 24.14-24 (MacRae)

. . . so that through the mercies of the Father
the *aeons* may know him and cease laboring in
search of the Father, resting there in him,
knowing that this is rest. Having filled
(EAYMOY2) the deficiency (ɰTA) *he* abolished the
form - the form of it is the world, that in
which he served.

177

The key word ΕΑΥΜΟΥϪ admits of being translated either
at the end of one sentence or at the beginning of the
next, with corresponding differences in meaning as
illustrated above. The continuation of the passage,
however, does not seem to warrant the interpretation
that the Father himself filled the ϢΤΑ, "the lack" or
"the deficiency." Rather, the lack vanishes of itself
when the Father is known. In this imagery, "completion," "knowledge," "unity," and "repose" eliminate
the lack.

Behind the elevated language of the *Gospel of Truth*
there is the familiar imagery of the fault of Sophia
and the apocalyptic end of the cosmos. The hypostatized Sophia does not appear in the *Gospel of Truth*;
in her place there is the hypostatized Planē, "error,"
which is responsible for all the disorder and insta-
bility in the universe as well as for the crucifixion
of Christ.

> This is the gospel of him whom they seek,
> which was revealed to those who are perfect
> through the mercies of the Father – the hid-
> den mystery, Jesus, the Christ. Through it
> he enlightened those who were in darkness.
> Out of oblivion he enlightened them. He
> showed (them) a way. And the way is the
> truth which he taught them.
>   For this reason ΠΛΑΝΗ was upset with him,
> persecuted him, oppressed him, and was
> brought to naught. He was nailed to a tree;
> he became a fruit of Gnosis of the Father
> which, however, did not perish when it was
> eaten. On the contrary, those who ate of it
> he caused to be joyful within the discovery
> (*Gos. Truth* 18.11-29).

In a fashion similar to the *Odes of Solomon*, the
trinitarian formulation can be presented with explicit
feminine elements.

> The Father reveals his breast. And his breast
> is the Holy Spirit. He reveals that of him-
> self which was hidden. That of himself which
> was hidden is his son (*Gos. Truth* 24.9-14).

The author interprets themes from both the Old and New
Testaments in ways that are both imaginative and allegorical. The parable of the lost sheep is important
to him for the number symbolism of ninety-nine and one
(31.35-32.17). The meaning of the Sabbath is that

"you (pl.) may say from the heart that you are the perfect day" (32.31-33). The division of male and female came about that "the warm pleroma of love" should come (34.30-31). All things come to pass through the will of the Father.

And it is in the will that the Father reposes and (in which) he is content. Nothing happens without him, nor does anything occur *without the will of the Father*. And his will is incomprehensible. His track is the will, and no one can know it, neither is it possible for anyone to perceive it so that he should understand it. But when he wills, that which he wills is there (*Gos. Truth* 37.19-31).

There is no direct reference to a benighted creator god. The author seems to be familiar with the gnostic myth of Sophia, Ialdabaoth, and the Immortal Man, but apparently has replaced Ialdabaoth by the feminine figure, Planē, a figure who also combines some traits from Sophia. Planē is described as being without root (17.29-30), existing in a fog (17.30-31), fashioning her own matter apart from truth (17.15-18), angry and persecuting the Savior (18.22-24), agitated, grieving, not knowing what to do (26.18-21). Planē is more than an abstraction here. She plays the mythological roles of forming the primeval matter ('υλη), of seducing the psychic ones (17.30-37), of warring against truth and the Father (26.18-31), and of course she is responsible for the crucifixion of the Savior. The very first reference to Planē makes it plain that this figure is more than an abstraction for our author. Jonas rightly points out that without acquaintance with the Sophia myth the passage would not be very meaningful to the reader.[22]

It was this ignorance of the Father which produced anxiety and terror. And anxiety congealed like a mist so that no one was able to see. Therefore, error (ΠΛΑΝΗ) was strengthened. She fashioned her own matter (2ΥΛΗ) out of vanity without knowing the truth. *She came into being in a plasma* preparing with power in beauty *the substitute for truth*.
    This was, however, no humiliation for him, the incomprehensible, inconceivable one. For

22. Cf. Jonas, *The Gnostic Religion*, pp. 313-15.

they were as nothing - the anxiety and the oblivion and *the plasma of the lie* - whereas the established truth is unchangeable, imperturbable, perfect in beauty. Therefore, despise *error* (ΠΛΑΝΗ).

Thus it was that having no root, she came into a mist with regard to the Father, being engaged in preparing works and oblivions and terrors in order that by means of them *she might entice those of the middle* and take them captive. The oblivion of *error* (ΠΛΑΝΗ) was revealed . . . . (*Gos. Truth* 17.9-37).

The translation given above follows Grobel's in making use of the personal pronouns "she" and "her" to emphasize the personified character of Planē. In line eighteen, ΑϹϢϢΠΕ ϨΕΝ ΟΥΠΛΑϹΜΑ is translated by us literally "she came into being in a plasma." The earlier translations render this by, "She was at work *upon a molded figure*" (Grobel); "It applied itself *to the modeling of a creature*" (Puech); "It set about making *a creature*" (MacRae). The literal translation here is perfectly intelligible; one can compare *Orig. World* 115.8-9, "lest the true man should come into his (the archigenetor's) *plasma* and rule over it."[23] The meaning seems to be that Planē, that is, the aeon Sophia, congeals and takes a solid molded form, the world. This "coming into being *in a plasma*" corresponds to the myth of the origin of Ialdabaoth as a final stage in the devolution of spirit. If this literal translation is correct and the text combines Planē-Sophia with Ialdabaoth, then the following reference (lines 24-25) to "*the plasma of the lie*" could also mean Ialdabaoth. Of course, the passage is not fundamentally mythological in tone, and the "plasma," the "mist," and "planē," are all meant as metaphors.

There are two other allusions to gnostic mythology in the passage. The first is to "the substitute for truth," ΤΧΒΒΙΟ ΝΤΙΤΜΝΤΜΗΕ (sic), which can be compared with "the opposed spirit," ΠΕΠΝΕΥΜΑ ΕΤϢΒΒΙΑΕΙΤ, literally "the variant spirit" in *Apoc. John* II.21.9; 24. 31-32; 26.20.[24] In the *Apocryphon of John* this "variant spirit" is the lust for intercourse which the

_____

23. Cf. also *Orig. World* 114.17; 124.21-22; 125.23-25; and *Hyp. Arch.* 96.34.
24. See S. Giversen, *Apocryphon Johannis*, pp. 268-69 for a good discussion on the "opposed spirit."

archon has implanted in mankind in order to disperse the spiritual element by procreation (*Apoc. John* 24. 26-32). Again, the passage in the *Gospel of Truth* places Planē in the role of the evil archon Ialdabaoth of mythological gnosticism.

The second allusion is to the psychics as "those of the middle." Planē is pictured as trying to entice them and take them captive exactly as the archon does in the *Apocryphon of John*.

Apocryphon of John II.26.36-27.8

In them (the psychics) the variant spirit has increased within them to cause them to go astray. And it weighs down upon the soul and entices her by the works of evil, and it casts her down into oblivion. And when she comes out (of the body) she is handed over to the authorities, who came into being through the *archon*, and they bind her with chains and cast her into prison.

These are the *psychic* ones who may be enticed and taken captive by the evil powers. The passage in the *Gospel of Truth* presumes an acquaintance with the gnostic doctrine of the three classes of mankind and the vulnerability of the *psychic* ones to the enticements of the world.

We have mentioned some typical gnostic feminine motifs in the *Gospel of Truth*, particularly the ꟼTA, the "lack" or the "fault," Sophia disguised as Planē, and the vulnerability of the *psychic* class, which in gnostic documents is often imaged as feminine. The *Gospel of Truth* does not express these feminine motifs in vivid detail; the presentation is almost uniformly on a more abstract plane. Yet we have tried to show that these motifs and their prejudices lie behind the more theological tone of this document.

The *Gospel of Truth* is important in the history of gnostic thought because good arguments can be presented for its date and connection with the Valentinian school. It should also be noted that the *Gospel of Truth* does not stand alone in this connection but must be considered along with the following document in codex one, *The Tripartite Tractate*. This is not the place to try to make an exact identification of these two codex one documents with a particular historical school of gnosticism; however, it should be pointed out that if

181

this Valentinian connection is warranted, then the
earlier mythological stage of gnosticism should be
dated to a period hardly any later than the first
Christian writings. For our purposes this means that
the feminine motifs with which we have been concerned
must not be thought of as secondary accretions within
rampant gnostic mythological speculation of the second
or third century of the Christian era, but that they
are intrinsic to the original formulations and belong
to a very early period. The opinion of Hans Jonas is
important on this question. He finds the Gospel of
Truth difficult reading, and quite implausible the
view that it could belong to an "immature stage of
Valentinianism." He writes of the Gospel of Truth:

> Lastly, the reductive picture it thus offers
> of the 'system' (with no mention of Sophia and
> demiurge, of the number and names of Aeons,
> etc.) does not justify the inference that it
> represents an incipient, still undeveloped, as
> it were embryonic stage of that speculation.
> It rather represents a symbolism of the second
> degree. But it is indeed significant that the
> inner meaning of the doctrine could be
> expressed, at least to the "knowing ones, in
> such abstraction from the lavish personal cast
> with which it was presented on the mythologi-
> cal stage.[25]

The reduction of the mythological presentation is
carried one step further in the Tripartite Tractate.
Here the creator of the fallen world is not the Archigenetor Ialdabaoth, nor Sophia, nor Planē, but a
"logos." Nevertheless, the mythological picture is
still clearly present. This logos is identified with
an aeon who sought "to understand the inconceivable."
The feminine aspect of the logos is not immediately
apparent but emerges in the course of the presentation.

Tripartite Tractate 75.17; 76.6,13,15,24;
77.11-78.21

> It occurred to one of the aeons to attempt
> to understand the inconceivable. . . . He set
> his hand to a work beyond his power . . . For
> this aeon was the last to be brought forth
> . . . and young in age . . . For not without
> the will of the Father was this logos begot-
> ten. . . . For the logos begot himself as a

---

25. Jonas, The Gnostic Religion, pp. 316-17.

perfect unity, to the glory of the Father who loved him and took pleasure in him. But those whom he wished to take as an establishment, *he begot in shadows, images, and likenesses*. For he was not able to bear the sight of the light, but he looked into the depth and he doubted. Therefore there was a division which caused great distress, and a falling away arising from the double-mindedness and the division, an oblivion and an ignorance on his part. . . . That which he brought forth from himself alone, as an aeon of unity, rushed upwards to that which is his own and to his kin in the Pleroma. He abandoned that which originated in the lack (*ŲTA*), those who came forth from him in a fantasy, because they were not his. For he was perfect when he brought forth by himself alone that which was brought forth, (but) *he became weak in the way of a woman's nature* which has been abandoned by its masculinity.

For from that which was lacking in himself exist those things which came into being from his thought and his arrogance. Because of this, that which was perfect of him abandoned him and ascended to those who were his own. It was existing in the Pleroma as a reminder for him.

Here we have the Sophia myth in a disguised form. There is no mention of a dramatic conflict with the arrogant archon, but rather the tragic split of the deity has been somewhat healed over. The feminine motifs are still there, and apparently the masculine savior is prepared to redeem his fallen partner. From other passages in the *Tripartite Tractate* it is apparent that this *logos* can also represent the God of the Old Testament, and he is not totally presented in a bad light.26 Fundamentally, however, the fallen state of the universe is still traceable to a *female archon* who wished to conceive by herself and in so doing not only

---

26. See *Tripartite Tractate* 90.14-95.22, where the Logos is described as "deficient," "stripping himself of that arrogant thought," and then being "entrusted with the administration (*OIKONOMIA*) of all those things that have been established" (95. 20-22). On the other hand, in 100.18-36, it is said that the Logos makes use of an Archon who is called "father," "god," "demiurge," "king," "judge," etc. to work and beautify the things below and to be used as a mouth for the things which will be prophesied.

lost her higher nature but also brought forth imperfect
souls in the forms of "shadows, images, and likenesses."

The *Tripartite Tractate* goes into considerable detail
with regard to the three classes of mankind. They are
described as "those of the image"; "those of the remembrance"; and "those of the likeness."[27] The terms
"image" and "likeness" apparently go back to the Genesis
creation story. The one are the perfect masculine
spirits; the other are the condemned hylics. The middle
class apparently is of a feminine order and the phrase
which is used of them, NA ΠMEEYE, "those of the remembrance," could just possibly once have been NA TMEEY,
"those of the Mother." We saw this confusion between
these two words in the *Song of the Woman* in *The Thunder*
(13.20).[28] In the *Tripartite Tractate*, a description
of the middle class of mankind as "those of the Mother"
would be logical and appropriate as the following
passage shows:

Tripartite Tractate 1.94.10-21

And it is these which took form with him, and
according to the image (EIKWN) of the Pleroma,
having their fathers who also are the ones
that gave them life. Each one of them is an
impress (XAPAKTHPION) of each one of the faces
which are forms of masculinity. They do not
have their origin *in the sickness which is
femininity*, but they are from this one who has
already left behind the sickness, possessing
the name "the Church."

Here we have a doctrine of "images" which is reminiscent of the "antopoi" in *Eugnostos* III.75.7-18, a class
of spiritual persons who are mirror reflections of the
face of the Father. Probably this doctrine has some
kinship with primitive ideas of guardian angels and
astral doubles. The elect are explicitly presented as
masculine, belonging to "fathers" above. The continuation of the Tractate makes it plain that this group is

---

27. Cf. *Tripartite Tractate* 118.14-23, "Mankind came to be in
three essential types, the spiritual, the psychic, and the
material, conforming to the triple arrangement of the Logos, from
which were brought forth the material ones and the psychic ones
and the spiritual ones. Each of the three essential types is
known by its fruit."
28. See footnote 11 for discussion of possible confusion between
MEEY, "mother," and MEEYE, "thought."

the pneumatic ones. If the pneumatic ones are masculine and have this special relationship with their "fathers," it would be logical enough for the second group, which here and elsewhere is termed "feminine," to be called "those of the Mother."

Although the *Gospel of Truth* generally avoids male-female imagery, there is one passage which seems to reflect an acquaintance with the doctrine that the soul is feminine and the breath of the spirit is the awakening force that heals their division.

Gospel of Truth 34.9-34

For it is not the ears that smell the fragrance, but (it is) the breath that has the sense of smell and attracts the fragrance to itself, and is submerged in the fragrance of the Father. It shelters it, then takes it to the place from where it came. The first fragrance which has grown cold is something *in a psychic form*, being like cold water which has [   ], being in earth that is not deep, of which those who look on it think it is earth. Afterwards it dissolves again; *if a breath draws on it, it becomes hot.* The fragrances, therefore, that have grown cold are from the division. For this reason [faith] came; *he abolished the division* and brought the warm pleroma of love in order that the coldness should not return but there should be the unity of perfect thought.

The soul and the spirit are not explicitly contrasted here. But the passage echoes the codicil of the *Sophia of Jesus Christ* where it is said of the *psychic* drop:

It cooled and slept on account of the oblivion of the soul. When it warmed with the breath of the great light of the male . . . (*Soph. Jes. Chr.* BG 120.1-6).[29]

The passage in the *Gospel of Truth* clearly alludes to the male-female division. The author compares the sleeping feminine element to earth which is not really earth because it can be awakened and heated when the breath draws on it, that is the moisture within it can

---

29. See pp. 90-91 for a discussion of "the breath of the great light of the male" in the *Soph. Jes. Chr.*, BG 120.4-6.

be enlivened. This, of course, must be taken to mean the *psychic* class of mankind which can attain to salvation when yoked with the *pneumatics*.

We have tried to show that Christian gnosticism made use of a number of pejorative feminine motifs in its mythological formulations. These include the concept of the fallen Sophia, the cosmological fault of the woman, and the imperfect feminine soul. These motifs persist even in the more abstract theological presentations of the *Gospel of Truth* and the *Tripartite Tractate*. It should not be thought, however, that these two documents, which we take to be illustrative of developed gnosticism, are completely negativistic with regard to feminine imagery. The ultimate goal of the soul is not to be thought of as masculine but as a unity which is neither male nor female. Thus the *Tripartite Tractate* can express the restoration of all things in Christ:

Tripartite Tractate 132.16-28

For when we confessed the kingdom which is in Christ, we escaped from the whole multiplicity of forms and from inequality and change. For the end will receive a unitary existence just as the beginning, where there is no male nor female, nor slave and free, nor circumcision and uncircumcision, neither angel nor man, but Christ is all in all.

Perhaps the chief characteristic of the Nag Hammadi documents is the boldness with which they make use of feminine imagery. Although the soul is often portrayed as feminine in a manner which is outrageous to modern sensibilities, there is at least one metaphor in the *Gospel of Truth* that shows that *even Jesus* can be considered as feminine:

Gospel of Truth 23.33-24.9

Thus the Word of the Father travels through the universe being the fruit of his heart and a facial aspect of his will. And he upholds the universe, choosing them, receiving the facial aspects of the universe, purifying them, causing them to return to the father, to *the Mother, Jesus of infinite gentleness*.

186

APPENDIX A

On the Origin of the World (II.5)[1]

(Cosmological Beginning)

[97][2] Since all the gods and men of the universe
(25) say that nothing existed before the Chaos, I shall
now demonstrate that they are all in error, and ignorant of the constitution of Chaos and its origin. And
I shall begin the proof (30) with the agreement of

---

1. The Coptic text of the codex thirteen version seems to have
been based on the same Coptic translation and differs only in a
few spellings, e.g. ЕΠΙΔΗ (cf. ЕΠΕΙΔΗ), ΛΛΑΥ (cf. ΛΛΑΥЕ), ΝΔЕ
(cf. ΔЕ).
2. Numbers in brackets denote page numbers; numbers in parentheses are line numbers.

[98] all men concerning Chaos that it is darkness. And it[3] is as something from a shadow; it was called darkness. But the shadow is as something from a force existing (5) previously. So it is obvious that it (force) existed before the Chaos came into being. And it (Chaos) followed the first force.

Let us now approach the truth. And that is also the first force from which came forth the Chaos. (10) And in this way we shall make manifest the immediacy of truth.

When immortal nature had been perfected from that which is limitless, then from Pistis an image flowed forth which is called Sophia. It (image)[4] willed, (15) and it became a force like unto the light which existed before it. And immediately her (Sophia's) will was manifest as a heavenly image, possessing an unimaginable magnitude, (20) being in the midst of the immortals and those who came into being after them, even as the heaven is a curtain separating mankind from that which is above. The aeon of the truth, however, has no shadow (25)〈within〉it, because the light which is without measure is completely within it. But its exterior is a shadow. And this they called darkness.

A power from within revealed itself upon the darkness. And the powers (30) which came into being afterwards called that shadow "the Chaos without bounds." The generations of the gods sprang up from it, and one and all followed after the first

---

3. The "it" is ambiguous. The antecedent seems to be "the darkness" which according to the argument is a dependent principle and not coeval with the light.
4. The NHL translation without warrant reads the errant Sophia of Valentinian theology into this passage: "〈She〉wished . . .".

[99] force. It revealed the Abyss from that Pistis of whom we spoke.

Then the shadow perceived that there was that which was stronger than herself. She became envious and when she had conceived (5) by herself, immediately she brought forth envy. From that day forth, the Arche of envy was manifest in all of the aeons and their worlds. And that envy was found to be as an abortion (10) in which there was no spirit. It came into being as the shadows in a great watery substance. Then wrath which came into being from the shadow was cast into a region of Chaos. From that day forth a watery substance (15) was manifest, and that which was locked within it flowed forth. It was manifest in Chaos. As with one who brings forth children, all their afterbirth falls away, so the matter which came into being (20) from shadow was cast aside and did not come forth from Chaos, but that matter was within Chaos being in a portion thereof.

And when these things had come to pass, then Pistis came and revealed herself over the matter of (25) Chaos which had been cast forth as an abortion in which there was no spirit,[5] for its entirety was darkness without limit and water without measure. But, when Pistis saw that which had come into being (30) through her fault,[6] she was disturbed. And the disturbance was manifest as a fearful force. It fled [down into] Chaos. And she turned to it and [breathed] into its face in the Abyss which is

---

5. It is the abortion, not Pistis, "in which there was no spirit." Cf. 99.9–10 and 115.5.
6. The "fault (ⲱϫⲧⲀ) of the women" is here identified with the "darkness" and a "watery substance."

[100] underneath all the heavens.

(First Narrative Section)

When Pistis Sophia wished that that which was without spirit should receive formal image and rule over matter and over (5) all of its powers, then was first manifest an archon out of the water, being in the form of a lion and an androgyne possessed of great authority. But he did not know (10) whence he had come into being. And when Pistis Sophia saw him moving within the depths of the waters, she spoke to him, "Young fellow, move over there,"[7] the interpretation of which is "Ialdabaoth." From that day forth (15) was manifest the Archē[8] of the word which attained unto gods, angels, and mankind. And that which came into being through the word was perfected, namely, the gods, and the angels, and mankind.

Now the archon Ialdabaoth was ignorant (20) of the power of Pistis and had not seen her face, but he had seen the image which had spoken with him in the water. And according to that voice he named himself Ialdabaoth. But the perfect ones (25) call him Ariel, because he is a lion in appearance. And after this had come to pass, there being authority in matter, Pistis Sophia made her way back to her light.

When that archon saw (30) his magnitude, and there was only himself which he saw, and he saw nothing else except water and darkness, then he thought that he alone was what existed. His thought perfected itself through the word.

---

7. The words are meant to be deprecatory.
8. The Archē is a feminine hypostasis, the equivalent of "Wisdom."

[101] It revealed itself as a spirit moving to and fro over the waters. And when that spirit revealed itself, the archon separated the watery substance to one side and that which was dry (5) to another side, and he created from matter a dwelling place which he named heaven. And the archon created from matter a footstool which he called the earth.

Afterwards (10) the archon thought within himself and he created through the word an androgyne. He (androgyne) opened his mouth and boasted of himself. And when he opened his eyes, he saw his father and he said to him, "I." (15) But his father called him "Iao." Again, he created a second son. He (second son) boasted of himself. He opened his eyes and said to his father, "E." His father called him "Eloai." Again, he created (20) a third son. He (third son) boasted of himself. He opened his eyes and he said to his father, "As." His father called him "Astaphaios." These are the three sons of their father.

Seven androgynes having masculine and feminine names were revealed from the Chaos. (25) The feminine name is the Pronoia Sambathas, that is, the Hebdomad. And the son called Iao - his feminine name is Lordship; (30) and Sabaoth - his feminine name is Godhead; and Adonaios - his feminine name is Kingship; and Eloaios - his feminine name is Envy; and Oraios - his feminine name is Riches; but Astaphaios - his feminine name

191

[102] is Sophia. These are the seven powers of the
seven heavens of Chaos, and they came into being as
androgynes according to the immortal type which existed
before them, according to (5) the will of Pistis so
that the image of that which existed from the beginning
should rule until the end. You will find the activity
of these names and the masculine powers in the *Annals
of Moses the Prophet.* (10) And the feminine names are
in the *First Book of Noraia.*

And since he had great powers, the Archigenetor,
Ialdabaoth, created by the word for each of his sons
heavens which were beautiful abodes, (15) and for
each heaven great glories seven times more choice,
with thrones and abodes, and temples, and chariots,
and spiritual virgins even invisible in their glory,
each one (20) having in his own heaven powerful armies,
divine, lordly, angelic, and archangelic, myriads
without number so that they should serve him. The history of these things you will learn more accurately
from the *First Logos* (25) *of Oraia.*[9]

And they were perfected from this heaven up (or
down) to the sixth heaven which is that of Sophia.
But heaven and earth were disturbed by the Quaker, who
is beneath everything. And the six heavens trembled;
(30) but the powers of Chaos knew who it was that was
destroying the heaven which was beneath them. And when
Pistis understood the abomination of the quaking, she
sent her breath and she bound him and cast him down
to Tartarus. (35) Since that day, the heaven and the
earth were established

---

9. Probably the same book previously referred to as "the *First
Book of Noraia.*" The scribe here gives the title in Greek:
λογοσ νωραιασ.

192

[103] by Ialdabaoth's wisdom (Sophia), who (*fem.*) *is beneath all the waters.*[10]

And when the heavens were established together with their forces and all their departments, the Archigenetor (5) lifted himself up and received glory from all his host of angels. And all the ⟨gods⟩ and their angels rendered unto him blessing and honor. And he himself rejoiced in his heart and boasted (10) of himself at all times saying to them, "I have need of nothing." And he said, "I am God, and there is none other existing beside me." Now when he said these things, he committed sin against all of the immortal ones who took notice[11] and watched (15) him. Indeed, when Pistis saw the impiety of the great archon, she was very upset. Without anyone seeing her, she spoke, "You are wrong, Samael," that is, the blind god;[12] "there is an immortal Light-man (20) who exists before you, who shall be revealed in your plasma.[13] He will trample upon you as a clay vessel which is stepped on, and you will go with those who belong to you down to your mother, the Abyss. For in (25) the consummation of your works the universal fault which was revealed from the truth shall be done away with, and it shall pass away and be as that which never came into being." And when Pistis said these things, she showed forth upon the (30) waters *her* majestic image, and thus she made her way back to her light.

(*Sabaoth Intrusion*)

But when Sabaoth,[14] the son of Ialdabaoth, heard the voice of Pistis, he sang a hymn to her, and he (35) damned his father [...]

---

10. The *NHL* translation has "the one which is beneath them all." *MMOOY* can be either "waters" or "them". The clause is possibly an anti-Sophia gloss; it lacks in the Subachmimic fragments published by C. Oeyen in *Nag Hammadi Studies*, vol. 6, p. 137.
11. Translating *ETXE OYW* as "who received a report," or "who took notice."
12. ΠΝΟΥΤΕ ΒΒΛΛΕ, the blind god." Cf. the erroneous improvement in *Hyp. Arch.* 87.3–4 and 94.26, ΠΝΟΥΤΕ ΝΒΒΛΛΕ, "the god of the blind ones."
13. The "plasma" is molded matter which becomes the arena of the struggle between light and darkness.
14. An intrusion featuring Sabaoth begins here and ends at 102.17.

[104] on the word of Pistis. He gave glory to her because she had taught them about the immortal man and
his light. And Pistis Sophia stretched forth her
finger; she poured forth light upon him (5) from her
own light as a condemnation of his father. Now, when
Sabaoth received light, he also received a great
authority over all the powers of Chaos. From that day
forth he was called (10) "the Lord of Hosts." He
hated his father, the darkness, and his mother, the
Abyss. He loathed his sister,[15] the thought of the
Archigenetor, who moved to and fro over the waters.

And on account of his light all the authorities of
Chaos envied (15) him, and when they had been thrown
into confusion, they waged a great war in the seven
heavens. Then Pistis Sophia saw the warfare and sent
Sabaoth seven archangels from her light. (20) They
snatched him up to the seventh heaven and constituted
themselves before him as deacons. Again, she sent to
him another three archangels, and she established a
kingdom for him above all of them, so that he should
be (25) over the twelve gods of Chaos. And when
Sabaoth took his place of rest in return for his
repentance, Pistis even gave him her daughter Zoe
with great authority so that she should (30) teach
him about all that which is in the Eighth.

And since he possessed authority, he first created
for himself an abode. It is large and exceedingly
glorious, being seven times greater than all those
(35) which are in the seven heavens. And in front

---

15. Cf. in *Hyp. Arch.* 95.17 the elliptic "he loathed her."

[105] of his abode he created a majestic throne upon a
chariot having four faces which are called Cherubim.
And the Cherubim have (5) eight forms in each of the
four corners. Some have the form of a lion; some the
form of a bull; some the form of a man; and some the
form of an eagle; so that all the forms make sixty-
four. (10) And there are seven archangels standing before him. He is the eighth one; he possesses authority.
All of the forms make seventy-two, for the seventy-two
gods received form from this chariot. (15) They
received form that they should rule over the seventy-
two languages of the nations. And upon that throne he
created yet other angels in the forms of serpents,
which are called the Seraphim, who praise him at all
times. (20)

Afterwards, he created an angelic church, thousands
upon ten-thousands without number, which is like unto
the church which is in the Eighth, and a first-born
one, who is called "Israel," that (25) is "the man who
sees God," and another,16 "Jesus, the Christ", who is
like unto the Savior who is above the Eighth, sitting
on his right hand upon an exalted throne. And on his
left (30) sits the Virgin, the Holy Spirit, upon a
throne praising him. And before her stand the seven
virgins and with them are thirty guitars together with
harps and

---

16. The NHL translation tries to identify "Jesus the Christ"
with "Israel": "and (also) having another name (sic)." The
Coptic text does this in such an awkward way that a literal
translation is needed to show that this is probably a
Christian addition which ends with two persons on the right-
hand throne. Cf. the parallel in Hyp. Arch. 95.31-35.

[106] trumpets, praising him. And all the hosts of angels praise and bless him. And he is sitting upon a throne in the light of a great cloud (5) which covers him over; and there is no one with him in the cloud except Sophia Pistis who is teaching him about all the things in the Eighth, in order that they should create the images of those things by which the kingdom will remain (10) with him until the consummation of the heavens of Chaos and their powers. But Pistis Sophia separated him from the darkness. She called him to her right hand. And the archigenetor she placed on her left hand. From that day forth the right hand has been called (15) "righteousness," and the left hand has been called "unrighteousness." Now, therefore, they all received a world assembled of righteousness and unrighteousness, which stands over every creature.

Now the Archigenetor of Chaos (20) upon seeing his son, Sabaoth, and the glory which was his, that it was more excellent than all of the authorities of Chaos, was filled with envy against him. And when he became angry, he begat death from his own death. It was placed over the sixth (25) heaven. But Sabaoth was delivered from that place, and thus was completed the number six of the powers of Chaos. Then death, being an androgyne, blended with its nature and begat seven androgynous sons. (30) These are their masculine names: Envy, Anger, Weeping, Sighing, Mourning, Crying, Groaning; and these are their feminine names: Hostility, Melancholy, Pleasure, Sighing, Cursing, Complaining, Contention. (35) They consorted with one another. Each one begat seven more, so that they make

[107] forty-nine androgynous demons. Their names and their activities you will find in the *Book of Solomon*. And opposed to these, Zoe, the one who (5) was with Sabaoth, created seven good androgynous powers. These are their masculine names: Contentment, Happiness, Joy, Truthfulness, Satisfaction, Loveliness, (10) Faithfulness. These are their feminine names: Peace, Gladness, Rejoicing, Blessing, Truth, Love, Faith. And from these, there are many (more) beneficent and innocent spirits. Their efficacies (15) and energies you will learn about from the *Patterns of Divine Destiny Which Are Under the Twelve*.[17]

(*Second Narrative Section*)

But the Archigenetor, when he saw the image of Pistis on the waters, was sorely grieved, (20) especially when he heard her voice which was like unto the first voice which had called him forth from the water. And when he understood that it was she who named him, he groaned and became ashamed of his (25) transgression. And when he truly understood that there was an immortal Light-man existing before him, he was greatly disturbed that earlier he had said to all the gods and their angels, (30) "I am God; there is none other existing beside me." For he was afraid lest they should understand that there was another existing before him and that they should renounce him.

But because he is unintelligent, (35) he was contemptuous of criticism, and he dared to say,

---

17. A reference to an astrological source book. The Sabaoth intrusion ends here.

[108] "If there is one existing before me, let him reveal himself[18] so that we might see his light." And
immediately, behold, a light came forth from the Eighth
which is above, penetrating all of the heavens, (5)
earthward. When the Archigenetor saw the light, that
it was beautiful and dazzling, he was astonished and he
was greatly ashamed. When that light was revealed, a
human image showed forth within it, which was exceedingly wondrous, (10) and no one saw it except the
Archigenetor himself and the Pronoia[19] who was with
him. But its light was visible to all the powers of
the heavens. Therefore were they all disturbed by it.

(*Pronoia Intrusion*)

Then the (15) Pronoia, when she saw that angel,
fell in love with him; but he despised her because she
was in darkness. And she wished to embrace him but
could not. When she was not able to fulfill her love
she poured forth her light upon the earth. From (20)
that day forth, that angel was called "the light-
Adam,"[20] the interpretation of which is "the blood-
man of light." And the earth spread out upon him, "the
holy Adaman," (25) the interpretation of which is "the
holy adamantine earth." From that day forth, all of
the authorities honored the blood of the virgin. And
the earth was purified on account of the blood of the
virgin. And even more was the water purified through
the image of Pistis (30) Sophia, she who was revealed
to the archigenetor in the waters.[21] Indeed, it is
correctly said, "through the waters," since the holy
water makes all things alive.

---

18. Cf. the parallel in *Hyp. Arch.* 94.27f.
19. In the narrative "the Pronoia" seems to be the syzygy of
the Archigenetor. Cf. "Pronoia Sambathas" in 101.27. An
intrusion in the narrative featuring Pronoia begins at 108.14
and ends at 111.28.
20. Cf. the parallel narrative of the naming of Adam in *Hyp.
Arch.* 88.13-17.
21. In this account, the image in the waters seems to be that
of Pistis Sophia rather than that of the Immortal Man. Cf.
Orig. World 103.30, "her majestic image" and 107.18-19, "the
image of Pistis," Cf. also *Hyp. Arch.* 87.13-14, "her image
appeared in the waters." *Apoc. John* II.14.23-34 has a
different account.

198

[109] It purifies.

From this first blood was manifested Eros, himself
an androgyne. His manhood is Himeros, being fire from
the light; (5) his femininity which is with him is a
blood-soul. She is from the substance of the Pronoia.
He is exceedingly beautiful in his beauty, possessed of
every grace beyond all of the creations of Chaos.
When all of the gods and their angels saw (10) Eros,
they fell in love with him. And when he was manifested
among them all, he set them on fire; as many lamps are
lit from a single flame, and that light individuates
them,22 but the lamplight does not diminish. And in
this way Eros (15) spread himself throughout the
whole creation of Chaos and did not diminish. Just as
out of the midst which is between the light and the
darkness Eros appeared, so, too, from the midst of
angels and mankind the intercourse of Eros was perfected. (20) In this way, the first pleasure sprang
up on the earth.

The woman²³ followed after the earth.
And marriage followed after the woman.
Generation followed after marriage.
Dissolution (25) followed after generation.

After Eros, the grapevine sprouted up from the blood
which had been poured forth upon the earth. Therefore,
those who drink of it are apt to acquire for themselves
the lust of intercourse. (30) After the grapevine, a
fig tree and a pomegranate tree sprouted up on the
earth, and all the other trees, according to their
kind, each having their seed within them from the

_____

22. For OYWT MMAY (sic) as "individuates them," cf. *Goↄ. Phiℓ.*
60.19, 31.
23. The *NHL* translation unaccountably introduces the poetic
quotation with "⟨the man followed⟩".

[110] seed of the authorities and their angels.

   Then righteousness created a beautiful paradise beyond the orbit of the moon and beyond the orbit of the
sun on (5) luxuriant earth which is in the East in the
midst of the stones.[24] And desire is found in the
midst of its beautiful, tall trees. And the tree of
immortal life, as revealed by the will of God, (10)
is on the north side of paradise so that it should
make immortal the souls[25] of the saints, those who are
coming forth from the plasma of poverty at the consummation of the age. And the hue of the tree of life
is like to the sun, (15) and beautiful are its
branches. Its leaves are like to those of the cypress
tree; its fruit is like unto clusters of white grapes.
Its height reaches unto the heavens, and beside it is
the tree of knowledge (Gnosis) possessing the power
(20) of God. Its glory is like unto the moon, dazzling
in brightness, and beautiful are its branches. Its
foliage is like unto the leaves of the fig tree. Its
fruit is like unto good, large dates. And this is on
the north side of (25) paradise so that it should
awaken souls from the sleep of the demons, in order
that they should come to the tree of life and eat of
its fruit and reject the authorities and their angels.
The efficacy (30) of this tree is written in the *Holy
Book*:

> Thou art the tree of knowledge (Gnosis) which
> is in paradise, from which the first man ate,
> awakening his mind. He loved his co-image,
> and he rejected

---

24. This description of paradise is reminiscent of the Samaritan
identification of "the East" with Mt. Gerizim and their particular
veneration for the north side of that mountain. "The stones" are
perhaps the sacred stones of passage removed from the Jordan and
placed on Mt. Gerizim according to the Samaritan text of Deut.
27:4.
25. The *NHL* translation incorrectly has "life" for МΨΥΧΗ (pl.),
"souls." The "souls of the saints" are not immortal until the
consummation of the age.

[111]   alien images. He detested them.

After this, there sprang up the olive tree which
would sanctify the kings and high-priests of righteousness, who would be (5) revealed in the last days. And
the olive tree had revealed itself in the light of the
first Adam on account of the anointing which they
received.[26]

And the first Psyche[27] fell in love with Eros who
was with her. She poured forth her (10) blood over
him and upon the earth, and from that blood first
sprang up on the earth the rose, from whose thorns is
gladdened the light which was to be revealed in the
thornbush. After (15) this also sprang up the beautiful, sweet-smelling flowers upon the earth, according
to their kinds, each from a virgin of the daughters of
Pronoia. When these fell in love with Eros, they
poured forth (20) their blood on him and upon the
earth.

After these things, all the vegetation sprang up
on the earth, according to its kind, each possessing
seed from the authorities and their angels. After
these things, the authorities (25) created from the
waters every beast, according to its kind, and every
reptile and bird, according to its kind, each possessing
seed from the authorities and their angels.[28]

(Third Narrative Section)

But before all these things, (30) when he (the Light-
man) was revealed on the first day, he remained on the
earth in this way for two days. He left the lower
Pronoia in heaven and he went up to his light, and
immediately darkness came upon the whole [world].

---

26. The text's ΕΤΟΥΧΙΤΥ is probably an overcorrection of an
earlier Achmimic ΕΤΑΥΧΙΤΥ, "which was received." The passage
explains that Adam and Eve were the first kings and high-priests.
27. "The first Psychē" is an allusion to the Greek myth of Psyche
and Eros.
28. The Pronoia intrusion ends here.

[112] Now Sophia who was in the lower heaven, when she wished, received authority from Pistis. She created great luminaries and all of the stars and placed them in the heaven so that they should (5) shine upon the earth. And they are perfected in the signs of the times, and in eras, and years, and months, and days, and nights, and instants, and all the rest of them. And thus the universe was set in order (10) under heaven.

But when the light-Adam wished to return to his light, that is, to the Eighth, he was not able to on account of the poverty[29] which was mixed with his light. Then he created for himself a great aeon, and in (15) that aeon he created six aeons and their six worlds, being seven times more excellent than the heavens of Chaos and their worlds. And all of these aeons and their worlds exist in that which is without limit (20) between the Eighth and the Chaos which is beneath it, for they belong to the world to which there is that poverty. If you wish to understand the pattern of these things, you will find it written in the *Seventh Cosmos of the Prophet Hieralias*. (25)

But before the light-Adam could make his way out of Chaos, the authorities saw him. And they mocked the Archigenetor because he had lied when he said, "I am God; there is none other before me." When they came to (30) him they said, "Is this the god who has destroyed our work?" He answered and said, "Verily, if you wish that he should not be able to destroy our work, then come, let us make a man from the earth according to (35) the likeness of our body and according to the image

---

29. The light-Adam's contamination (the "poverty") here seems to be the prototype for the "fault of the woman" of the later myth. His worlds are specifically said to be below the Eighth. Cf. the account in *Apoc. John* II.14.5-13, where the Light-man (the Son) brings Sophia up to his realm in the Ninth, "until her fault should be corrected."

[113] of that one, and it will serve us; so that if
that one should see his image he will fall in love
with it and no longer destroy our work, and those begotten from the light we shall make servants of ours
(5) for all the ages of this aeon. But all this came
to pass according to the Pronoia of Pistis in order
that the Man should be revealed opposite his image and
condemn them in their own plasma, and their plasma (10)
<become> a display of light.

(*Eve Intrusion*)

   Then the authorities took knowledge that they should
make the man.[30] (But) Sophia Zoe, she who is by the
side of Sabaoth, anticipated them, and she mocked their
decision: "They are blind in their (15) ignorance"—
they created against themselves—"and they do not know
what they are about to do." Therefore she anticipated
them and created first her man, so that he should
instruct their plasma. As it was to be despised by (20)
them, so shall it also save them.

   Now the begetting of the Instructor came to pass in
this way. When Sophia had cast forth a light-drop, it
floated upon the water. Immediately, (25) the man was
made manifest, being androgynous. That drop took its
first form as a feminine body. Afterwards, she took
her bodily form in the image of the mother which had
been revealed. She was completed in twelve months.
(30) An androgyne[31] was born whom the Greeks call
"Hermaphrodites." But its mother in Hebrew called her
"the Living Eva," that is, "the Instructoress of Life."
And her son is the begotten one (35) who is the Lord.
Afterwards, the authorities

---

30. The Eve intrusion, which seems to be designed to show that
Eve was created before Adam, begins here and ends with the *Song
of the Woman* in 114.7-15.
31. The *NHL* translation erroneously takes this to be a *second*
androgyne, Seth, and the previous androgyne to be Eva, its mother.
The confusion is focussed on 113.32, ΤΕΥΜΑΑΥ ΝΔΕ Ν2ΕΒΡΑΙΟC, lit.,
"its (androgyne's) Hebrew mother." The sense of the passage is
that the Greeks and the Hebrews call this *one* androgyne by
different names: "Hermaphrodite" and "the living Eva."

[114] called him "the Beast" in order to deceive their
creatures. The interpretation of "the Beast" is "the
Instructor." For they found that he was wiser than all
of them.

Now Eva is the first (5) virgin who gave birth without a man.[32] She is the one who played her own doctor.
Therefore, it is said of her that she said,

> I am a portion of my mother and
> I am the Mother.
> I am the woman and
> I am the maiden. (10)
> I am the one who is with child; (and)
> I am the doctor.
> I am the consoler of the labor pains.

> The one who begat me is my husband; and
> I am his mother; and
> he is my father and my lord.
> He is my power.
> That which he wishes he speaks.
> With propriety I exist, but (15)
> I have begotten a child with the lord.[33]

(Fourth Narrative Section)

Now these things were revealed in the Will to the
souls of Sabaoth and his Christ, which are to come into
the plasma of the authorities. And on account of these,
the holy voice spoke, "Increase and multiply. Be lord
(20) over all creation." And these were taken captive
according to fate by the Archigenetor and thus locked
within the prisons of plasma until the consummation of
the aeon.

And at that time (25) the Archigenetor made a
decision for those with him concerning the Man. And
then each one of them cast his seed into the midst of
the navel of the earth. From that day forth the seven
(30) archons molded the Man making his body like unto
their body but his image like unto the man which had
been manifested to them. His plasma came into being,
piece by piece, from each one of them. And their leader
made (35) his brain and marrow. Afterwards, he was
manifest as the one before him and he became

204

[115] a psychic man, and they called him Adam, that is "father," according to the name of him who was before him.

But when they had completed Adam, he put him in a vessel because he had taken (5) form like an abortion in whom there was no spirit. On this account, when the great archon considered the words of Pistis he became afraid lest the true man should come into his plasma and rule over it. Therefore, he (10) left the plasma for forty days without soul and went his way and left him.

On the fortieth day, Sophia Zoe sent her breath[34] into Adam, in whom there was no soul. He began to move upon the earth (15) but was not able to stand upright. And when the seven archons came and saw him they were greatly disturbed. They came up to him, grasped him, and said to the breath which was within him, "Who are you? And (20) whence art thou come to this place?" He answered and said, "From the power of the Man, I have come for the destruction of your works." When they heard this, they gave honor to him because he had given them rest from the fear and anxiety which was (25) in them. Then they named that day "the day of rest," because they rested on it from their troubles. But when they saw that Adam was unable to stand upright they rejoiced. They took him away and placed him in paradise and (30) went their own way back to their heavens.

After the day of rest, Sophia sent her daughter Zoe, who is called Eva, as an Instructoress to awaken Adam in whom there was no soul, (35) in order that those whom he would beget should become vessels of the light. Now when

---

32. The *Song of the Woman* (cf. *The Thunder* VI.13.15-14.9 and *Hyp. Arch.* II.89.16-17) extolls virginal birth. The *NHL* translation "Eve is the first virgin not having a husband" is nonsensical. The Coptic sentence cannot end here but includes the verb "ACϢAMICE, probably corrupt for EϢACMICE, "who gave birth."
33. Translating NX̄OEIC "with the lord": cf. MMOOY in 113.19-20. Cf. Gen. 4:1.
34. Sophia imparts the life-giving breath. Cf. the more biblical "and he breathed into his face" (Gen. 2:7) in *Hyp. Arch.* 88.3-4. Cf. also the account in *Apoc. John* II.19.25-27.

[116] Eva saw her co-image lying there, she took pity on him and she said, "Adam, live, rise up upon the earth." Immediately her word became effective, and immediately Adam (5) arose and opened his eyes. And when he saw her, he said, "Thou shalt be called 'the Mother of the Living', because thou art the one who gave me life."[35]

Then the authorities were informed that their plasma lived and stood upright, (10) and they were greatly disturbed. They sent seven archangels to see what had happened. They came to Adam, and when they saw Eva speaking with him, they said to one another, "Who is this Light-man (fem.)? For truly she appears like unto that image which (15) was manifest to us in the light. Come now, let us seize her and cast our seed on her so that she shall be defiled and no longer be able to return to her light, and those whom she shall bring forth will be subordinate (20) to us. And let us not tell Adam that she is also[36] one of us, but let us bring a forgetfulness over him and teach him during his sleep that she came forth from his rib, in order that the woman should be (25) subordinate and he should be lord over her."

Then Eva, because she was powerful, laughed at their decision. She cast mist upon their eyes, and she left her image secretly there with Adam and entered into the tree of knowledge and remained there. (30) But they followed after her, and she revealed to them that she had entered into the tree, and had become a tree. And when they became exceedingly terrified, they fled away ⟨blind⟩.

And afterwards, when they sobered up from their shock, they came up (35) to Adam, and upon seeing the image of herself

---

35. Cf. the parallel in *Hyp. Arch.* 89.11-15. The allusion is to Gen. 3:21.
36. Translating Sah. AN as Ach. AN, "also."

[117] beside him, again they were disturbed thinking that this was the genuine Eva, and they waxed bold, coming up to her and seizing her. They cast their seed upon her. They did it by (5) trickery, not only defiling her physically but also abominably defiling the seal of her voice which had first spoken with them, saying: "What is it to you (pl.) that those who speak out should be defiled? (10) Because 'by the *word* they are begotten in the consummation of the age by the true man.'" And they were deceived not knowing that they had defiled their own bodies. It is the image which has been defiled in every way (15) by the authorities and their angels.[37]

And she became pregnant first with Abel by the chief archon, and other offspring she brought forth by the seven authorities and their angels. But all this came to pass according to the Pronoia of the (20) Archigenetor, in order that the first mother should beget within herself all the seed which is mixed and yoked to the destiny of the cosmos and to her (Pronoia's) plans and righteousness. A system came into being (25) concerning Eva so that the plasma of the authorities should become a display of light. Then it will condemn them through their plasma.

Now the first Adam of light is spiritual. He was revealed (30) on the first day. The second Adam is psychic. He was revealed on the fourth day, which is the one called "Aphrodite." The third Adam is earthy, that is, (35) "the law-man," who was revealed on the eighth day, that is the

---

37. This sentence reads like an editorial gloss.

[118] day of rest from anxiety, which is called "the day of the sun." And the generation of the earthy Adam increased and perfected itself. It brought forth from itself all the history of (5) the psychic Adam. But of the universe it remained in ignorance. After this I will freely say that when the archons saw him and the one (fem.) who was with him deceiving themselves in ignorance like cattle, they rejoiced heartily. (10)

And when they understood not only that the immortal man would transgress[38] against them, but also that they were about to be terrified again by her who had become the tree, they were disturbed and said: "Can this be the true man who blinded us and (15) taught us of her who was defiled, who (fem.) appears like unto him, and might they overpower us?"

Then the seven took counsel together. They went up to Adam and Eve and said to him in terror: "Every tree which is in Paradise was created (20) for you to eat of the fruit thereof, but keep yourselves from the tree of knowledge. Do not eat from it. If you eat, you will die." After they had given them a great fright, they went away to their authorities. (25)

Then along came he who was wiser than all of them, whom they called "the Beast," and when he saw the[39] image of their mother, Eva, he said to her: "What is it that God said to you (pl.), 'Do not eat from the tree (30) of knowledge?'" She answered: "He said not only 'Do not eat from it' but also 'Do not touch it, lest you die.'" He said to her: "Do not be afraid. Certainly you (pl.) will not die. For [he knows] that if you (pl.) eat

---

38. The *NHL* translation renders ΠΑΡΑΒΑ literally, "pass by" rather than the New Testament meaning "transgress." Cf. Mt. 15:2-3.
39. The Coptic text mistranslates Gen. 3:2 "Why (τί) did God say to you . . ." as "what (τι) is it that God said to you . . ." Cf. the similar *Hyp. Arch.* 89.34. The same error occurs in 120.1 (cf. Gen. 3:14).

[119] from it, your mind will be enlightened, and you will become like the gods knowing the difference which exists between evil and good men. (5) For he said this to you because he is envious[40] lest you eat from it."

And Eva trusted herself to the words of the Instructor. She gazed upon the tree. She saw that it was beautiful and very tall. She fell in love with it. She took from (10) its fruit and she ate. She gave to her husband and he also ate. Then their mind was opened. For when they had eaten, the light of knowledge (Gnosis) shone upon them. And when they had clothed their shame, they knew that they had been naked (15) of knowledge (Gnosis). And when they reflected, they saw that they were naked, and they fell in love with each other. And when they saw that their makers were in the forms of beasts, they loathed them and became more understanding.

Then the archons, when they learned that they had (20) transgressed their commandment, came with quaking of the earth and great threatening into Paradise and approached Adam and Eve to see the outcome of this assistance. Then Adam and Eve were sorely distressed (25) and hid themselves under the trees which are in Paradise. And, since the archons knew not where they were, they said: "Adam, where art thou?" He said: "I am over here. And I hid myself from fear of you when I was ashamed." But they spoke to him out of their (30) ignorance: "Who is it that told thee of the shame which thou hast clothed, unless thou hast eaten of the tree?" He said: "The woman whom thou (sic) gavest me, she is the one who gave to me and I ate." And then [they said to her,]

---

40. Cf. the exact Coptic of this editorial gloss in *Hyp. Arch.* 90.7-8.

[120] "What is it that thou hast done?" She answered and said, "The Instructor is the one who provoked me, and I ate."

Then the archons went up to the Instructor. Their eyes were blinded by him. (5) They were not able to do anything to him. They cursed him because they were powerless. Afterwards, they went up to the woman and cursed her and her children. After the woman, they cursed Adam and the ground for his sake, together with the fruit. And all things which they made (10) were accursed. There is no blessing with them. It is not possible for them to bring forth good from evil. From that day forth the authorities understood that truly there is one stronger than they. They would not have known unless (15) their commandment had not been kept. They brought a great envy into the world simply because of the immortal man.

And when the archons saw that their Adam had come to another kind of knowledge (Gnosis), they wished to tempt him, and they assembled (20) together all the domestic and wild beasts of the earth and the birds of the heavens. They brought them to Adam to see what he should call them. And when he saw them, he named their creatures, and they were greatly disturbed because Adam had awakened (25) from all his trauma.[41] They gathered together in council and they said: "Behold, Adam has become like one of us, that he should understand the difference between light and darkness. Now, (beware), lest he be misled as with (30) the tree of knowledge and also go to the tree of life and eat from it and become immortal and be lord and reject us and despise us and all our glory. After that he would judge (35) us and the world. Come, let us cast him

---

41. ΑΓШΝΙΑ, lit., "anguish, agony, struggle."

[121] out of Paradise, down to earth, the place from which he was brought forth, so that he, from now on, shall not be able to know anything more than we." And thus they cast Adam and his wife (5) out of Paradise. And even this did not satisfy them, but since they were afraid they went to the tree of life and surrounded it with great terrors of fiery beasts, which are called "the Cherubim," and they placed (10) in the midst of them a flaming sword turning at all times with terrible threatening so that no earthly creature should ever approach that place.

And after these things, when the archons envied Adam, they desired to lessen (15) his span of life, but they were not able to do so because of the Destiny which had been decreed at the beginning. For their individual times had been determined - a thousand years according to the revolutions of the luminaries. And when the archons were not able (20) to do this, each one of the evil-doers subtracted ten years, and the total of this time was nine hundred and thirty years - and these are in sorrow and weakness and temptations (25) of evil. And thus from that day forth human life went downhill until the consummation of the age.

Then Sophia Zoe, on seeing that the archons of darkness had cursed her co-images, was very upset. (30) And when she came forth from the first heaven with all her powers, she drove those archons from their heavens and cast them down to the sinful cosmos, so that they should become like (35) evil demons there, upon the earth . . . .

211

[122] [She created a sign that should endure]⁴² the
thousand years of paradise in their world, a creature
with a soul, which is called the Phoenix. It dies and
gives birth to itself as a witness (5) to their judgment, because they dealt unrighteously with Adam and
his generation unto the consummation of the age. There
are three men and there are ⟨three⟩ generations until
the consummation of the world - the spiritual aeon, the
psychic, and the earthly. Thus it is with (10) the
three Phoenix birds of paradise. The first is immortal;
the second lives a thousand years; of the third it is
written in the *Holy Book* that he shall be consumed.
Thus, there are also three baptisms - the first is (15)
spiritual, the second is with fire, and the third is
with water.

As the Phoenix is revealed as a witness to the
angels, so also the crocodiles of Egypt became a witness to those who go down (20) into the waters of baptism of a true man. The two bulls of Egypt possess
the mystery of the sun and the moon, which exist as
witnesses of Sabaoth, because Sophia has placed the
world in their charge.⁴³ From (25) the day that she
created the sun and the moon, she sealed off her
heaven until the aeon. And the worm which is begotten
by the Phoenix bird is also a human.⁴⁴ It is written
concerning it that "the righteous shall sprout up like
the Phoenix bird." (30) The Phoenix appears first of
all alive and then dies, and then again rises up, being
a sign of him who has been revealed at the consummation
of the age. These great signs have been revealed (35)
only in Egypt. In no other land are there

---

42. Here the narrative is interrupted by an excursus on Egypt,
featuring the Phoenix and the crocodiles of the Nile. The
narrative resumes at 123.2.
43. Lit., "Sophia has brought the world down to them (sun and
moon)." Under the jurisdiction of Sabaoth, the sun and moon
stand as observers of earth.
44. Translating *AN* as "also."

[123] signs that it is like unto the divine paradise.

(*Fifth Narrative Section*)

Let us now return to the archons of whom we have spoken, so that we should continue the proof. For when the seven archons (5) had been cast out of their heavens down to earth, they created for themselves angels, that is, hordes of demons to wait upon them. And these taught mankind innumerable errors both magical and chemical, and the worship of (10) idols with the pouring out of blood upon altars and temples, and sacrifices and drink-offerings to all the demons of earth, having as their co-worker that Destiny which came into being according to agreement among the gods of unrighteousness (15) and of righteousness. And thus when the universe fell into confusion, it came to error, just as throughout all time. For all mankind upon earth served the demons from the foundation of the earth until the consummation - the angels (20) serving righteousness and mankind serving unrighteousness - so the universe turned to confusion in ignorance and oblivion. All of them erred until the advent of the true man. This should suffice for you (25) for now.

(*Apocalyptic Ending*)

Now[45] we shall come to our world so that we should complete its analysis and organization more exactly. Then it will be evident how Pistis[46] of the hidden things has been found <in> the invisible things (30) from the foundation unto the consummation of the age.

And now I come to the main point concerning the immortal man. I shall speak concerning all those that belong to him - why there are the (different) classes in these places. A host (35) of mankind came into being [from Adam] -

---

45. The Christian ending begins here.
46. For the teaching that personified Pistis is revealed "in the hidden things," cf. *Eugnostos* III.74.16-19 and the *Sophia of Jesus Christ* III.98.15-20, and BG 90.9-12.

213

[124] the one who had been molded. And because of matter, as soon as the world was completed, the archons became masters over it, that is, they held it in ignorance. What is the reason? (5) It is this. Since the immortal Father knows that a fault came into being from the truth within the aeons and their world; therefore, when he wished to dispossess the archons of destruction through their own plasma, he sent your images down into (10) the world of destruction - these are the blessed, innocent, little spirits. They are no strangers to knowledge (Gnosis), for the complete knowledge (Gnosis) is as an angel who is manifest before them. This one is not powerless before the Father to give them (15) knowledge (Gnosis). {for the complete knowledge (Gnosis) is as an angel who is manifest before them. This one is not powerless before the Father to give them knowledge (Gnosis).} 47

As soon as they appear in the world of destruction, they first show forth (20) the stamp of indestructibility for judgment against the archons and their powers. Now when the blessed ones became manifest in the plasma, the authorities envied them. And the authorities on account of envy mixed their seed with them that they should (25) defile them. But they were not able to do so.

Now the blessed ones, when they became manifest in light,48 manifested themselves in different ways, and each one of them from his own land showed forth his knowledge (Gnosis) to the visible church (30) in the plasma of destruction. They found that she (the church) has every seed because of the seed of the authorities which was mixed [with hers]. For the Savior created each one of them all, and the spirits of these (35) [are clearly] elect and blessed.

---

47. A scribal dittography.
48. One could also translate 2NNOYOEIN (sic), "in their lights." Cf. the similar spread of Eros in 109.11-21.

[125] And they differ among themselves according to election; and there are many others who are kingless and more elect than all who came before them, so that there are four races. There are three which belong to the (5) kings of the Eighth, but the fourth race is kingless and perfect, being above all the rest. For these shall enter into the holy place of their Father, and they shall refresh themselves in rest, (10) in an eternal, ineffable glory and in unceasing joy. They are kings in this mortal world, and they are like the immortals. They shall judge the gods of Chaos and their powers.

Now the Logos, who is above (15) all things, was sent forth for this purpose alone that he should preach concerning that which was unknown. For he said, "There is nothing hidden which is not revealed, and that which is unknown shall be known."49 But these were sent forth (20) that they should manifest that which is hidden of the seven authorities of Chaos and their impiety, and thus they have condemned them to death. For when all the perfect ones revealed themselves in the plasma (25) of the archons and when they showed forth the truth which cannot be imitated, then they shamed all the wisdom of the gods. And their Destiny also came under judgment, and their power (30) was extinguished. Their lordship was dissolved and their Pronoia became as that which [had never been] honored.

Now before the consummation [of the age], the whole universe will tremble with a great thunder.50 Then (35) the archons will mourn, [crying out over] their

---

49. Cf. Mt. 10:26 and *Gos. Thom.* 81.13-14, 21-22.
50. Here begins a standard apocalyptic conclusion.

[126] death. The angels will lament as humans,[51] and the demons will weep for their times, and their people will lament and wail over their death. Then the aeon (5) shall begin, and they will be afflicted. Its kings shall be drunk with the fiery sword, and they shall wage war against one another so that the earth shall be drunk with the blood which is poured forth. And the seas will be afflicted with (10) this war. Then the sun will be darkened, and the moon shall lose her light.[52] The stars of heaven will be displaced from their courses, and great thunder shall come forth from a great power, which is above (15) all the powers of Chaos, from the place of the feminine[53] firmament.

After that one (fem.) has created the first force, she will take off the wise flame of Epinoia and she will clothe herself with mindless fury. (20) Then she will drive out the gods of chaos whom she created with the Archigenetor. She shall cast them down to the abyss. They shall be wiped out by their unrighteousness. For they will become like fire-spewing volcanoes (25) and shall devour one another until they are destroyed by their Archigenetor. And when he has destroyed them he will turn against himself, and destroy himself until he is no more, and their heavens shall tumble upon one another, (30) and their powers shall burn for another aeon. They shall be annihilated and his heaven shall fall into pieces. His [universe] shall itself fall down to earth, [so that the earth will not] be able to bear up with it, and they shall together fall [down] into the abyss, (35) and the [abyss] shall be destroyed. The light will [cut off the] darkness and blot it out. It will become as that

---

51. NNOYPWME is ambiguous, and can be translated literally "as a man," or "for their men." Cf. ZNNOYNOϬ (sing.) in line 14.
52. Cf. Mt. 24:29.
53. The feminine power is probably Pistis Sophia.

[127] which never came into being, and the force which the darkness followed after[54] will be dissolved, and the fault[55] shall be torn out by its roots in darkness. And the light shall make its way (5) back to its root, and the glory of the unbegotten shall be revealed, and it shall fill all the aeons when the prophecy and history of those who are kings shall be manifest and fulfilled through those who are called (10) the perfect ones.

And those who have not been made perfect within the unbegotten Father shall receive a glory in an aeon[56] and in an immortal kingdom. But they shall not ever enter kinglessness. For it is necessary that each one go (15) to the place from which he came. For each one shall show forth by his actions and his knowledge (Gnosis) his own nature.

---

54. Or "the force within which the darkness dwelled." Cf. the beginning of the tractate (98.4,15) where this force (EPTON) is described.
55. The "fault of the woman."
56. NNOYEOOY and 2NNOYAIWN are ambiguous; they could be translated as plurals: "their glories," and "in their aeons."

APPENDIX B

The Thunder, Perfect Mind (VI.2)
(The Divine Barbelo or Perfect Mind)[1]

(Introduction)

13.2   I have been sent from the power, and
       I came to those who think on me, and
       I was found among those who sought after me.
       Behold me, ye who think on me, and
       Ye hearers, hear me.

13.8   Ye who gaze upon me, receive me to yourselves.
       Do not banish me from before your eyes,
       And let not your voices despise me nor your
           listening.
       Be not unmindful of me anywhere or any time.
       Beware! Do not be unmindful of me.

(Song of the Woman)

13.15 For I am the first and the last.
       I am she who is honored and she who is disgraced.
       I am the harlot and the holy one.
       I am the woman and the maiden.
       I am ⟨the mother⟩ [2] and the daughter.

13.21 I am the members of my mother.
       I am the barren one and many are her children.
       I am she whose wedding(s) are many, and I have
           not married.
       I am the midwife and she who does not deliver.
       I am the solace of my labor pains.

_____

1. Reading *TEBPONTH* as an abbreviation for *TBAPBHΛW NNOYTE*, "The
Divine Barbelo." See pp. 173-74.
2. The Coptic text has *TMEEYE*, "the thought," using the feminine
article "*T*" which indicates the original reading, *TMEEY*, "the mother," in the Achmimic dialect.

13.27   I am the bride and the bridegroom.
        The one who begat me is my husband, and
        I am the mother of my father,
        And the sister of my husband,
        And he is my offspring.

13.33   I am the slave of him who prepared me, and
        I am the mistress over my offspring, and
        It is he who [begat me] before all time
        In a kind of conception, and
        He is my offspring in due time.

14.4   My power comes forth from him.
        I am the rod of his power in his youth, and
        He is my staff in my old age.
        And whatever he wishes
        Comes to pass from me.³

(Poetic discourse)

14.9   I am the silence which is unattainable,
        And the Epinoia who provokes many thoughts.⁴
        I am the voice of her whose sounds are many,
        And the word whose images are many.
        I am the saying of my name.

14.15   Why do you love me, you (who) hate me,
            and (why do) you hate those who love me?
        Those who deny me, confess me,
            and those who confess me, deny me!
        Those who speak truth about me, lie about me
            and those who lied about me,
            speak the truth about me!
        Those who know me, be ignorant of me
            and those who knew me not,
            let them know me!

14.26   For I am the knowledge and the ignorance.
        I am the shame and the boldness.
        I am shameless and I am ashamed.
        I am strong and I am fearful.
        I am war and peace.

---

3. Translating MMOEI as agential. The alternative translation is
"Whatever he wills happens to me."
4. The gnostic "επινοια" provokes the "νουσ" in man. ΠΕΣΡΠΜΕΕΥΕ
means "her causing thought," (a subjective genitive).

219

14.32　Give heed to me!
　　　　I am she who is condemned and she who is great.
　　　　Give heed to my poverty and my riches.
　　　　Do not be arrogant to me when I am cast out upon
　　　　　　the earth,
　　　　And you will find me among those who are to come.

15.5　　And do not look upon me on the dung-heap, nor
　　　　　　go and leave me cast out,
　　　　And you will find me among the kingdoms.
　　　　And do not look upon me when I am cast out among
　　　　　　those who are condemned and in humble places,
　　　　And do not mock me,
　　　　And do not cast me down to those who are cut off
　　　　　　harshly.

15.15　But I, I am compassionate and I am heartless.
　　　　Beware!
　　　　Do not hate my obedience and do not love my
　　　　　　self-control.
　　　　In my weakness do not despise me, and do not
　　　　　　fear my power.
　　　　For why do you disdain my fear and curse my pride?

15.25　And I am she who exists in every fear.
　　　　And (I am) strength in trembling.
　　　　I am she who is weak, and
　　　　I am well in a pleasant place.
　　　　I am senseless, and I am wise.

15.31　Why have you hated me in your counsels?
　　　　Because I will be silent among those who are
　　　　　　silent?
　　　　But I shall appear and I shall speak.
　　　　Why, then, have you hated me, Greeks?
　　　　Because I am a barbarian among the barbarians?

16.3　　For I am the Sophia of the Greeks [5]
　　　　　　and the Gnosis of the barbarians.
　　　　I am the judgment to the Greeks
　　　　　　and to the barbarians.
　　　　I am she whose images are many in Egypt
　　　　　　and she who has no image among the barbarians.
　　　　I am the one who has been hated in every place
　　　　　　and she who has been loved in every place.
　　　　I am she who is called Life
　　　　　　and you have called me Death.

_____

5. Probably with the meaning of condemnation to both Greeks and
barbarians.

16.13   I am she who is called Law
        and you have called me Lawlessness.
    I am she whom you have pursued
        and she whom you have caught.
    I am she whom you have scattered
        and you have assembled me.
    I am she before whom you have been ashamed
        and you acted shamefully to me.
    I am she who does not celebrate,
        and I am she whose celebrations are many.

16.24   I am godless,
        and I am she whose gods are many.[6]
    I am she upon whom you have thought,
        and you have wounded me.
    I am unlearned,
        and they learn from me.
    I am she whom you have despised,
        and you think of me.
    I am she from whom you have hidden,
        and you are manifest before me.

16.33   But when you hide yourselves
        I myself will appear,
    For [when] you [appear],
        I myself will hide from you.
    Those who have [...] to it [...]
        [...] senselessly [...]
    Take me [...] understanding from grief,
        and take me to yourselves from
        understanding [and] grief.
    And take me to yourselves from condemned
        places and from ruin, and plunder among
        the good as well as among the condemned.

17.16   Out of shame take me to yourselves in
        shamelessness,
    And from shamelessness and shame put to
        shame my members within you.
    And make your way towards me.
    You who know me, and you who know my members,
        Strengthen the mighty
    Among the first small creatures.

---

6. Reading NECNOYTE (pl.), "her gods." The unreconstructed text, ΠECNOYTE, is singular.

17.24   Make your way back to childhood and do not
          despise it
        Because it is little and a small thing.
        And do not reject some of the mighty in some
          places
        On account of smallnesses.
        For the small are known from the mighty.

17.33   Why do you curse me and honor me?
        You have bruised and you have been merciful.
        Do not separate me from the first ones,
          those [...] and do not cast out anyone [...]
          [do not] reject anyone [...] reject you,
        And [... know] him not [... him], that
          which belongs to me [...].
        I know the [first ones and] those after them
          know [me].

18.9   But I am the mind of [...] and the refreshment
          [...].
        I am the knowledge of my seeking,
        And the finding of those who seek after me,
        And the command of those who ask of me,
        And the power of the powers is in my "gnosis."

18.15   The messengers have been sent by my Logos[7]
        And the gods of the gods (are) by my counsel[8]
        And the spirits of all men exist with me
        And the feminine (spirits)
        Exist within me.

18.20   I am she who is honored and blessed
        And she who is despised scornfully.
        I am peace, and war has come into existence
          on account of me.
        I am an alien (f.) and a citizen.
        I am being and she who has no being.

---

7. The passage is corrupt. Perhaps the words "the messengers
(literally, "*oϧ* the angels") . . . Logos" are a Christian interpolation. Cf. 21.15-16 NNAΓΓEΛOC (sic) MN̄ NENTAYTAOYOOY "of the angels
and those who have been sent." In both passages, the erroneous
NNAΓΓEΛOC may indicate a pronunciation "eng·angelos."
8. Perhaps the beginning of this line should be reconstructed AYW
NNOYTE 2ENNOYTE< NE> "and the gods are divine . . .".

18.28   Those who originated from my intercourse are
             ignorant of me and those who exist in my
             being are the ones who know me.
          Those who are close to me are ignorant of me
             and those who are far way from me are
             they who have known me.
          On the day when I am close to [you I am far
             away] from you, and
          On the day when I [am far away] from you,
             [I am close] to you
          [I am...] within, [I am...] of the natures.

19.6   I am [...] of the creation of the [spirits],
          [...] request of the souls.
          [I am] control and [...].
          I am the yoke and the loosing.
          I am the residence and I am the moving.
          I am the one descending,[9] and they come up to me.

19.14   I am the judgment and acquittal.
          I am sinless, and the root of sin is within me.
          I am the outward lust, and inward self-control
             exists in me.
          I am the audibleness which everyone receives
             and the word which cannot be understood.
          I am a mute (f.) unable to speak,
             and great is the quantity of my words.

19.25   Hear me gently and learn about me rigorously.
          I am she who cries out {upon the face of
             the earth} and I am cast down upon the
             face of the earth.
          It is I who prepare the bread and my mind
             within; I am the knowledge of my name.
          I am the one who cries out, and it is I who
             listen.
          I appear and [...] wander about [...] seal
             of my [...].

20.5   I am [...] the defense [...].
          I am the one called Truth and violence [...].
          You honor me [...] and you whisper against me
             [...] victorious (f.) over them.
          Judge them before they judge you
          Because it is from you that the judge and
             the partiality originate.

---

9. ΠΙ is to be read as Π·ΕΙ, "the coming (down)."

20.14   If you are condemned by this one, who will
acquit you? Or,
If you are acquitted by him, who will be
able to detain you?
For that which is inside of you is that which
is outside of you;
And he who fashions the outside of you is he
who stamped you on the inside.[10]
And that which you see outside of you, you
see inside of you.
It is manifest, and it is your garment.

20.26   Hear me, listeners, and learn about my sayings,
you who know me.
I am the audibleness which is received
everywhere;
    I am the word which cannot be understood.[11]
I am the name of the sound and the sound of the
name.
I am the meaning of the writing and of the
spacing.
And I [...].

(*Christian Ending*)

21.4   [...] the light [...] listeners [...] to you.
He is [...] the great power.
And [...] it will not shake the name [...] he
who created me.
And I shall tell you his name.
Look, then, at his sayings and (at) all the
scriptures which have been fulfilled.

21.13   Therefore, give heed, listeners, and ye
angels also, and those who have been sent,
and ye spirits who have risen from the dead:[12]
I am he who alone exists, and there is
no one who shall judge me.

---

10. Cf. Gos. Thom., II.48.14-16. Lines 20-22 may be a Christian
interpolation.
11. Cf. the almost identical wording in 19.20-23. Perhaps the
Christianized ending begins with this repetition.
12. The passage is in the nature of an oath which summons supernatural
witnesses, i.e., unborn spirits sent to earth as well as the spirits
of the dead. The XE in line 18 introduces the witnessed statement.

21.20   For there are many pleasant modes which exist
         in innumerable sins, and some uncontrollable
         things, and some damnable passions, and
         pleasures which last for a little while—
         which are controlled until they cool and
         flee down to their graves.[13]

21.29   And I shall be found there, and they will live
         and not die again.

_____

13. The passions are personified as evil spirits which return (lit.
"flee down") to their graves when they are controlled.

Index of Authors

Ancient

Basilides, 2
Clement of Alexandria, 13, 28
Dositheos, 2
Epiphanius, 30, 31, 32, 169, 170
Hippolytus, 5, 6, 12, 30, 32
Homer, 36, 43
Ignatius, 61
Irenaeus, 1, 2, 12, 17, 30, 32, 53, 54, 55, 60, 62, 63, 72, 74, 75, 76, 77, 79, 95, 115, 181, 182

Justin Martyr, 61, 62
Philo, 14, 15, 40, 47
Plato, 1, 40
Plotinus, 2, 13, 104
Pythagorus, 85
Tertullian, 6, 100
Valentinus, 2, 5, 6, 72

Modern

Anz, W., 12
Bagatti, B., 61
Bergman, J., 15
Berdyaev, N., 40
Bethge, H.-G., 116, 126, 127, 130, 133, 148, 165
Böhlig, A., 22, 24, 25, 26, 27, 31, 93, 94, 96, 100, 145
Bousset, W., 113
Bullard, R., 94, 95, 108, 118, 121, 141, 143, 146, 148, 149, 158
Bultmann, R., 25, 113, 114
Burkitt, F.C., 12, 173
Conzelmann, H., 15
Daniélou, J., 26, 111
Dart, J., 1
Drijvers, H.J.W., 13
Dungan, D., 99
Foerster, W., 3, 6, 31
Giversen, S., 33, 173
Goodenough, E.R., 47, 123
Grobel, K., 169, 180
Haardt, R., 26
Harnack, A., 12
Helmbold, A., 27, 28
Horsley, R., 14, 118
Jewett, P.K., 40
Jonas, H., 11, 12, 78, 85, 104, 111, 114, 115, 175, 179, 182
Jung, C.G., 40
Kasser, R., 25

Klijn, A.F.J., 36
Koester, H., 13
Krause, M., 2, 36, 51, 52, 95
Labib, P., 22, 24, 25, 36, 93
Layton, B., 95, 96, 108, 145, 148, 150, 151
Leisegang, H., 12
Lidzbarski, M., 113
MacDonald, J., 34
MacRae, G., 25, 26, 31, 36, 84, 177, 180
Mack, B., 15
Mead, G.R.S., 95
Mueller, D., 161
Munck, J., 12
Nagel, P., 95, 149
Nock, A.D., 12
Oeyen, C., 95, 146
Orbe, A., 26
Parrott, D., 51, 53, 59, 72, 73
Pearson, B., 2, 119
Peek, W., 159
Pétrement, S., 12
Puech, C., 180
Quispel, G., 12, 61, 111, 112, 157, 162, 175
Reitzenstein, R., 113
Ringgren, H., 15
Robinson, J.M., 13, 15, 25, 26, 27, 59, 93
Robinson, W.C., 36, 37
Rosenstiehl, J.-M., 123

226

Rudolph, K., 25
Schenke, H.-M., 26, 93, 95
Schmidt, C., 12
Schuré, E., 5
Solmsen, F., 161
Suggs, J., 14
Tardieu, M., 165

Till, W., 51, 52, 68, 149, 173
Wilson, R. McL., 3, 12, 17, 51
Wintermute, O., 116, 126, 127,
  130, 133, 148
Wisse, F., 24, 36, 37, 38
Yamauchi, E., 12, 13, 25, 26,
  111, 114

Scripture Passages

Genesis
1:1	61
1:22	148, 149
1:26	40
2:7	73, 90, 91, 144, 154
2:15	138
2:15-17	141
2:16-17	138
2:17	142, 143
2:24	8, 42, 74
3	141
3:3, 4	138, 142
3:5-7	139
3:9-15	140
3:16	8, 42
3:20	131, 132, 147, 148
3:23	140
3:24	91
4:1	132, 162
12:1	44

Job
| 26:14 | 169 |
| 29:18 | 100 |

Psalms
6:6-9	39
45:10-11	43
91:12	
(LXX)	100

Proverbs
1-9	15
8:22-23	59
8:27	61
8:30	61

Isaiah
45:5	115
46:9	115
47:8-10	115

Jeremiah
| 3:1-4 | 40 |

Hosea
| 2:2-7 | 40 |

Ezekiel
| 16:23-26 | 40 |

Matthew
| 24:29 | 122 |

John
12:29	169
14:17	122
14:26	122, 135
26:14	169

I Corinthians
| 5:9 | 38 |
| 11:3 | 41, 42 |

Ephesians
4:6	122
5:23	42
6:12	109, 150

I Timothy
| 2:14 | 41 |

Hebrews
| 1:3 | 58 |

I John
| 2:20 | 122 |
| 2:27 | 122 |

Revelation
| 1:8 | 164 |
| 6:1 | 169 |

Subject Index

Abyss (see Chaos), 5, 16, 149, 153–54, 170
Adam, 5, 16, 22, 91, 102, 113, 118–119, 138–40, 145, 154, 171
Adamantine earth, 118–19, 144–45
Androgyne, original, 17–18, 29, 39–41, 46, 74, 80, 85–86, 91, 99,
    116–18, 129, 186
Anti-Semitism, 114–15
"Antopoi" (light projections), 87–88, 103, 105, 126, 184
Aphrodite, 43–44
Apis and Mnevis, 133–34
Apocalyptic, 17–18, 122, 170, 178
Archē, 54, 58, 60, 165, 172
Aretalogies, 4, 15, 158–62

Baptism, 133
Barbelo, 2, 7, 10, 165–75
Blind god, 110–13, 147, 150–51, 153
Blood of the virgin, 129
Breath of the male, 5, 185
Bridal chamber, 17–18

Chaos (See Abyss), 103, 108, 116, 124–25, 135, 167, 170
Christianization, 3–4, 7–10, 97, 108, 122, 128, 135, 152, 174
Church, 17, 128
Church fathers, 2, 11–13

Disciples, 18–19, 83
Duad, 6

Eden, paradise of, 5, 16, 29, 102, 138–41
Eidea, 55–58
Eighth sphere, 17, 98, 101, 112, 114, 128, 134, 155, 166, 172
Eleleth, 107–108, 136
Epinoia, 122, 170
Eros, 129
Eve
  birth of, 83, 99, 130–31
  salvific, 8, 10, 16, 28, 32, 35, 47, 84, 99, 102, 110, 117–120,
    136–37

Father
  Christian, 10, 16, 104–105, 108, 135, 151–52, 156, 157, 176–80,
    183–86
  of the All (universe), 4–5, 17, 54, 70–71, 135, 169
  second, 54
  will of, 7, 45, 48–49, 135, 152, 179

Fault
   of Sophia, 5-7, 67-68, 71, 74-76, 81, 83, 86, 124-26, 178
   of the universe, 103, 105, 125-26, 186
   of the woman, 10, 75, 86, 124, 177-78, 181, 183-84, 186
Flood, 23, 31-32, 107
Forefather, 54-55

Gnostic approach, 21
Gnostic motifs, 141, 151-56
Gnosticism, 11-14, 181-82
   Christian, 5-6, 8, 186
   definition, 11-13, 85, 111-15
   Jewish, 13, 21, 35-36, 61, 114-15, 162
   pre-Christian, 12, 24-26, 123, 162
Gnosis, 5, 8-9, 13-14, 16, 24, 27-30, 102, 106, 125-26, 139, 141,
   166, 178
Gnostics, 2, 6, 9, 11-14, 24

Homer's Odyssey, 36, 43

Ialdabaoth, 5, 6, 9, 16, 76, 80, 82, 98, 100-101, 112, 115-16,
   125, 135, 154, 174, 179-80
Image
   of God, 40, 56, 155, 184
   of Immortal Man, 100-101, 112-13, 155
   of Pistis Sophia, 100, 129, 135, 155
Immortal Light-man, 4-6, 52, 89, 99-102, 112-14, 124, 155-56, 179
Imperishability, 5, 109-10, 135, 137, 152
Instructoress, 16, 99, 101, 137-41
Isis, 7, 14-15, 116, 131-32, 158-61, 164
Israel, 128

Jewish motifs, 3, 13, 151-52
Jesus
   Christ, 6-9, 14, 18-19, 63, 98-99, 128, 136, 178-79
   Savior, 4, 9, 156, 176, 186

Kingless Generation, 4, 10, 24, 54, 87-92, 126

Male
   as master, 8-9, 163
   seed, 4, 9, 42, 48
Marriage, patrilocal, 43-44
Mary Magdalene, 18-19
Mary Mother of Jesus, 18, 121
Masculine additions, 81, 88, 90, 92, 130
Micheu, Michar, Mnesinous, 26
Monad, 5, 166
Mother
   as creator, 5, 6, 31-32, 62, 68, 158-59, 168
   as revealer, 57

235

Ninth sphere, 129
Noah, 23, 136, 155
Norea (Noraia), 16, 32, 106-107, 110, 121, 136-37, 144, 146
Norea source, 144

Pantheism, 7, 164, 168-69
Parthenogenetic conception, 6, 33, 35, 49, 68, 71, 125, 162, 183
Passwords, 78, 114
Peter, 19
Phoenix, 100, 133
Pistis, hypostatized faith, 64-66, 98, 100-101, 112-14, 123-28, 134
Pistis Sophia, 9, 64, 152-54, 100, 112, 114, 124, 128-29
Planē (error, folly), 7-8, 81, 86, 115, 136, 176-81
Plasma, 73, 156, 179-80
Pneumatics, Psychics, Hylics, 10, 14, 72, 118, 126, 184-86
Pronoia, 99, 101, 129, 152, 167
Psyche and Eros, 45-46
Psychics (see Pneumatics), 179, 181
Pythagoreans, 5

Redeemed redeemer, 113-14
Remythologization, 11, 182

Sabaoth, 17, 98-101, 128, 133-34, 150, 152
Sahidic biblical texts, 141-42, 144, 148-50
Saklas, 23, 29, 32-33
Samaritans, 34, 36
Seir, Mount, 107
Serpent, 117, 137-38, 140-41
Seth, 22, 132, 137
Sethians, 2, 8, 23, 25, 28, 30-32, 137
Silence, 67, 78-79
Solomon, 33-34
Song of the woman, 10, 99, 130-32, 147-48, 157, 162, 163-64
Son of Man, 4, 52
Son of the Son of Man, 52
Sophia
  breath of, 16, 73, 118-19, 154
  as creator, 6, 16, 55, 110, 133-34
  fallen, 4, 6, 9, 15, 53, 64, 71, 74-75, 81, 84, 86, 123-24, 134, 186
  generic, 86, 166
  as mother, 15-16, 32, 69, 117, 186
  myth of, 5, 7, 15, 179, 182-83
  salvific, 4, 15
  as revealer, 15, 73
  varied roles, 4-8, 14-15, 53, 64-71, 123, 137, 154
  as wisdom, 7, 14-15, 30, 115

Soul
  the, 21, 37–41, 67, 72, 76–78, 80, 103–104
  as bride, 4, 8, 36–37, 41–44, 49, 74
  fallen, 8–9, 48, 71, 81, 181–86
  womb of, 4, 37, 39, 48–49
Source for *Orig. World*, 97
Sun and moon, 133
Syzygy, 4, 59, 63, 66, 67, 69, 71

Tabitha, 123
Tartarus, 16, 116, 144–46
Tree of Knowledge, 5, 102, 138–39
Tree of Life, 102

Valentinians, 2, 5–6, 62, 181–82
Veil, cosmic, 69–70
Virgin, undefiled, 16–17, 34, 119–21, 136

Water, 129

Yesseus, Mazareus Yessedekeus, 26

Zoe, Sophia, 16, 101, 110, 119, 128, 137, 153

AUTHOR'S BIOGRAPHICAL SKETCH

Born in downstate Illinois in 1931, Rose Horman
Arthur served as a teaching member of the Sisters
of Divine Providence from 1949-69. She has received
three degrees in the field of religious studies: the
B. S. from St. Louis University; the M. A. from St.
Mary's Graduate School of Theology in Notre Dame; and
the Th. D. from the Graduate Theological Union in
Berkeley, California.

While pursuing doctoral studies, the author directed the Center for Women and Religion which she had
helped to found at the Graduate Theological Union.
During 1973-79 she served as education specialist,
television teacher, and researcher in American Samoa.
Upon completion of her thesis regarding feminine mo-
tifs in the Nag Hammadi documents, she taught in the
New Testament Department at Harvard Divinity School
as a Research/Resource Associate in Women's Studies.
She then became Coordinator of Academic Affairs and
Acting Executive Director of the Chicago Cluster of
Theological Schools. Along with other duties, she
organized the Women's Studies Program and serves as
Assistant Professor of Women and Religion at Meadville
Lombard Theological School.